Make America Meme Again

D1452949

Mitchell S. McKinney and Mary E. Stuckey
General Editors

Vol. 45

The Frontiers in Political Communication series
is part of the Peter Lang Media and Communication list.
Every volume is peer reviewed and meets
the highest quality standards for content and production.

PETER LANG
New York • Bern • Berlin
Brussels • Vienna • Oxford • Warsaw

Heather Suzanne Woods
and Leslie A. Hahner

Make America Meme Again

The Rhetoric of the Alt-Right

PETER LANG
New York • Bern • Berlin
Brussels • Vienna • Oxford • Warsaw

Library of Congress Cataloging-in-Publication Data

Names: Woods, Heather Suzanne, author. | Hahner, Leslie A., author.
Title: Make America meme again: the rhetoric of the alt-right /
Heather Suzanne Woods and Leslie A. Hahner.
Description: New York: Peter Lang, 2019.
Series: Frontiers in political communication; vol. 45 | ISSN 1525-9730
Includes bibliographical references and index.
Identifiers: LCCN 2018044668 | ISBN 978-1-4331-5974-9 (hardback: alk. paper)
ISBN 978-1-4331-8205-1 (paperback: alk. paper)
ISBN 978-1-4331-5975-6 (ebook pdf) | ISBN 978-1-4331-5976-3 (epub)
ISBN 978-1-4331-5977-0 (mobi)
Subjects: LCSH: Right-wing extremists—United States.
Memes—Political aspects—United States. | Social media—Political aspects—United States.
White supremacy movements—United States. | White nationalism—United States.
Presidents—United States—Election—2016. | Trump, Donald, 1946–
Classification: LCC HN90.R3 W66 2018 | DDC 320.56/90973—dc23
LC record available at https://lccn.loc.gov/2018044668
DOI 10.3726/b14436

Bibliographic information published by **Die Deutsche Nationalbibliothek**.
Die Deutsche Nationalbibliothek lists this publication in the "Deutsche Nationalbibliografie"; detailed bibliographic data are available on the Internet at http://dnb.d-nb.de/.

The paper in this book meets the guidelines for permanence and durability of the Committee on Production Guidelines for Book Longevity of the Council of Library Resources.

© 2019, 2020 Peter Lang Publishing, Inc., New York
29 Broadway, 18th floor, New York, NY 10006
www.peterlang.com

All rights reserved.
Reprint or reproduction, even partially, in all forms such as microfilm, xerography, microfiche, microcard, and offset strictly prohibited.

Printed in the United States of America

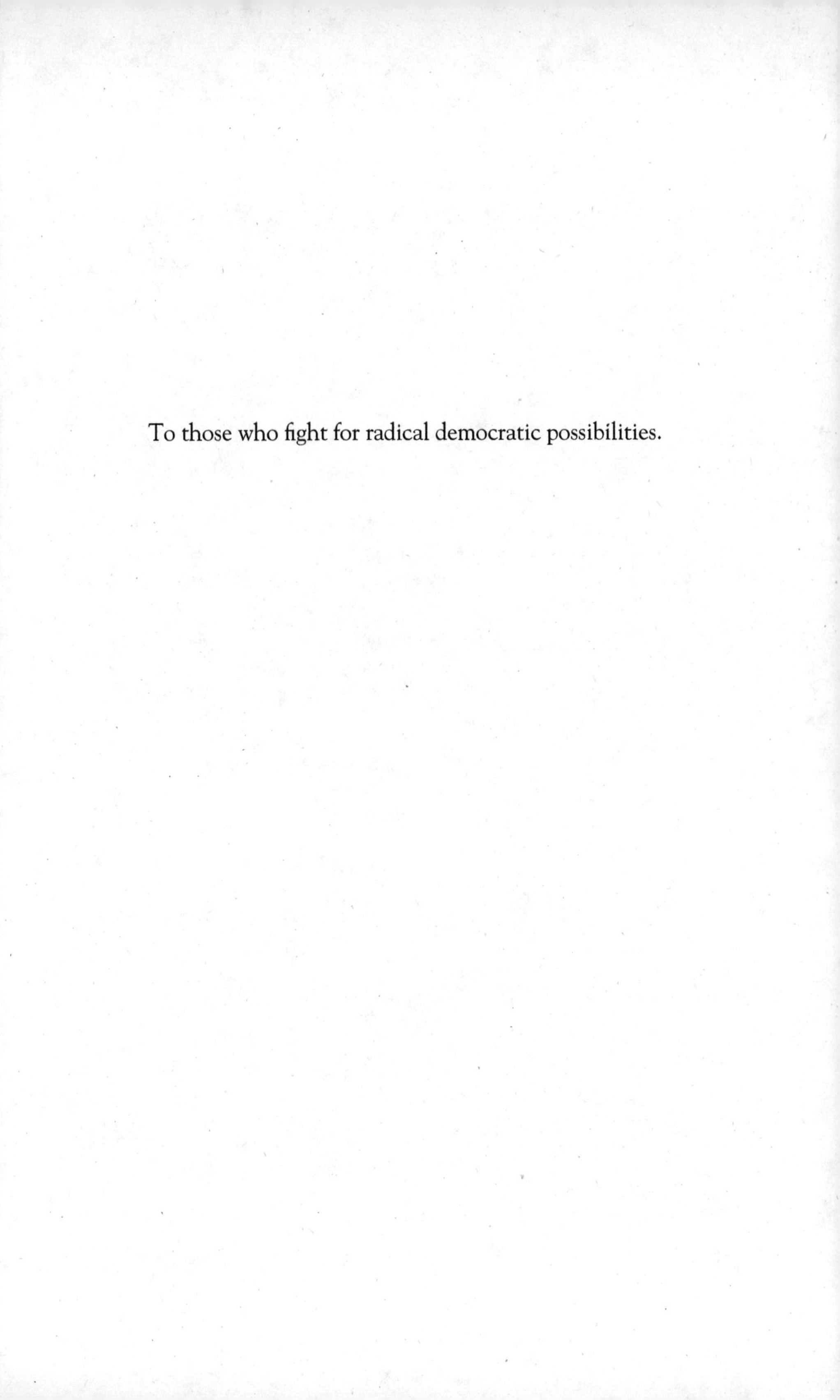

To those who fight for radical democratic possibilities.

CONTENTS

FIGURES

ACKNOWLEDGMENTS

This project began over a series of frenetic text messages, each attempting to make sense of the new landscape of digital propaganda. Both of us were trying to understand how our mediated friends and family members could fall so easily for obviously dubious persuasive tactics. As more information unfolded, we found that we, too, had been courted by such communiqués—this time by (at least) targeted messages from Russia's Internet Research Agency. We also discovered that we were compelled to name and analyze what was happening—we could not sit idly by and not use our skills to help citizens grapple with ongoing information wars. Our individual areas of expertise, historical uses of propaganda, visual rhetoric, digital ecosystems, and algorithmic amplification, enabled us a certain level of know-how, but also provided us enough background information to underscore how much more we, and the general public, needed to learn about the new landscape of psychological operations. We have learned much over the course of this project. There is still much to discover and we hope that this project is a beginning, one that invests in areas of research that require ongoing and robust analysis.

We have quite a few folks to thank for helping us complete this project. First, we would like to thank Kathryn Harrison, who saw potential in this project and kept us invested in the work and the vision of Peter Lang and the

Frontiers in Political Communication series. We are also deeply indebted to Mitchell S. McKinney and Mary E. Stuckey. Both of these editors devoted themselves to bettering this project and understood our goals and insights—sometimes better than we did. This project is stronger from their astute guidance and energetic support.

Colleagues at both of our home institutions have enabled the success of this book. At Baylor, Scott Varda was a precise editor who dropped everything to help us when we needed it. He is a champion of good scholarship and we could not have finished this project without him. Fielding Montgomery and Alden Conner contributed significant time and effort to helping us finish this project. David Schlueter facilitated our efforts by finding us resources and time to do the work. Martin J. Medhurst, as always, offered his wisdom and insights whenever we needed it. The College of Arts and Sciences also supplied Leslie Hahner with leave time to engage this book. Theresa Varney Kennedy, Kara Poe Alexander, and Beth Allison Barr bettered early work for this project through their wonderful advice. The women's writing group started by Lisa Shaver buoyed this endeavor when it could have rested in the doldrums of Leslie Hahner's associate professorship. At Kansas State University, the intellectual community comprised of Soumia Bardhan, Soo-Hye Han, Tim Shaffer, Travis Smith, William James Taylor (JT), Darren Epping, and Craig Brown inspired deep thinking about communication's democratic possibilities. Alex McVey critiqued early (and also late) drafts of several chapters, and challenged us to carefully imagine a future, mediated politics. Greg Paul and Melissa Winkel supported the project logistically, often in pivotal, behind-the-scenes ways. Jakki Mattson provided critical research for chapters one and four, while also serving as a sounding board for ideas. Colene Lind and Sarah Riforgiate gave really good advice. Natalie Pennington was a thoughtful interlocutor and advocate. Joe Koehle shared dank memes (and how to find them). At the University of North Carolina, Chapel Hill, Kumi Silva provided excellent advice (as always).

We are also thankful to scholars across our field who helped us through productive conversations and advice. We are particularly grateful to Heather Ashley Hayes, Casey Ryan Kelly, Ryan Milner, Damien Pfister, Jonathan Carter, Rachel Winter, Emily Winderman, Atilla Hallsby, and Dustin Greenwalt. As well, Jennifer Coates Millard was an astute and rigorous copyeditor for early work in this project. We are likewise grateful for the legal services and advice of John Cook, who is brilliant and helpful, as per usual.

This project is inspired by our students. It could not exist without the scholarly fruit harvested from the relationships between teachers and students. In particular, students from Heather Woods' Contemporary Rhetorical Theory graduate class and undergraduate classes in Rhetoric in Western Thought and The Rhetoric of Social Movements studied memes alongside us, participating in the struggles and delights of rhetorically engaging an emerging genre of political discourse. Calvin Horne and Jeremy Williams shared with us several of the memes referenced in this volume. Students in Leslie Hahner's Theories and Methods of Visual Communication supplied astute observations about digital propaganda. We have also learned from one another as teacher and student, each occupying both roles in various ways throughout our tenures. We continue to learn from our students and endeavor to give them our very best insights on pressing matters. This work has helped us reach toward that end and reminded us to continually wrestle with the ever-changing conditions of late capitalism. Ultimately, then, we dedicate this project to those who would fight for radical changes in the worlds in which we live, to the people's victory over hegemonic interests. We are far from that future, but we can use our rhetorical skills to invent new pathways toward it.

INTRODUCTION

ALT-RIGHT MEMES AND NETWORKS OF PUBLIC DISCOURSE

Heading into the 2018 midterms, a number of heavy-hitting financiers began to invest in the persuasive power of viral media. The *New York Times* reported that a wealth of enterprising liberals were raising money to fight for voters via those modes of communication at the forefront of political campaigns—spreadable content.[1] New organizations such as Stand Up America joined forces with older social media groups such as The Other 98 % and Civic Ventures to generate social media dispatches that might bolster democratic candidates and issues. Reid Hoffman, one of the creators of LinkedIn, and Mark Pincus, of Zynga, founded Win the Future, a group aiming to turn "user-generated" messages into Washington, D.C. billboards.[2] Social media users formed Facebook groups, Twitter hashtags, and Tumblr feeds to sway constituents. Companies hired meme designers to fashion aspiring viral messages.[3] Such efforts demonstrate how the battle for public opinion and political candidacies is focused on harnessing the opportunities of social media. Such investments follow the 2016 election in which conservative, often vicious, memetic imagery played a significant part in the outcomes. Indeed, the vast majority of viral social media messages toward the end of the election were either pro-Trump or anti-Clinton.[4] Post-election, bolstering the reach of digital content entrenches the battle to win the hearts and clicks of voters.

These entrepreneurial efforts are predicated on the unprecedented outcomes of the 2016 election—a contest that has come to be known aptly as the meme election.[5] During this period, a number of actors deployed prolific amounts of visual internet memes to benefit presidential candidates and political parties. Memes were far more influential to public discourse than scholars have begun to grasp fully. Yet, memes, as we will show, became one of the most important persuasive channels for the contest and the political machinations that followed. That status rests predominantly on the role of the Alt-right, who became a pernicious force during this time based largely on those who fashioned memes on 4chan and reddit. While we cannot know if Alt-right memes swayed voters, these images nevertheless created a significant impact on public culture during the election. Because of the shocking and hateful tenor of Alt-right memes, these discourses became a regressive force on public culture, ultimately stultifying exchange. For his part, Donald Trump benefitted from these tactics and, as we will show, demonstrated his support in numerous ways. Such claims do not discount the massive impact of third party candidates, voter-suppression, or Russian propaganda on the outcomes of the election, but rather underscore another way voters were addressed during the contest and in the months that followed.

The Alt-right has become a significant social force in recent years, generating an incredible amount of attention and interest through innovative media tactics, especially those visual memes deployed in the months leading up to the presidential election. 4chan is an imageboard while reddit is a digital forum; both are places where users can post under a pseudonym or anonymously on a variety of topics.[6] Of course, 4chan is popularly known as the birthplace of memes and a wide swath of creative content. Reddit has followed suit as a place for invention and discussion. Each site boasts millions of users, totaling over 350 million in April of 2018.[7] In recent years, the Alt-right on both 4chan and reddit began using memes as tactical propaganda. The apotheosis of this mode of visual engagement seemed to be the 2016 election. Users associated with Alt-right message boards launched a massive meme campaign to promote the election of Donald Trump and impede Hillary Clinton's chances of victory. In this context, memes refer to concepts and images that spread virally across culture, largely through social media platforms. In their most popular instantiation, visual memes are used for humor, political claims, visual short hands, and more. In a number of boards on 4chan and reddit, visual, static memes became a crucial site for advancing not simply the election of Trump but engendering a significant shift in public culture. The

Alt-right made tactical use of memes to create a public presence and attract new members.

The Alt-right (with attempts at rebranding using the title the New Right) is a loose collection of social media users and boards, public personalities, and content platforms that often adopt libertarian or far right advocacy. The Alt-right commonly espouses claims, including but not limited to, support for white supremacy, opposition to feminism, rejection of identity-based rights, exclusive immigration policies, and an abhorrence of political correctness. The Alt-right capitalizes on those modes of communication prominent in the digital sphere. Major personalities identified with the Alt-right include Richard Spencer, Milo Yiannopoulos, and YouTuber PewDiePie. YouTube alone has enabled Alt-right figures to attract an audience of millions.[8] Content platforms such as Breitbart have helped legitimize the views of the Alt-right. Recent research suggests that the headlines of Breitbart and similar news agencies "successfully set the agenda for the conservative media sphere, but also strongly influenced the broader media agenda, in particular coverage of Hillary Clinton."[9] In select forums and boards, 4chan and reddit users often refer to the election of Donald Trump as a result of meme magic—the tactical use of memes supposedly changed mainstream culture and politics. The election of Trump—and the belief that their memes played a role—has resulted in these boards continuing to use memes to push an agenda. On our view, the most significant tactic of the Alt-right is its use of memes to both lure mainstream devotees and direct larger public discussions. Memes are the nodal points in the ecosystem of this far right collective. The rise of Alt-right digital media, then, is of serious concern in that discourses emerging from this stance play a prominent role in public culture.

The memes developed on Alt-right boards do not stay in these enclaves but travel outward across social media platforms, indicating the reach and significance of such modes of address. In the months leading up to the 2016 election, memes created on 4chan and reddit moved rapidly from these locales to mainstream sites such as Facebook and Twitter. A specific image of Pepe the Frog, the poster symbol of the Alt-right, even traveled from these discussion boards to candidate Trump's Twitter feed.[10] During the campaign, Trump retweeted several extremist images developed on 4chan and reddit.[11] Of course, these retweets should not be surprising. Donald Trump's campaign team had staffers monitor reddit and 4chan boards, communicate with users, and direct effective content to the social media director.[12] Such patterns have not abated since the election. In early July 2017, President Trump retweeted a GIF that showed him pummeling a figure of CNN (See Fig. I.1). The GIF was created by a reddit user who "had a history of tweeting anti-Semitic and racist memes."[13] In this way, Alt-right memes are now part of presidential public address and comprise a significant number of messages on most social media platforms.

Figure I.1: Can't Stop the Trump Train.

Memes are an exemplary persuasive mechanism for the Alt-right insofar as this imagery is especially compelling for its target audience and helps to proliferate an Alt-right agenda, even as insiders disagree about its specific goals. Angela Nagle argues in *Kill All Normies* that the collective is a contentious group that is often "warring and sectarian" such that a committed political ideology is difficult to codify.[14] Yet, the Alt-right congeals and converts through its mediated tactics.[15] In particular, the social media strategies of the Alt-right have influenced the way politics informs public culture. Of its media tactics, memes are the tactic *par excellence* as they have the most social traction. As these images traveled from message boards to the mainstream, memes flagged the work of the Alt-right and generated journalistic coverage. Such coverage helped to legitimize the Alt-right and provided a mainstream platform for its views.[16] Memes operate as palpable propaganda for the Alt-right. Douglas Haddow acknowledges that viral short hands have often been used for persuasive effect.[17] Yet, as Haddow notes, "What's novel here is an inversion of control—political memes are no longer rare flashes of uncensored personality or intensely manicured visual messages. They are now born from the swamps of the internet in real time, distributed from the bottom up."[18]

Moreover, memes have attracted those who do not consider themselves ideologues but are instead invested in the irreverence of the Alt-right or memes generally. Memes are a gateway for the radicalization of outsiders to far right advocacies. Nagle argues that "the alt-right today could never have had any connection to the mainstream" without "the image- and humor-based culture of the irreverent meme factory of 4chan and later 8chan that gave the alt-right its youthful energy, with its transgression and hacker tactics."[19] Memes enabled the Alt-right considerable suasory power in terms of recruitment and attracting media attention. Memes are not just one part of how the Alt-right communicates—they are the most important rhetorical tool it uses.

Yet, memes as part of the Alt-right arsenal have not received significant scholarly attention. Though there have been numerous studies on Anonymous, 4chan, and reddit, as well as robust attention given to memes and virality as a whole, the dramatic outcome of the 2016 election marks the importance of investigating the Alt-right's influence on public culture.[20] A few books and a growing collection of journal articles are at the fledgling stages of research seeking to understand the culture of the Alt-right and the tactics used by its members.[21] Patent in popular journalism and scholarship on the topic is a diminution of the work of memes or a lack of sophisticated engagement with their suasory role. Those who write about Alt-right memes often do so by attempting to decode "meme magic" as a manifestation of chaos magic. They identify ritualistic interpretations of memetic symbols on particular message boards.[22] Others will write about the culture of these sites and how specific ideological patterns structure broader public tactics, sometimes referencing memes.[23] There is little dedicated work on Alt-right memes as persuasive tactics in and of themselves, especially as these memes change the contours of public discourse. Such focus is necessary, especially if we heed Nagle's insight that the Alt-right rarely congeals around a singular or coherent ideology. Instead, the work of memes is important precisely because these images can be disarticulated from their creators, who may or may not espouse a particular political viewpoint, who nevertheless fashion memes that impact public culture in rather important ways. Memes are not simply one tactic for the Alt-right—they are the primary rhetorical mechanism grounding its broader work and linking outsiders to its radical views. To grasp how this collective has been successful, there must be a robust interrogation of the rhetorical work of memes.

This volume analyzes the memes of the Alt-right from their development on the boards of 4chan and reddit to their circulation across mainstream media sites. We argue that Alt-right memes impact public culture by stultifying discourse and thereby shaping the ways publics congeal. More specifically, memes are the mechanism that helps proliferate white nationalism and exclusionary politics by spreading algorithmically, often in ways that are difficult to identify easily. We focus on several boards, but dedicate most of our attention to two specific sites: politically incorrect or /pol/ on 4chan and r/the_donald/ on reddit. Our goal is to analyze the persuasive principles used to design memes, with the understanding that memes are generated in these sites to target and lure outsiders to the worldviews of those on 4chan and reddit. Thus, we explore the work of these memes in galvanizing political candidates and issues, as well as spreading extremist, often racist, views. Memes are not simply humorous short hands, or pithy assertions, but play a significant role in the machinations of politics and the ways the public comes to understand and respond to their government and compatriots. To grasp the radicalization of the American electorate, scholars must engage at the forefront of politics. At the present juncture, that forefront is the rhetoric of memes. Memes are part of an overarching shift in public culture that requires scholarly consideration. The Alt-right has capitalized on memes as a mode of public address. Our goal is to analyze the architecture of the persuasive communiqués that have helped build the Alt-right agenda.

The Rhetoric of Memes

This project begins by taking memes seriously as rhetorical images that are designed to move audiences and ultimately shape the larger culture. Rhetorical studies have traditionally focused on meaningful modes of public address—presidential speeches, social movements, and public debate. To study these events rhetorically was to analyze their persuasive principles or the means through which the speaker or movement responded to an exigence to sway an audience. Today, the study of rhetoric also examines how forms of address shape public culture. In this way, rhetoric shapes both a specific audience response and the larger culture in which audiences are immersed. Images, including memes, are significant to the ways audiences are rhetorically addressed and moved. Members of 4chan and reddit understand memes as modes of communication that promulgate their views both inside and outside their enclaves. As Whitney Phillips notes, users sometimes refer to their skills as "knowing how to rhetoric."[24] Memes employ particular features that aim to persuade viewers. Our goal is to interrogate both the suasory features board users espouse and the actual ways memes work as rhetorical devices. Thus, we use our training as rhetorical critics to understand the principles users proclaim as significant to their methods just as we analyze the functional mechanisms that make some memes travel far and reach broadly.

Memes are crucial means of rhetorically addressing audiences within this cultural milieu. Their visual variations and quick replication enable memes to reach a wide set of viewers. Memes are efficient as images that can quickly disseminate a political agenda. Internet memes are constructed and reconfigured hundreds of times with one still image or GIF providing the visual foundation for its considerable afterlife. In the narrow sense, these images are rhetorical insofar as they can be designed to persuade audiences for a particular purpose. For instance, Occupy Wall Street (OWS) memed the image of Lieutenant John Pike pepper spraying Occupy protestors at UC Davis. Many of the memes created by OWS provided a visual synecdoche of the ideas motivating the movement: a figure of the state overpowering a larger, defenseless group of students.[25] Memes are fashioned with particular rhetorical features to charm audiences into replication or in an attempt to induce other specific actions. Ryan M. Milner argues that memes are multimodal texts that are appropriated, possess resonance, existing as collective phenomena that are spreadable.[26] Building on earlier studies, Limor Shifman suggests that memes that circulate widely are more likely to exhibit six features that abet virality: "*positivity*, *provocation of high-arousal emotions*, *participation*, *packaging*, *prestige*, and *positioning*."[27] Milner and Shifman delineate the general qualities of memes and the mechanisms that facilitate their speedy circulation. Put into the language of rhetorical studies, these scholars demarcate the mechanisms that invite the audiences' admiration (likes, hearts, retweets, etc.) of memes and drive replication.

Yet, memes are also rhetorical in a broader sense insofar as they become a propagandistic means of affectively impacting both audiences and culture. These images are cunning because memes typically conceal their status as persuasive texts. As Shifman writes, the meme works "as a living and changing entity that is *incorporated in the body and mind of its hosts*."[28] When rhetorical texts such as these precipitate embodied or pre-conscious residuals, scholars read them as creating affective resonance. Eric S. Jenkins maintains that memes illustrate how "affective capacities" structure the "encounter between viewers/rhetors and images."[29] In this sense, memes are both direct forms of persuasion but also modes of rhetorical address that may work more obliquely. It is important, then, for scholars to analyze the specific ways that memes function as selected images or modes of address that travel across the media landscape. Sometimes, memes are obvious attempts to persuade the populace. In other instances, memes conceal or hide their rhetorical work, even as they sway viewers.

Alt-right memes are a unique instantiation of this overarching visual form, exhibiting features and circulatory patterns that indicate a rhetorical difference from other memes. While the images may employ some of the attributes outlined by Milner and Shifman, they usually exhibit other qualities. To wit, high arousal emotions and appropriation are significant to Alt-right memes but positivity and prestige are not essential to their virality. Moreover, these basic features do little to indicate the motivated reasons for why Alt-right memes travel in particular patterns. For instance, President Trump retweeted a meme designed in reddit. The meme was a political cartoon of a train emblazoned with a Trump logo (See Fig. I.1). The train collided with a human figure, stamped with the CNN logo. The caption read: "Fake News Can't Stop the Trump Train." As it relates to the categories outlined by Shifman, the image was an appropriation, it aroused high emotions, it was a collective phenomenon, and it was a multi-modal, spreadable meme. Yet, these basic characteristics say very little about the rhetorical resonance of this image. This image is both a dog whistle to Alt-right audiences and an alienating image to liberal viewers. Moreover, these basic categories fail to detail how this image polarizes audiences or the modes through which it marks white supremacy—and how those actions facilitate its travels. By exploring the specific rhetoric of Alt-right memes, we may better understand their circulation and the ways they shape the larger culture.

Memes certainly play a pivotal role in public life and may generate larger outcomes than popularly imagined. Milner argues that memes facilitate individual expression and participation in larger collectives, especially for those who may be disenfranchised from mainstream forms of communication.[30] In this sense, memes broaden access points and generate inventional opportunities for outsiders. Other scholars suggest that memes are a resource from which participants can fashion arguments, new modes of activism, and other modes of public engagement.[31] Memes, then, are not simply pithy images or rote modes of communication. Instead, they are tools that can be deployed in a multitude of ways. It is their flexibility that allows them to be used as novel rhetorical resources.[32] Insofar as the meme can be redesigned, appropriated, and deployed for new audiences, it affords a multiplicity of rhetorical possibilities. The considerable participation in the creation and circulation of memes suggests that a meme can reach a broad set of audiences, a potentiality that serves as the ground for its rhetorical finesse.

Memes are also rhetorically important to the temporality of public attention given the speed of their circulation. Like much viral media, memes are known for incredibly quick propagation and movement. The speed of the meme is part of its rhetorical power. Shifman contends that virality itself is a form of persuasion, noting that Elihu Katz's and Paul Lazarsfeld's understanding of "personal influence" indicates how viral content travels through affinity routes—your friends, family, and contacts. Building on the work of W. Lance Bennett and Alexandra Segerberg, Shifman writes that "memes play an important role" in the "coordinated actions" of social movements in that they are "personalized, adapted by individuals to tell their own stories."[33] For Bennett and Segerberg, it is the largescale network that creates a social movement with new and effective advocacy. The network facilitates the breadth and speed of the meme's travels. The meme often begins in smaller, digital enclaves and then spreads virally to a whole host of other sites via the wealth of network nodes. The relationships that build that network may engender a sympathetic viewpoint or interpretation of viral content, thereby shaping the ways publics encounter and understand memes.

Overall, memes are important rhetorical texts that use their flexibility and circulation to move audiences. For social movements and users on networks, memes present significant opportunities for advocacy, creativity, and investment. The specific features of memes are often deployed by creators for a variety of rhetorical purposes. In these ways, memes can operate rhetorically as explicit or implicit means of audience identification, resonance, or persuasion. Yet, while scholars are beginning to grasp how memes open up the advocacy possibilities of social movements and individuals, those same rubrics for analysis may not apply to Alt-right memes. By interrogating the specific ways that Alt-right memes are designed, travel, and shape audience response, we glean a stronger understanding of the current political climate and the ways these memes stultify public discourse.

Memes and Public Culture

Memes play a significant role in public culture, one predicated on the creation and maintenance of social identities and values. Shifman writes that memes facilitate the "construction of group identity and social boundaries."[34] Carl Chen concurs and suggests that memes developed by 4chan users are participating in their own public sphere, identifying a particularly positive outcome from the creative process: "increasing diversity in taste, creating a unified identity, and expressing political agendas."[35] For a number of scholars, memes mark the creative and interactive processes of the collective.[36] Memes, as fashioned in digital enclaves, are images that highlight the values of the group, their identities, and the negotiated processes of participation. We explore these aspects of meme creation in chapter one, describing how board culture contributes to the development of memes and the standards that privilege certain expressions over others.

Yet, memes are not simply important to the collectives working in 4chan and reddit but also respond to and shape a larger set of values and principles—those of public culture. When we refer to a public culture, we mean the available repertoire of social practices that structure discourse, affective investments, patterns of thinking, and daily practices. Robert Hariman and John Louis Lucaites suggest culture is "a distinctively coherent set of social practices" as they are articulated through "habituation."[37] When it comes to digital public cultures, that coherence is a bit more difficult to theorize. Nathan Rambukkana argues that the "form and matter" of network "assemblages can take on different emergent qualities based on the particular actants that are at work in shaping each…unique and individual event."[38] Memes are specific modes of rhetorical address that shape public culture. In this sense, memes are one mode of emergent possibility. They are not simply reflections of the culture of 4chan and reddit—though they are related to such sites of origin. Instead, memes are active and responsive rhetorical texts that play a part in the ongoing negotiations of public culture.

Memes emerge alongside the digital public that shapes and is shaped by their creation. Memes are fashioned through robust digital participation, a mode of invention that indicates how these images are a key way communities and publics congeal. Nissenbaum and Shifman argue that memes "function as part of a culture, contributing to the set of ideas around which communities gather and act."[39] As we detail in chapter one, users on 4chan's /b/ board indicate their adherence to community norms and protocols by developing memes that speak to the culture in which they are immersed. Similarly, users of forums on both reddit and 4chan must follow community patterns if they are to feel included, if they seek their memes to be valued, or if they seek to avoid ridicule.[40] Certainly, users on /pol/ and r/the_donald/ are policed in terms of their ability to fashion memes that stay in keeping with the standards of the board. The community of users comes together via memetic discourse, among other discourses, by speaking to the larger trends and values of the board. Memes thereby articulate and reify the normative culture of users. Yet, memes are also sites of creation. Norms are not static but modified over time. Memes are a key place where innovation is essential to both community membership—one must be able to build on the standards to show competence—but also to the success and growth of that board.[41] Invention is a form of social capital such that users must create novel memes that nevertheless remain wedded to community standards.[42] The constitution of the public on these boards is predicated on the juxtaposition between stability and change.

Memes are also sites of public investment through their circulation outside of their digital origins into the mainstream. Some memes speak to insiders on 4chan and reddit and often focus on working with or innovating community standards. Memes designed for external audiences operate differently. Kate M. Miltner maintains that once memes move to the mainstream, the social capital they once held diminishes for insiders as that same capital increases for outsiders. LOLCats memes, for example, become rejected "by the collectives that created them" once they are a technology for anyone.[43] For memes designed specifically for publicity or propagandistic purposes, the shift in their value remains; however, their capital for persuading the masses is increased for users on the boards. That is, if a meme is successful at moving from the original board to the mainstream and is heavily circulated, that meme becomes one to imitate. The image still articulates what is valued and persuasive, but now the public constituted by the meme's circulation is broader. However, this wider public remains somewhat tethered to the norms enunciated on the original boards. That is, while social media users may spread or remake the meme for different purposes, the circulation of Alt-right memes often traces the aesthetics and attitudes of their creators. Such memes remain indebted to the patterns of their conception and may suture such communicative tactics to novel re-creations.

The circulation of Alt-right memes is the cardinal feature of their impact on public culture. The travels of memes are what enables the articulation and re-articulation of values and standards from 4chan and reddit to the larger public. Memes become points of recognition for particular Alt-right arguments and manifestations of its public presence. Alt-right memes, then, travel with the specter of Alt-right advocacies, unless the original memes are changed dramatically. Previous studies of memes and imagery have indicated that the circulation of these visuals opens up their constitutive possibilities.[44] Memes are highly manipulable imagery that can be changed and redirected toward new political and social realities. As such, these images are difficult to theorize as indebted to the goals of their creators. Their circulation often ensures they are a radical image, always open to reinterpretation and reuse. Ariella Azoulay writes that photography's temporality is one of "an ever-expanding series of encounters."[45] The same is true of memes, which renew in each click the possibilities indexed by their creation and re-creation. Yet, with Alt-right memes in particular, their circulation often echoes and reifies the claims designed to travel with them. Many of these memes remain imbued, marked by the imprint of the Alt-right, especially when the meme circulates without visual editing. In part, as we explore in chapter two, those goals are entrenched given the responses of the Alt-right. Nearly any attempt to resignify an Alt-right meme by outsiders is often minimized by the subsequent proliferation of extremist memes. In this sense, the Alt-right fights back against attempts to redeploy its imagery by inundating social media with memes. While radical possibilities of rhetorical invention remain with more general memes, Alt-right memes often iterate the advocacy of extremists.

Users of 4chan and reddit design memes as purposeful rhetorical devices—memes help to organize political actions and recruit new devotees. In August 2016, white supremacists protested the removal of a statue of Confederate General Robert E. Lee in Charlottesville, South Carolina. In the course of their demonstration, three people died and many were injured. The incident sparked national interest in how these young, largely millennial men became radicalized as white supremacists. Certainly, many of the protestors present at the rally were attracted to the cause for a variety of reasons. But, as explained by those at the protest, memes were often the method of organizing and attracting new adherents. *Vice* interviewed feature writer Robert "Azzmador" Ray of The Daily Stormer, a white supremacist website, who explained that their physical presence meant "that we are showing to this class of parasitic, anti-white vermin that this is our country."[46] He continued to say that the demonstrators were "stepping off the internet in a big way."[47] They had been organizing, specifically by "spreading our memes."[48] For some members of the Alt-right, memes became a method to organize and create new white supremacists. One of the main organizers at Charlottesville, Christopher Cantwell, claimed he turned from libertarianism to the Alt-right because it "had better memes."[49] One young man at the rally even indicated that he was compelled to join the demonstration given that it was fun to "say white power."[50] Once the violence at the rally proved fearsome to this young man, he removed his Vanguard America shirt (an internet-purchase t-shirt supporting a white supremacist group), and tried to proclaim that he wasn't truly a white supremacist.[51] Here, visual memes and memetic imitation become a tactic for both earnest adherents to the Alt-right but also provide cover for those who wish to enact white supremacy, even as they disavow their complicity.

Memes also become a way to brand the Alt-right such that like-minded folks have a way to proliferate their ideas and to recognize those with whom they align. Pepe the Frog is a useful case study here—an exemplar we analyze fully in chapter two. Pepe was not initially an Alt-right symbol. Yet, users on 4chan and reddit transformed him into a poster-child for the Alt-right and white nationalism more generally. When that symbol appeared on mainstream sites, users found their viewpoint sanctioned. For instance, it was considered a triumph by 4chan and reddit users in /pol/ and r/the_donald/ when candidate Trump retweeted a Pepe image. In this instance, a viral image rewarded the branding work of the collective. Likewise, when other social media users posted or retweeted Pepe, those posts became a way to identify affinities. Yet, such recognizability was also important to counter responses. When Hillary Clinton reviled Pepe as a symbol of white nationalism, that same moment is a marker of memetic spread. The meme has been codified and traveled to further sites. Eliciting a response from Clinton—regardless of what she said—demonstrated the efficacy of the Alt-right: it had made her respond to a frog meme. In this sense, recognizability is key to the spread of the Alt-right brand and pernicious perspective.

Alt-right community building necessarily divides insiders from outsiders. The rhetorical work of the meme is to attract those who can identify with the meme and sow division from outsiders. The first goal is to create an image that might make extremist ideas more palatable to moderate or mainstream individuals. A humorous or often satiric image entices audiences to consider Alt-right claims or to at least spread those viewpoints to others. Memes become the place where Alt-right ideas are noticed and debated—a mode of engagement that mainstreams the advocacies of the far right. Whereas older generations of Nazis, Klansmen, and related far right political viewpoints used rallies, books, or other modes of communication, the Alt-right speaks to general audiences through memes. As we detail throughout this volume, memes are designed with a host of rhetorical features to prompt identification with the Alt-right. Just as memes draw likeminded folks together, memes can also separate citizens by pitting them against one another. 4chan and reddit meme generators use these images to distinguish themselves from liberals and drive a wedge between liberals and moderate conservatives, sometimes even moderate liberals. Alt-right memes regularly vilify the left as absurd actors who seek the destruction of the country. The ways liberals are depicted by these memes redefine the lines of insiders and outsiders, using memes to delineate a collective identity based on crafting liberals as enemies of the good.

Additionally, 4chan and reddit users deploy memes to anger leftist social media users. As we analyze in chapter five, the goal is to entrench leftist disaffection, to stir a reaction such that the left alienates mainstream voters. Some memes thus anticipate leftist response to shift the grounds of debate such that audiences might focus on the supposed hegemony of left-wing demands. Often, these tactics appropriate formerly leftist tools for this purpose. With the ideological tools of the left now deployed by the right, the left is to be without recourse, to erode their so-called safe spaces. The objective is to reposition the left as the establishment that must be railed against by those who claim to be disenfranchised by a progressive agenda. Such memes have succeeded if they anger liberals to respond with vitriol and outrage. The larger the reaction, the more successful the demonstration.

If scholars are to understand the rise in both publicity and numbers for the Alt-right, we must study its memes and the rhetorical principles they demonstrate. Memes are the gateway to a more vicious advocacy. These images organize the Alt-right and collect adherents who might otherwise consider themselves dissimilar to neo-Nazis. The basic function of a meme is to proliferate, to create fertile ground for this extremism. For the last thirty years, memetic theory has suggested that memes work by spreading virally.[52] Memes employ an evolutionary impulse—the goal of the meme is to infect and spread. As Davi Johnson writes, the "meme is self-replicating, at least up to a critical threshold, because the more adopters it infects, the more others will be exposed to it."[53] While a meme can be any viral phenomenon—an idea, a habit, a fashion trend—visual internet memes work by spreading through online networks of distribution. When a meme is seen, retweeted, or shared via social media, it has fulfilled its evolutionary principle. The users of /pol/ and r/the_donald/ understand the basic circulation of memes and employ them to disseminate ideas and invite action.

Alt-right memes play upon the networks fueling virality. For instance, many meme makers create an image displaying an oppositional stance. Audiences who replicate that image may understand themselves as adopting a renegade perspective—a small part of the defiance that is the Alt-right. It is this resistant posturing that fuels the meme's ability to spread quickly and reach far. Memes are thus rhetorical images that influence insiders on message forums but, more importantly, are tactically used to convince mainstream audiences to find affinity with far right claims. Given this, scholars must engage with the tactical elements of meme creation and distribution. These images are fashioned with ideas about audience persuasion and adaptation in mind. The goal is to use affective appeals, stretched reasoning, simplistic claims, and other tactics to move audiences toward extreme positions. If these rhetorical appeals are successful in initiating the meme's circulation, its continued proliferation is more likely. The ultimate result is that the Alt-right attracts a wider audience. By engaging with such rhetorical strategies, scholars might discover the viral force of these images. Memes are not simply heavily circulated images nor ritualistic activities. They are best studied as visual and verbal appeals designed to persuade a broad set of audiences. The rhetorical action of memes is both to normalize and generate devotion to extremism but also to organize and congeal the Alt-right and its modes of publicity.

This book analyzes how Alt-right memes impact public culture by precipitating investment in dangerous ideals and stultifying political discourse. Memes structure and organize the Alt-right as a recognizable group. By announcing the norms and attitudes of the group, memes aid in tabulating an Alt-right collective. The rhetorical actions of memes also help to lure devotees to the Alt-right. Those actors who are attracted to the Alt-right because they have "better memes," as with Cantwell and others, are radicalized in their political actions or enabled to dissociate themselves from white supremacy or extremism by assuming a playful stance toward it. Additionally, the use of memes to declare and circulate particular claims directs the nature of public discourse. As memes such as Pepe the Frog take center stage in public discourse, the nature of discussion remains bound to extremist claims of white supremacy and more. That is, even if actors (e.g., politicians, journalists) repudiate the claims of the Alt-right, they are nevertheless moored to the Alt-right via the imposition to respond to the assertions and ideas of the collective. Public discourse is thereby stultified, or at least unproductive, when public figures and the people are compelled to respond to memes. As we will discuss in chapters two and four, the massive public attention given to memes shifts the focus and flow of public discourse. These memes are capable of radically changing the topics addressed by politicians, journalists, and the public. In these ways, Alt-right memes have both stagnated and directed the nature of discourse within public culture.

Framework of the Book

In this volume, we use rhetorical criticism to understand the ways memes have contributed to the current political climate. Our training in rhetorical criticism enriches contemporary discussion on memes of the Alt-right and on the suasory power of the Alt-right. Although there have been a few scholarly investigations on this topic, there is a dearth of scholarly inquiry on the memes of the Alt-right. Rhetorical analysis supplies a necessary investigation into the principles that fuel the replication and spread of these memes. Specifically, rhetorical analysis illuminates the persuasive mechanisms the Alt-right uses to attract new members and direct public attention and conversation. Memes are not simply one aspect of the Alt-right's public address, they are the linchpin of the organization and the images provoking proliferation of its messages. Investigation of the specific operations of persuasion and resonance enable us to have a stronger understanding of how the Alt-right has grown, as well as the principles that can be redeployed for new political realities and modes of public discourse.

Our work predominately examines two boards on 4chan and reddit most readily associated with the memes of the Alt-right: 4chan's /pol/ or politically incorrect and reddit's r/the_donald/. These forums are not the only ones where memes of the Alt-right are created and circulated, and we may at times discuss other sites and images, including associated boards and journalistic coverage of relevant histories and events. However, the majority of discourses on publicizing the agenda of the Alt-right have emerged from these two sites.[54] Focusing on these two boards also allows us to specify the norms and strategies of those interacting, and the tensions entailed. To be sure, the Alt-right is not a cohesive whole. In the same way, users on these boards are not strict ideologues that articulate a singular worldview. There is ample disputation and conversation on what is needed to organize an Alt-right agenda and the best ways to create and circulate memes. Similarly, the nature of discussion on these boards changes quickly such that even public figures of the Alt-right—for instance, Christopher Cantwell who spoke to *Vice*—are often rebuked for their ineffectiveness, even moments after being celebrated. Studying these two boards with nuance and sophistication is our goal. We account for the general discussion and the memes created while we attend in detail to significant objections and opposition. Doing so allows us a stronger sense of the nature of their rhetorical work and the ongoing ways board users respond to changing exigencies.

The time period under consideration spans from mid-2016 and continues into the middle of 2018. Our narrow time span centers the analysis on the actions and events that have enabled the Alt-right to develop a considerable public presence. Foremost among these events is the 2016 election, which witnessed users of 4chan and reddit engaging in a calculated campaign to meme Donald Trump into the White House. We therefore begin our analysis by studying the early memes that marked the Alt-right's importance and set the tone for how the group and the larger public would come to understand the stakes of such imagery. Our interrogation continues by examining the ongoing significance of memes to the public presence of the Alt-right. We attend to the influence of memes as they appeared on President Trump's Twitter feed, the memetic generation of the demonstrations in Charlottesville, and a whole host of other moments that indicate a correspondence between memes and the publicity of the Alt-right. In a relatively short time-span, the Alt-right has taken up a considerable amount of space in public discourse. Our investigation follows this explosive moment and grapples with its persistent influence.

To engage with the memes of the Alt-right and their persuasive impact, we employ our training as rhetorical critics. That is, we analyze the suasory principles evident in both the memes proper and the ways rhetorical operations are discussed and debated. Our collection methods follow general protocols for social media research. We study the images themselves, their circulation, and the practices (e.g., imageboard discussions) that give rise to memes.[55] We use screen shots and other methods of saving textual data to provide a basis for analysis. When available, we use existing data sets or collect information from the circulation of particular hashtags, images, and the like. Given that the specific content on 4chan and reddit decays very quickly (often within twenty-four hours), our methodology captures relevant information and images such that we may analyze the initial moment of creation (or re-creation) and the image's afterlife off the board. Given the way data withers on these boards, and the fact that the Alt-right uses a multiplicity of social media to convey messages, we are limited to the data we can digitally reap as we engage in on-the-ground research. Yet, our research methods collect data until we reach a point of saturation: when the claims we assert are proven significant through patterns of discourse. Using this data set, we are then able to interrogate the rhetorical principles users espouse as important to the Alt-right production of memes and its agenda more broadly.

Yet, we also employ our rhetorical training to compare and contrast the persuasive intent of users and the actual rhetorical machinations that either impede or effectuate the work of memes. Certainly, not all memes created on /pol/ or r/the_donald/ are viral media that proliferate an Alt-right agenda. Only some memes are capable of being picked up and circulated rapidly for a broad set of audiences and some circulate only internally within certain forums or boards. Even if users attempt to create each meme as a viral phenomenon, not every meme is potent as such. Moreover, just as meme generators insist that their memes work with one particular goal or tactic in mind, that assumption may not materialize in the circulation or uptake of the meme. As such, we analyze the compelling rhetorical functions of these memes—an assessment that may sometimes align with or deviate from the stated intentions of board users. As Edwin Black claimed in 1965, rhetorical judgment does not simply examine the text on its own but in relationship to the interactions between rhetor and audience.[56] Given that the rhetorical situation engendered by the circulation of memes may enable a radical interpretation, we must not simply consider a single relationship between rhetor and audience but a multitude of perspectives as related to a meme. Jim Ridolfo and Dànielle Nicole DeVoss have characterized texts that assume a multiplicity of audiences through the concept of "rhetorical velocity," wherein the assumption of appropriation is key to rhetorical invention.[57] In this sense, we employ rhetorical criticism to understand the ways these memes proliferate and the modes of address that allow a successful meme to be appropriated (shared, retweeted) and spread quickly.

The chapters that follow map out the rhetorical strategies at stake in Alt-right memes and how these images structure the agenda and principles of the Alt-right and subsequently, impact public culture. After an initial chapter that lays out the important histories of the digital sites we study and of memes specifically, the remaining chapters attend to the ways memes amplify the Alt-right and embolden its rhetorical finesse. We begin by explaining the role of memetic iconicity in constituting the Alt-right and shaping how this, often haphazard and contentious, group works. The next two chapters explain the messaging strategies of memes outside their digital enclaves such that they normalize extreme views. We pay particular attention to the ways these images mark a resistant posturing to interrupt and reposition mainstream values. We then turn to memes that alienate and silence the opposition, such that nearly any response is absurd or ineffectual. We conclude by offering an assessment of what happens to public culture when memes drive political and cultural discussions. Our goal with this arrangement is to follow Alt-right memes from their participatory creation, to their circulation, and conclude by considering the ramifications for these memes for public culture. The advantage of this approach is that it offers a conceptually rich account of the persuasive principles of meme invention and circulation.

To better grasp the radicalization of increasingly substantial portions of the American populace, we must attend to the rhetorical work of memes. Without an understanding of how moderates can be moved to the extreme (and perhaps back again) through the stealthy influence of memes, we cannot predict nor manage what will happen when the next set of propagandists uses memes for their own purposes. If democratic *praxis* can be radically shifted through the work of these digital images, scholars must begin to take stock of how memes persuade, influence, and entice audiences. We must begin, then, by attempting to understand how these digital sites birthed memes and the ramifications of that origination for the rise of the Alt-right.

Notes

1. Kevin Roose, "Political Donors Put Their Money Where the Memes Are," *New York Times*, August 6, 2017, https://www.nytimes.com/2017/08/06/business/media/political-donors-put-their-money-where-the-memes-are.html.
2. Roose, "Political Donors."
3. Francesca Wallace, "Gucci Just Hired Professional Meme Makers, Are Now Making Memes," *Vogue*, March 20, 2017, http://www.vogue.com.au/fashion/news/gucci+memes+brand+hires+professional+meme+makers,42220; Peter A. Berry, "Professional Meme Maker Claims Interscope Hires Him to Help Promote Artists," *XXL Magazine*, July 31, 2017, http://www.xxlmag.com/news/2017/07/professional-meme-maker-claims-interscope-hires-him-promote-artists/.
4. Walid Magdy and Kareem Darwish, "Trump vs. Hillary Analyzing Viral Tweets during US Presidential Elections 2016," *ArXiv*, October 2016, https://arxiv.org/pdf/1610.01655.pdf.
5. Ryan M. Milner and Whitney Phillips, "Dark Magic: The Memes That Made Donald Trump's Victory," *US Election Analysis 2016*, http://www.electionanalysis2016.us/us-election-analysis-2016/section-6-internet/dark-magic-the-memes-that-made-donald-trumps-victory/; Rodney Taveira and Emma Balfour, "How Donald Trump Won the 2016 Meme Wars," *The Conversation*, November 29, 2016, http://theconversation.com/how-

donald-trump-won-the-2016-meme-wars-68580; Dawn Chmielewski, "Internet Memes Emerge as 2016 Election's Political Dog Whistle," *USA Today*, September 30, 2016, https://www.usatoday.com/story/tech/news/2016/09/30/internet-memes-white-house-election-president/91272490/; Alana Levinson, "Meet the 'Meme Scientists' Who Tracked This Election's Crazy Viral Phenomena," *Splinter*, November 8, 2016, https://splinternews.com/meet-the-meme-scientists-who-tracked-this-elections-cra-1793863563.

6. Emily van der Nagel and Jordan Frith, "Anonymity, Pseudonymity, and the Agency of Online Identity: Examining the Social Practices of r/Gonewild," *First Monday* 20, no. 3 (2015).
7. "Advertise – 4chan," accessed April 20, 2018, http://www.4chan.org/advertise; "Upvote Your Advertising," accessed April 20, 2018, https://www.redditinc.com/advertising/.
8. Tom Whyman, "Why the Right Is Dominating YouTube," *Vice*, March 18, 2017, https://www.vice.com/en_us/article/3dy7vb/why-the-right-is-dominating-youtube.
9. Yochai Benkler *et al.*, "Study: Breitbart-Led Right-Wing Media Ecosystem Altered Broader Media Agenda," *Columbia Journalism Review*, March 3, 2017, https://www.cjr.org/analysis/breitbart-media-trump-harvard-study.php.
10. Adam Serwer, "It's Not Easy Being Meme," *The Atlantic*, September 13, 2016, https://www.theatlantic.com/politics/archive/2016/09/its-not-easy-being-green/499892/.
11. Caroline Simon, "5 Times Donald Trump Has Engaged with Alt-Right Racists on Twitter," *Business Insider*, July 9, 2016, http://www.businessinsider.com/donald-trump-alt-right-2016-7.
12. Ben Schreckinger, "World War Meme," *Politico*, March 3, 2017, http://politi.co/2mPM37L.
13. Garet Williams, "Donald Trump Jr. Is Fanning the Flames of the #CNNBlackmail Story," *Vox*, July 5, 2017, https://www.vox.com/policy-and-politics/2017/7/5/15921816/cnn-blackmail-donald-trump-jr-reddit-wrestling-gif-alt-right.
14. Angela Nagle, *Kill All Normies: Online Culture Wars from 4chan and Tumblr to Trump and the Alt-Right* (Winchester, UK: Zero Books, 2017), 12. Nagle's work has faced charges of plagiarism and sloppy reporting. The limited arguments we use from her have not faced such criticism. See Charles Davis, "Sloppy Sourcing Plagues 'Kill All Normies' Alt-Right Book," *The Daily Beast*, May 19, 2018, https://www.thedailybeast.com/kill-all-citations-sloppy-sourcing-plagues-kill-all-normies-book-on-sjws-and-the-alt-right; "5 Big Problems with Kill All Normies," *libcom.org*, May 24, 2018, https://libcom.org/blog/5-big-problems-angela-nagle-kill-all-normies-24052018.
15. Nagle, *Kill All Normies*, 12.
16. Benkler *et al.*, "Study: Breitbart-Led Right-Wing Media Ecosystem Altered Broader Media Agenda"; Niko Heikkilä, "Online Antagonism of the Alt-Right in the 2016 Election," *European Journal of American Studies* 12, no. 2 (2017).
17. Douglas Haddow, "Meme Warfare: How the Power of Mass Replication Has Poisoned the US Election," *The Guardian*, November 4, 2016, https://www.theguardian.com/us-news/2016/nov/04/political-memes-2016-election-hillary-clinton-donald-trump.
18. Haddow, "Meme Warfare."
19. Nagle, *Kill All Normies*, 13.
20. See, for example, Luke Goode, "Anonymous and the Political Ethos of Hacktivism," *Popular Communication* 13, no. 1 (2015): 74–86; Vyshali Manivannan, "Attaining the Ninth

Square: Cybertextuality, Gamification, and Institutional Memory on 4chan," *Enculturation*, October 10, 2012, http://enculturation.camden.rutgers.edu/attaining-the-ninth-square; Gabriella Coleman, *Hacker, Hoaxer, Whistleblower, Spy: The Many Faces of Anonymous* (Brooklyn, NY: Verso Books, 2014); Noah Hampson, "Hacktivism: A New Breed of Protest in a Networked World," *SSRN Scholarly Paper* (Rochester, NY: Social Science Research Network, 2011); Asaf Nissenbaum and Limor Shifman, "Internet Memes as Contested Cultural Capital: The Case of 4chan's /b/ Board" *New Media & Society* 19, no. 4 (2017): 483–501; Nagle, *Kill All Normies*; Matthew Trammell, "User Investment and Behavior Policing on 4chan," *First Monday* 19, no. 2 (2014); Lee Knuttila, "User Unknown: 4chan, Anonymity and Contingency," *First Monday* 16, no. 10 (2011); Laine Nooney *et al.*, "One Does Not Simply: An Introduction to the Special Issue on Internet Memes," *Journal of Visual Culture* 13, no. 3 (2014): 248–52; Heidi E. Huntington, "Pepper Spray Cop and the American Dream: Using Synecdoche and Metaphor to Unlock Internet Memes' Visual Political Rhetoric," *Communication Studies* 67, no. 1 (2016): 77–93; Ryan M. Milner, "Pop Polyvocality: Internet Memes, Public Participation, and the Occupy Wall Street Movement," *International Journal of Communication* 7 (2013): 2357–2390; Akane Kanai, "Sociality and Classification: Reading Gender, Race, and Class in a Humorous Meme," *Social Media + Society* 2, no. 4 (2016): 1–12; Limor Shifman, "The Cultural Logic of Photo-Based Meme Genres," *Journal of Visual Culture* 13, no. 3 (2014): 340–58; Jacqueline Ryan Vickery, "The Curious Case of Confession Bear: The Reappropriation of Online Macro-Image Memes," *Information, Communication & Society* 17, no. 3 (2014): 301–25; Kate M. Miltner, "'There's No Place for Lulz on LOLCats': The Role of Genre, Gender, and Group Identity in the Interpretation and Enjoyment of an Internet Meme," *First Monday* 19, no. 8 (2014).

21. See, for example, Yochai Benkler *et al.*, *Network Propaganda: Manipulation, Disinformation, and Radicalization in American Politics* (New York: Oxford University Press, 2018); Stephanie L. Hartzell, "Alt-White: Conceptualizing the 'Alt-Right' as a Rhetorical Bridge between White Nationalism and Mainstream Public Discourse," *Journal of Contemporary Rhetoric* 8, no. 3 (2018): 6–25; Kory A. Riemensperger, "Pepe's Power: Internet Memes, Constitutive Rhetoric, and Political Communities" (MA Thesis, Wake Forest University, 2018); Nagle, *Kill All Normies*; Matthew N. Lyons and Bromma, *Ctrl-Alt-Delete: An Antifascist Report on the Alternative Right* (Montreal, Quebec: Left Wing Books, 2017); George Michael, "The Rise of the Alt-Right and the Politics of Polarization in America," *Skeptic* 22, no. 2 (2017): 9–18; Evan Malmgren, "Don't Feed the Trolls," *Dissent* 64, no. 2 (2017): 9–12; Benita Heiskanen, "Meme-ing Electoral Participation," *European Journal of American Studies* 12, no. 2 (2017); Niko Heikkilä, "Online Antagonism of the Alt-Right in the 2016 Election"; Paul Mihailidis and Samantha Viotty, "Spreadable Spectacle in Digital Culture: Civic Expression, Fake News, and the Role of Media Literacies in 'Post-Fact' Society," *American Behavioral Scientist* 61, no. 4 (2017).
22. Milner and Phillips, "Dark Magic"; Abby Ohlheiser, "'We Actually Elected a Meme as President': How 4chan Celebrated Trump's Victory," *Washington Post*, November 9, 2016, https://www.washingtonpost.com/news/the-intersect/wp/2016/11/09/we-actually-elected-a-meme-as-president-how-4chan-celebrated-trumps-victory/; Schreckinger, "World War Meme"; Haddow, "Meme Warfare: How the Power of Mass Replication Has Poisoned the

US Election"; Paul Spencer, "Trump's Occult Online Supporters Believe 'Meme Magic' Got Him Elected," *Motherboard*, November 18, 2016, https://motherboard.vice.com/en_us/article/pgkx7g/trumps-occult-online-supporters-believe-pepe-meme-magic-got-him-elected.

23. See, for example, Dale Beran, "4chan: The Skeleton Key to the Rise of Trump," *Medium*, February 14, 2017, https://medium.com/@DaleBeran/4chan-the-skeleton-key-to-the-rise-of-trump-624e7cb798cb; Sophia A. McClennan, "Forget Fake News—Alt-Right Memes Could Do More Damage to Democracy," *Salon*, July 8, 2017, http://www.salon.com/2017/07/08/forget-fake-news-alt-right-memes-could-do-more-damage-to-democracy/; Heikkilä, "Online Antagonism of the Alt-Right in the 2016 Election."
24. Whitney Phillips, *This Is Why We Can't Have Nice Things: Mapping the Relationship between Online Trolling and Mainstream Culture* (Cambridge, MA: MIT Press, 2015), 126.
25. Huntington, "Pepper Spray Cop and the American Dream"; Jack Bratich, "Occupy All the Dispositifs: Memes, Media Ecologies, and Emergent Bodies Politic," *Communication and Critical/Cultural Studies* 11, no. 1 (2014): 64–73.
26. Ryan M. Milner, *The World Made Meme: Public Conversations and Participatory Media* (Cambridge, MA: MIT Press, 2016).
27. Shifman, *Memes in Digital Culture*, 26.
28. Shifman, *Memes in Digital Culture*, 56.
29. Eric S. Jenkins, "The Modes of Visual Rhetoric: Circulating Memes as Expressions," *Quarterly Journal of Speech* 100, no. 4 (2014): 462.
30. Milner, *The World Made Meme*, 217; Heather Suzanne Woods and James Alexander McVey, "#BlackLivesMatter as A Case Study in the Politics of Digital Media: Algorithms, Hashtag Publics, and Organizing Protest Online," *Teaching Media Quarterly* 4, no. 1 (2016).
31. Leslie A. Hahner, "The Riot Kiss: Framing Memes as Visual Argument," *Argumentation and Advocacy* 49, no. 3 (2013): 151–67; Huntington, "Pepper Spray Cop and the American Dream"; Bratich, "Occupy All the Dispositifs."
32. Heather Suzanne Woods, "Anonymous, Steubenville, and the Politics of Visibility: Questions of Virality and Exposure in the Case of #OpRollRedRoll and #OccupySteubenville," *Feminist Media Studies* 14, no. 6 (2014): 1096–98; James Alexander McVey and Heather Suzanne Woods, "Anti-Racist Activism and the Transformational Principles of Hashtag Publics: From #HandsUpDontShoot to #PantsUpDontLoot," *Present Tense* 5, no. 3 (2016).
33. Shifman, *Memes in Digital Culture*, 128; W. Lance Bennett and Alexandra Segerberg, *The Logic of Connective Action* (New York: Cambridge University Press, 2013).
34. Shifman, *Memes in Digital Culture*, 100.
35. Carl Chen, "The Creation and Meaning of Internet Memes in 4chan: Popular Internet Culture in the Age of Online Digital Reproduction," *Habitus* 3, no. 1 (2013): 15.
36. Noam Gal, Limor Shifman, and Zohar Kampf, "'It Gets Better': Internet Memes and the Construction of Collective Identity," *New Media & Society*, 18, no. 8 (2016): 1698–1714; Ryan M. Milner, "FCJ-156 Hacking the Social: Internet Memes, Identity Antagonism, and the Logic of Lulz," *The Fibreculture Journal* 22 (2013): 62–92; Ryan M. Milner, "Media Lingua Franca: Fixity, Novelty, and Vernacular Creativity in Internet Memes," *AoIR*

Selected Papers of Internet Research 3 (2013); Milner, "Pop Polyvocality"; Bennett and Segerberg, *The Logic of Connective Action*; Paolo Gerbaudo and Emiliano Treré, "In Search of the 'We' of Social Media Activism: Introduction to the Special Issue on Social Media and Protest Identities," *Information, Communication & Society* 18, no. 8 (2015): 865–71; Paolo Gerbaudo, "Protest Avatars as Memetic Signifiers: Political Profile Pictures and the Construction of Collective Identity on Social Media in the 2011 Protest Wave," *Information, Communication & Society* 18, no. 8 (2015): 916–29.

37. Robert Hariman and John Louis Lucaites, *No Caption Needed: Iconic Photographs, Public Culture, and Liberal Democracy* (Chicago, IL: University of Chicago Press, 2007), 26.
38. Nathan Rambukkana, "#Introduction: Hashtags as Technosocial Events," in *Hashtag Publics: The Power and Politics of Discursive Networks*, ed. Nathan Rambukkana (New York: Peter Lang, 2015), 2.
39. Nissenbaum and Shifman, "Internet Memes as Contested Cultural Capital," 485.
40. Kelly Bergstrom, "'Don't Feed the Troll': Shutting down Debate about Community Expectations on Reddit.Com," *First Monday* 16, no. 8 (2011); Benjamin D. Horne, Sibel Adali, and Sujoy Sikdar, "Identifying the Social Signals That Drive Online Discussions: A Case Study of Reddit Communities," *arXiv*, May 7, 2017, https://arxiv.org/abs/1705.02673; James Meese, "'It Belongs to the Internet': Animal Images, Attribution Norms and the Politics of Amateur Media Production," *M/C Journal* 17, no. 2 (2014); Noam Gal, Limor Shifman, and Zohar Kampf, "'It Gets Better;'" Kanai, "Sociality and Classification;" Trammell, "User Investment and Behavior Policing on 4chan."
41. Kevin Howley, "'I Have a Drone': Internet Memes and the Politics of Culture," *Interactions: Studies in Communication & Culture* 7, no. 2 (2016): 155–75; Najma Al Zidjaly, "Memes as Reasonably Hostile Laments: A Discourse Analysis of Political Dissent in Oman," *Discourse & Society* 28, no. 6 (2017): 573–94; Bratich, "Occupy All the Dispositifs"; Vickery, "The Curious Case of Confession Bear."
42. Nissenbaum and Shifman, "Internet Memes as Contested Cultural Capital"; Milner, "Media Lingua Franca."
43. Milner, "There's No Place for Lulz on LOLCats."
44. Bennett and Segerberg, *The Logic of Connective Action*; Miltner, "There's No Place for Lulz on LOLCats"; Shifman, "The Cultural Logic of Photo-Based Meme Genres"; Bradley E. Wiggins and G. Bret Bowers, "Memes as Genre: A Structurational Analysis of the Memescape," *New Media & Society* 17, no. 11 (2015): 1886–1906.
45. Ariella Azoulay, *Civil Imagination: A Political Ontology of Photography* (New York: Verso, 2015).
46. Vice, *Charlottesville: Race and Terror*, YouTube, August 14, 2017, https://www.youtube.com/watch?v=RIrcB1sAN8I.
47. Vice, *Charlottesville: Race and Terror*.
48. Vice, *Charlottesville: Race and Terror*.
49. Christopher Cantwell, "Radical Agenda EP331 – Naming the Hate," *Christopher Cantwell*, July 19, 2017, https://christophercantwell.com/2017/07/19/radical-agenda-ep331-naming-hate/.

50. Max Londberg, "White Supremacist in Charlottesville, Va., Says He 'Just Came Here for the Fun,'" *Kansas City Star*, August 16, 2017, http://www.kansascity.com/news/nation-world/article167641112.html.
51. C. J. Hunt, "A Charlottesville White Supremacist Stripped Down to Escape Protesters and We Got It on Video," GQ, August 16, 2017, https://www.gq.com/story/charlottesville-white-supremacist-strips-to-escape-protestors.
52. Richard Dawkins, *The Selfish Gene*, 40th Anniversary Edition, Oxford Landmark Science (Oxford: Oxford University Press, 2016); Susan Blackmore, *The Meme Machine* (Oxford: Oxford University Press, 1999).
53. Davi Johnson, "Mapping the Meme: A Geographical Approach to Materialist Rhetorical Criticism," *Communication and Critical/Cultural Studies* 4, no. 1 (2007): 42.
54. "Alt-Right," *Know Your Meme*, n.d., accessed September 1, 2017, http://knowyourmeme.com/memes/cultures/alt-right.
55. Martin Hand, "Visuality in Social Media: Researching Images, Circulation and Practices," in *The Sage Handbook of Social Media Research Methods*, ed. Luke Sloan and Anabel Quan-Haase (Thousand Oaks, CA: Sage, 2017), 215–31.
56. Edwin Black, *Rhetorical Criticism: A Study in Method* (Madison: University of Wisconsin, 1978), 62.
57. Jim Ridolfo and Dànielle Nicole DeVoss, "Composing for Recomposition: Rhetorical Velocity and Delivery," *Kairos* 13, no. 2 (2009).

· 1 ·

THE ORIGINS OF ALT-RIGHT MEMES AND THEIR PROLIFERATION

In spring of 2016, *Politico Magazine* published an essay entitled "World War Meme." In it, author Ben Schreckinger describes the power of the meme to sway the election for the highest office in the United States: that of the presidency. "There is no real evidence that memes won the election," Shreckinger writes, "but there is little question they changed its tone, especially in the fast-moving and influential currents of social media."[1] Yet, before memes even reached social media sites such as Facebook, Twitter, and Instagram, many of them were created in enclaved websites. These websites, including 4chan and reddit, were memetic laboratories where users would experiment with persuasive memetic texts and later unleash some on the world. For many meme generators in these locales, the Great Meme War would unseat the liberal Democratic Party and install a new conservative, populist leader in its place. As Schreckinger puts it,

> The fighters in the Great Meme War took their intimate knowledge of this ecosystem and weaponized it, genetically engineering pro-Trump and anti-Clinton supermemes they designed to gain as much mainstream traction as possible. The staging ground was an anonymous message board called "/pol/"—the "politically incorrect" section of 4Chan, which was founded in 2003 to host discussions about anime and has since evolved into a malignant hive mind with vast influence over online culture.[2]

The Great Meme War was fought in many theatres, both online and offline. The initial weapons—ideologically charged memes—were produced in counterpublic enclaves and then disseminated rapidly to the masses.[3] During the 2016 election, memes fashioned on these sites travelled rapidly and widely across multiple platforms, bringing with them pointed political messages about hot-button issues such as immigration, health-care reform, and civil rights in America. Ultimately, these memes became weaponized by the Alt-right who continued to deploy them long after the election.

The circulation of memes both in and outside these sites is a rhetorical phenomenon worthy of serious scholarly inquiry, in part because memes were one of the most significant rhetorical forms of the 2016 election cycle. These images have retained their significance in the months following. To investigate the influence of memes, we must analyze the places from which they emanate. Against those who would characterize 4chan and reddit as chaotic free-for-alls where anything goes, we treat them as sites of purposeful, rhetorical innovation. This chapter explores the history of 4chan and reddit and provides a roadmap for grasping the creation and proliferation of memes within these and other digital sites. The chapter lays out the chronological development of 4chan and reddit as networked sites influential to public culture, and in particular, to the development of Alt-right memes. It proceeds in three parts. In part one, we begin by introducing 4chan, the website most (in)famous for spawning the hacktivist collective Anonymous and now well-circulated memes such as LOLCats. We examine how 4chan's inventional functions helped birth Alt-right memes. In part two, we describe the rise of social news aggregator site reddit that similarly played a role in the growth of Alt-right imagery. Although each of these websites is distinct, they share several structural characteristics that predispose their utility as so-called meme factories. Both reddit and 4chan thrive off of the anonymity/pseudonymity requisite of the sites, serve simultaneously as producers, hosts, and disseminators of memetic content, and constantly negotiate an ambivalent, antagonistic relationship with the public sphere. In the third part of the chapter, we outline our approach to memes as rhetorical artifacts that are both cultural products and productive of culture. We conclude by describing how memes transition from pithy internet jokes to tactical persuasive messages, a topic that receives more extensive treatment in chapter four.

4chan: A Site of Enclaved Rhetorical Invention

Sometimes called the "rude, raunchy underbelly of the internet," 4chan is a web-based community where public culture is produced and negotiated, in large part through the creation and dissemination of memes.[4] Memes function as a shared vernacular for users. Adroit use of memetic content demonstrates in-group status.[5] Memes also serve as the symbolic apparatus from which shared culture is managed. While we focus our analysis in this book on the sub-board /pol/ as the site of memetic creation and imitation, it's worth outlining fundamental characteristics of 4chan because it structurally predisposes certain types of posts—and therefore certain modes of communication—over others. In particular, the simple format of the website combined with its status as an imageboard facilitates the development of memes, which serve a multitude of functions, including internal information transmission, communication of one's insider status, and the dissemination of 4chan culture beyond the boards themselves.

4chan is an imageboard, divided into some 70 sub-boards, each with a different focus, community, and set of formal and informal rules. With the exception of a landing page linking to rules, FAQs, and information for the press, these boards comprise the entirety of the public face of the website. In part because of their topical orientation, the boards all inflect a different set of communication standards. The boards' names are linked to an associated URL, demarcated by a forward slash and an abbreviation of the name of the board. For instance, /co/ (or, URL 4chan.org/co/) is for the discussion of comic books; /pol/ stands for "Politically Incorrect," where 4chan users discuss politics; and /b/, which stands for "random," is the part of 4chan often described as the place where "anything goes" (e.g., where other boards send trolls and other troublemakers to perform their various mischief). Users may access these sub-boards one of two ways, either by directly linking to them through a URL, or by clicking through a hyperlinked menu displayed at the top of website.

The design of 4chan imageboards can best be described as stark simplicity: the website has few bells and whistles.[6] On the boards, the image is presumed a superior mode of communication; while text does constitute a significant portion of the communicative exchange that occurs on 4chan, oftentimes users will post images (either related or unrelated) to accompany their text. The original poster—more colloquially and somewhat disparagingly known as "OP"—begins a chain of posts. 4chan users may reply to the post, creating a chronological thread in response to OP. Importantly, these posts live or die based on user engagement; the boards are set to feature the most engaging posts at the top of the front page of each board. Those posts that see little to no action are algorithmically bumped off the front page. Although users have the ability to navigate to later pages, posts or threads that exist beyond the first and second pages are functionally ghost-towns. Unless they are revitalized through users posting, they slide down more pages and effectively disappear.

On 4chan, nothing good (or bad) can ever truly stay on the boards. Posts functionally vanish after a significant lack of engagement, demonstrating what scholars and cultural commentators have elsewhere called the "ephemerality" and "impermanence" of the site.[7] While this design feature promotes lively communication for users, the structural prioritization of some threads over others as well as the non-static nature of the site poses a problem for scholars wishing to outline a conclusive history of the imageboards. As Whitney Phillips and others have noted, due to the ephemeral nature of the site, a thorough, complete history of 4chan is difficult—if not impossible—to report.[8]

We do not attempt to construct a complete history of 4chan, but instead focus on the site's relationship to public culture. We do draw upon those histories that have been pieced together via informal documentation on encyclopedic sites such as Wikipedia and Know Your Meme.[9] We also employ scholarly work on 4chan and our own participant observation. Because we are interested in tracing how memes move from enclaved spaces such as 4chan, we choose to use a chronological approach to document events that have shaped the culture of 4chan since its initial development, focusing on events that molded 4chan boards as cultures and content creators. We also highlight moments in the imageboard's history when the community's content spilled beyond its gate-kept walls. As we will show, these moments of rupture also demonstrate how the site functions as integral to meme creation and dissemination. We do not mean to suggest that this is the sole history relevant to this site. We choose to accent particular events because they reveal two important characteristics about the website: first, that the site is a complex network and, second, that the networked nature of the site encourages content produced on the platform to disseminate beyond it. By network, we mean that 4chan exists alongside and interdependent with other content-producing and -disseminating websites, and that these websites are nodal points within a web of information flows. Moreover, these websites are connected through (and sometimes against) varying degrees of publicity and counterpublicity that characterize their user base. Ultimately, our timeline demonstrates the rhetorical valence of 4chan in public culture by showcasing how this site has continually grappled with its influences, and a series of increasingly sophisticated attempts to harness 4chan's memetic capacity outward.

Like its current manifestation, 4chan's beginning was heavily networked, facilitated by the transition of users from other sites to the newly formed imageboard. There is some debate as to the precise date of 4chan's creation. Some scholars suggest that 4chan was created in 2004.[10] Phillips, on the other hand, argues that 4chan was introduced a year earlier, in 2003, by a teenaged Christopher Poole, known elsewhere on the internet by his pseudonym "moot."[11] Know Your Meme and Wikipedia support Phillips' claim, maintaining that moot envisioned a simple imageboard that would serve as an English-speaking version of Japanese imageboards.[12] Poole, an avid anime fan, developed the simple imageboard modeling sites such as Futaba Channel (or 2chan), where users could discuss anime, manga, and a variety of other topics.[13] Like Futaba, 4chan revolves around the sharing of images and also features discussion boards siloed according to topic. In this way, 4chan is a product of a specific genre of internet sub-culture. The site shares distinctive design and cultural features with both Futaba and Something Awful, another predecessor that appears to have influenced 4chan's aesthetic and cultural feel.

Prior to its creation, Poole was a frequent user of an influential, comedic website called Something Awful (SA), which preceded 4chan's development by 15 years.[14] SA emerged in 1999 and became one of the original sites where internet culture was fashioned and propagated.[15] Moot frequented the site, which, in addition to boasting comedic content, had forums where subcommunities developed and mischief was planned. It is highly likely that SA impacted the structure of 4chan, which both extended and pivoted away from SA.[16] It is significant that many of 4chan's initial users came from SA, as this rambunctious site likely played a key role in 4chan as a site for trolling and activity that has been referred to as the "lulz." SA was home to some of the earliest internet memes, including the now well-established meme "All your base are belong to us," a phrase and phenomenon drawing attention to the poor translation of a phrase from non-English languages to English.[17] SA, like 4chan and reddit after it, is known for producing highly influential content (that content would now be considered viral). The construction of the forums and users' engagement within them creates the cultural conditions necessary to design internal memes and then radiate them outward to wider publics. Like 4chan, SA's reputation as a "meme factory" relies on its members' engagement, and in particular, their innovative use of popular culture to fashion sticky content for external broadcast.[18]

According to internet lore, 4chan's creator moot belonged to a SA subforum community quite descriptively called "Anime Death Tentacle Rape Whorehouse" or ADTRW. One SA internet historian describes ADTRW as a place to keep unwelcome subthreads.[19] The author suggests that the forum was not created "until a certain group posts a lot of threads about the same stupid shit that we give them their own forum. Then we hope and pray they all post there and stay the hell away from us normals."[20] As this description and the name of the forum suggest, ADTRW was a space not only for discussing anime, but for joyfully flaming and trolling in community with other like-minded flamers and trolls. ADTRW's enclaved status is central to its (im)proper functioning on SA. A place to keep "a certain group" "the hell away from us normals," ADTRW's inherent alterity served as a perfect entry point for moot's 4chan, which became an enclaved site set aside from the rest of the internet for board users to discuss things in peace using their own discursive norms and cultural practices. 4chan began as a "content overflow site" for material produced on ADTRW, and grew from there.[21]

4chan speaks to diverse enclaved publics. While the board began as a site for discussing Japanese anime, 4chan quickly expanded to its present seventy boards, each with a different focus of conversation. The wide range of topics abets its popularity, attracting users to the site in the thousands. As Lee Knuttila notes, "the user base has grown from a small community of site creator Christopher Poole's friends to a massive collective of nearly 18 million unique site visitors with over 730 million page views a month."[22] The website is a well-trafficked and quite productive corner of the internet. Phillips, citing data provided by moot, states that "the site is host to 60,000 overall users at any given moment and 10,000 on the front page of /b/ alone."[23] Those users create and recycle significant content, including posts, images, and, of course, memes. Tim Bavlnka points out that "As of February 1, 2013, 4chan has accumulated 1,149,144,201 total posts and over 100 gigabytes of content."[24] For this, Bavlnka hails 4chan as "one of the largest and most notorious Internet communities."[25] At the time of this writing, 4chan's FAQ page claimed that the website "serve[s] more than 100 *terabytes* of data per day, and over 680 million pageviews to more than 22 million unique visitors per month."[26] For a majority of the time since its birth, the website remained notorious and largely separate from the rest of the internet. However, every so often, content would spill from the boards into the greater digital public sphere.

Perhaps the most popular meme to emerge from 4chan to mainstream discourse is "LOLCats," elsewhere known as "cat macros," featuring cats in funny poses overlaid by white text captions. For Limor Shifman, LOLCat memes are an exemplar of what she calls an "egalitarian meme," or a widespread meme with no discernible "founding" image and one that leans on a template or associated genre.[27] Before LOLCats had broad cultural appeal, widespread distribution, and their own website, "I Can Haz Cheezburger," LOLCats were exchanged on 4chan on Saturdays, also known as Caturday. Caturday is a ritual practice of posting funny images of cats, especially LOLCats, on 4chan, and in particular, on /b/.

LOLCats highlights the importance of trolling as a cultural norm on 4chan. According to Know Your Meme, the rise of Caturday as an internal cultural phenomenon on 4chan's /b/ occurred sometime in the middle of the aughts, with 4chan users participating in Caturday in 2006.[28] The popular website I Can Haz Cheezburger first began publishing LOLCat memes in 2007.[29] As Phillips notes, the birth of LOLCats is inextricably tied to 4chan and the trolling culture endemic to it. She contends that "a significant percentage of popular memes… originated within or amplified by subcultural trolls, particularly those associated with 4chan's /b/ board. In fact, the act of trolling and the act of making memes were so interconnected during this period that the existence of memes on a given page or forum almost guaranteed that trolling had been afoot."[30] Trolling helped define the culture of the group and developed evolving standards by which memes were seen as effective. Caturday, for instance, shared relevant content as well as funny pictures of cats. As memes developed, a vernacular appropriate to Caturday emerged. Users could perform their membership in the enclave by appropriately using the vernacular, which was a humorous approach to broken English. Building on the trolling culture of the site, 4chan users who deviated too far from the accepted language of the intertextual artifact would be shamed and told to "lurk moar" rather than actively post content. Caturday remains an important tradition on 4chan, although its luster has dulled because so-called normies have hijacked (and, later corporatized) the once sacred text used to determine belonging on the boards.

As the LOLCats meme moved to the mainstream, it became a resource for building public culture beyond 4chan. Although Shifman notes that "to produce and understand LOLCats, users need to master LOLspeak," the widespread dissemination of LOLCats enabled more opportunities for non-fluent LOLlinguists to participate in building the meme.[31] Moreover, because the meme requires a specific format, and because no one owns the particular image upon which the meme is based, LOLCats spreads quickly and to more popular audiences, who, modeling the basic structure of the meme, can participate in constructing new memes, propagating them further. This effect has been documented by Phillips, who describes "waves of corporate encroachment" on meme culture, as well as "the mainstreaming of the web" that "resulted in a dizzying influx of novice users."[32] The effects of this circulation were two-fold. On one hand, newbie normies wrested a prized cultural tradition from the reclusive, exclusive 4chan communities, issuing the meme beyond the reproach of its initial creators. On the other hand, new users propagated 4chanian form and content outward, where counter-cultural ideas could become mainstream.

The LOLCats meme template is a prime example of how material that begins on enclaved sites such as 4chan and reddit are transmitted outward, often with mixed feelings for board users. Since their initial development and circulation, scholars have described LOLCats as one of the oldest internet memes and as one of the "most popular and enduring."[33] LOLCats have become so ingrained in the internet cultural milieu that they are imminently recognizable for many people on the internet. Miltner describes the "cultural resonance" of the LOLCat memes and their later iterations, which have led to corporate product spinoffs, including a TV show and a Bible translation.[34] The diffusion of LOLCats to outsiders was met with ambivalence by users on the boards. Of course, memes by nature propagate. As more and different types of users interact with and share the meme, both the meme itself and the content contained within it are more widely distributed. The influence of the meme increases, and along with it, its rhetorical significance and power. Yet, Caturday began as a ritual process of belonging and culture-building for those endemic to the enclaved site of 4chan. Moreover, deft use of the meme was a sign that users understood the culture and language of the site enough to create content to reproduce the culture. If 4chan users were displeased when a novice user bumbled the cat macro, widespread popular misuse by normies off the site was unforgivable. The popularity of LOLCats demonstrates the antagonism and ambivalence of 4chan's networked status as well as its role as a producer of content for the mainstream. Caturday is not the only mimetic content to slip from the counterpublic to general publicity, to the chagrin of some 4chan users.

Anonymous and Networked Influence

To grasp the rhetorical tactics of 4chan users, it is important to attend to the actions of the hacker group that was spawned, in part, from this site. The ambivalence and hostility often expressed by Alt-right members can be indexed by analyzing an earlier 4chan collective: Anonymous. In early 2008, Anonymous emerged from the internet ether as a formidable assemblage willing and able to take on major targets.[35] Anonymous is a decentralized group of human and non-human agents whose primary function is to agitate, and at times, to advocate for causes agreed upon—at least temporarily—by the collective. Notoriously elusive by virtue of its anonymity, "Anonymous resists straightforward definition as it is a name currently called into being to coordinate a range of disconnected actions, from trolling to political protests."[36] Bolstered by the anonymity encouraged by the boards of 4chan, varying masses of individual 4chan users, dubbed "anons" would use the site as a counterpublic enclave for stirring up trouble. Often, trouble would take the form of an antagonistic attack, or "raids" for which the site became (in)famous. These raids were a performance of shared collectivity, often leveraging the affordances of the site against significant targets. Success required users to band together to participate in any one particular action. Large raids drew more firepower from 4chan's "anons." However, bigger raids also meant more publicity and visibility on the boards. Though increased visibility lends legitimacy to the raids, increased attention also involves more risks for anons.

One of the first targeted, political raids that captured public scrutiny was called Project Chanology, a response to a promotional video shot by the Church of Scientology.[37] The video had been leaked and became available for public viewing. The 2008 video depicted an incoherent Tom Cruise waxing poetic about the virtues of Scientology. In the video, Cruise issues statements that are nonsensical and unclear at best, including sentences that are missing parts of speech.[38] Overall, it was an embarrassing video for Scientologists, prompting *Wired* to call it a "heaven-sent extra helping of the weirdness [of] Tom Cruise" for "wiseasses" looking for a chuckle.[39] The Church of Scientology worked quickly to rectify the humiliating situation, issuing numerous copyright violation claims to force video hosting sites to take it down for a brief period of time.

The quick removal of the Cruise video did not sit well with a particular group of internet denizens who found the video intensely amusing and the rapid takedown of said video unamusing. Anonymous, whose amorphous but technology-forward actions tends toward a libertarian ethics of free speech and circulation, responded with pranksterish vitriol.[40] The Church of Scientology answered with similar causticity, calling anons terrorists and threatening legal action. Anonymous reacted with a dual attack on the Church's physical and digital locales. In an impressive assemblage of agitational rhetoric, Anons pranked the Church of Scientology with phone calls, all-black faxes, and unwanted pizza deliveries.[41] Anons also took to the streets in protest of the church.[42] The church countered by calling Anonymous religious bigots and cyber terrorists and again, leveraging lawsuits.[43] The actions garnered media attention for each attack and counterattack. Project Chanology demonstrated that given an appropriate target, users from 4chan could be convinced to work together toward a particular end. Its success recruited more anons and prompted more raids for Anonymous.[44]

But 4chan users—the original anons—expressed ambivalence about the collective's newfound popularity and protest-based action.[45] As Gabriella Coleman notes, "Homeostasis is not, exactly, the preferred state of Anonymous—certainly not before Chanology, and definitely not after."[46] Some saw the trolling actions of Anonymous to be a direct extension of the cultural capacities of the site. Others saw the publicity tactics of Anonymous as a rejection of the anonymity of the site and a move toward incorporating the enclave into the mainstream.[47] Since much of 4chan's cultural ethos opposes mainstream forms of communication in favor of subcultural activity, Anonymous' success may have been read as a blow to the very heart of 4chan itself. Adding insult to injury, Anonymous eschewed typical characteristics of a movement. As a decentered, supposedly leaderless consortium of individuals whose roster changed with every operation, Anonymous was difficult for the public to understand.[48] Those intrigued by Anonymous' actions tried to comprehend Anonymous by grappling with the place where it originated. As a result, a bright and oftentimes unforgiving light was shown on 4chan—a community of people defined by their alterity. These types of investigations rarely portrayed 4chan or Anonymous with accuracy.[49] For these reasons, reports such as these were perceived as an attack on 4chan by normies who just didn't get it. Already somewhat militant, disgruntled, and reclusive, some 4chan users responded by turning even more inward to the site itself.

Understanding the networked structures of Anonymous is key for the work of some 4chan boards, especially in the ways users engage the deliberative process to create collective action and invent novel methods of redress. The memetic creation we analyze leading into the 2016 election and beyond is indebted to this history. Tactical online actions are empowered by the structure of the site and the values of many users on the boards, who are often antagonistic to the mainstream. The more users who participate in collective action, the greater the tactical force of the whole in terms of garnering publicity and emboldening the work of others. But, these campaigns are often misunderstood by outsiders who tend to demonize the site and all users by painting them with a single brush.[50] Similar modes of invention and action emerged from reddit. Yet, while this site shows affinities with the modes of communication on 4chan, it is also unique in its history and norms of dialogue.

Reddit as Meme Factory: More Than a News Aggregator

Reddit entered into a crowded media landscape in 2005, just two years after 4chan was founded. The site followed closely on the heels of popular platforms Facebook and Digg, each of which launched in 2004. Twitter would premier just a year after reddit began amassing users. In the early years, reddit was a small community featuring few forums, known on the site as "subreddits." Then, just three years after its founding, reddit experienced a veritable explosion of new subreddits developed on the site. Now the 7th biggest website in the US, overtaking similar news aggregation sites such as Digg, reddit invites users to actively participate in the community-driven subreddits for which the site is known.[51] Like 4chan, reddit users produce massive amounts of content. Recent reports suggest that the 240 million monthly active users of reddit compose well over 300,000 posts each day.[52]

Much like 4chan, reddit is a heterogeneous collective, with a relatively diverse community (in interest or affinity, if not in identity). As a networked site where content flows from numerous external sources, a multitude of publics form, at once coalescing around and creating discourse specific to the reddit community. As such, there is likely to be heterogeneous opinions within subreddits and on the site as a whole. At times, the communities demonstrate antagonism against one another.[53] Other times, the communities band together in rejection of the established leadership. For instance, 2015 saw the reddit "blackout," in which hundreds of subreddits were effectively taken offline in protest of administrative changes at reddit.[54] Nevertheless, there are structural and affinity-based aspects of the site that bear consideration in understanding how the patterns of communication therein impact the culture of subreddits and a broader public culture.

A social news aggregator site, reddit relies upon user participation in the form of content sharing and upvoting or downvoting of content. Similar to 4chan, user engagement correlates with popularity, and downvoted content is bumped farther down the forum until it eventually reaches relative obscurity. Unlike 4chan, which assumes anonymity as the standard, reddit operates on a pseudonymous model, wherein users pick a name during account creation and can then acquire "karma," a sign of status in the community.[55] Users may operate under many pseudonyms. Since signing up for reddit requires very little information, one can also create a "burner," or throw-away reddit account, and use it for a very short period of time, or intermittently. Those who create, manage, and use the site suggest that reddit's pseudonymity allows people to express themselves more freely than other websites that require one's "real" name (Facebook and Google are examples of websites that require users to use one account under a legitimate name). Reddit, colloquially known as "the front page of the internet," has experienced significant success despite controversy both inside and outside of the company.

The site was developed by Steve Huffman and Alexis Ohanian, who met at the University of Virginia. Huffman, a computer scientist and engineer, and Ohanian, an entrepreneur, sold the company quickly after its launch. In 2006, Condè Nast—the mass media company that manages more than twenty magazines including *Vogue*, *The New Yorker*, *GQ*, *Wired*, and *ars technica*—acquired the company. While the specifics of the deal are not clear, the *New York Times* reported that Condè Nast exchanged some $20 million dollars for the site.[56] The sale of reddit to Condè Nast was met with some ambivalence by both reddit users as well as Huffman and Ohanian; Ohanian sometimes expressed regret about selling the company so early but also celebrated its purchase. In a *Bloomberg* interview with Huffman and Ohanian, Huffman noted that, upon reflection, "I'm not actually certain reddit would have survived… without" the acquisition by Condè Nast, which, Huffman later argued, helped transition reddit to a viable company.[57] Huffman and Ohanian enjoyed significant privileges after the acquisition, remaining with the company for three years after the sale. For some, however, the acquisition began a long downslide into corporatism that muddied the ethos of "community" for which the site was known.

In 2011, reddit was "spun off" as an independent subsidiary run by Condè Nast's parent company, Advanced Publications.[58] By most accounts, Advanced Publications used a *laissez-faire* approach to operations, prompting Ohanian, who remained on the board of reddit, to suggest that "For the most part, we were given a ludicrous level of autonomy."[59] The changes that were made by Advanced Publications appeared largely managerial. Then, in 2012, reddit returned to "truly a private, independent company after receiving outside investment."[60] During this time, Yishan Wong took over the position of CEO in 2012, a position he would hold for two years. Wong began his tenure as CEO as reddit began to gain its footing on an international stage.

Some five years after its launch, reddit experienced dramatic growth, cementing itself as a site where publics formed based on interest or affinity. The explosion of subreddits in early 2008 and 2009, evidenced both a glut of new users and attracted a massive number of digitally savvy audiences to engage with that new content, both on and off the site, for good and for ill.[61] In 2010, users organized the first global meet up day, in which those who had known each other online met in person, perhaps for the first time.[62] This trend would continue in the following years. In early 2011, reddit celebrated a major milestone: February witnessed the first time the site had reached over a billion page views per month.[63] "There are only about 100 sites on the entire Internet that get a billion pageviews in a single month, and now reddit can put on its smoking jacket and join that exclusive club," a reddit announcement read.[64] Several months later, reddit nearly doubled that number, jumping to 1.8 billion pageviews per month in October. October also saw reddit overcome Twitter in unique monthly visitors by some 28 million users.[65]

The material structure and layout of reddit holds rhetorical consequences because it implies who and what may be part of the reddit community. The affordances of reddit's design aesthetic are also its limitations. That is, to an outsider, reddit's design may appear obtuse. Yet its design aesthetic conveys important messages about what reddit values: namely, the production of content and the communities that make that production possible. Simultaneously both austere and a little cluttered, reddit is similar to 4chan in that the website is quite simple in its design: a header full of links to subreddits (subcommunities organized by interest or affinity), a long list of blue-links with associated up/down voting arrows, and a few basic ads or internal announcements across the top and sides of the website. For the uninitiated (or for those who are used to interacting with richly developed websites), reddit may appear both impenetrable and unwelcoming: a wall of blue text and symbols that, while perhaps intuitive to some, may alienate others. Indeed, the user experience on reddit has been compared to "peering into a bowl of spaghetti."[66] Once a would-be user moves beyond the barebones aesthetics (described by the same tech commentator as having "all the graphic appeal of Craigslist, which is to say, not much"), they access what users describe as a community of communities, all organized according to interest.[67] Here, users' "empirical" or offline identity comes second, if it is ever revealed at all.[68] Reddit spokesperson Anne Soellner has described it as a place where people are organized "around passion points" rather than "around your personal identity."[69] The identity of the community—rather than the individual—is foregrounded. As such, each of these communities may modify the aesthetic features of the site with static images and headers even as the overall vibe of the site remains the same.

From a rhetorical perspective, reddit's aesthetic simplicity serves several functions, the most visible of which is prompting the user to engage with the content rather than the site itself. Reddit leadership sees the site as a "platform" to facilitate engagement among users rather than a "publisher," which disseminates content in a top-down way.[70] The structure of the site is subtly persuasive; the argument forwarded by the design aesthetic is that the site is simply a host for the conversations that happen on it. Responsibility for the content on the site, the communication that happens with it, and the communities that form as a result, remains with users who actively create reddit. Framing reddit as an egalitarian platform where users determine content and culture is not only a branding move, but one that affords reddit's leadership a *laissez-faire* relationship with some of the more offensive content to be found on reddit. Moreover, this rhetorical framing-cum-design aesthetic gels well with the founders' and administrators' hands-off approach to the website. Reddit has notoriously sidestepped the question of regulating content found on the site, preferring instead to have communities (and the moderators who oversee them, sometimes several at a time) set the parameters for community engagement. As Soellner notes, "each community can govern that community itself, so that they have much stricter rules or no rules at all. They can govern rules such as speech or how users to relate to one another."[71] Users are responsible for moderating both content and their reaction to it. Co-founder and CEO Huffman notes that "Our mission is to make reddit as welcoming as possible….There's a lot of work we're doing…connecting people with their home on reddit."[72] Although Huffman here espouses inclusion, the logic of this argument tacitly condones toxic cultures. Moreover, the implicit warrant of Soellner's message is this: if users find content offensive, then they should locate their communities elsewhere. Additionally, the rhetorical pivot away from "publisher" to "platform" alters the legal responsibility of reddit: whereas publishers may be responsible for the content "published" on their sites, "platforms" have a more libertarian ethos, providing cover when content becomes offensive, violent, or otherwise problematic.

Reddit's leaders and administrators also argue that the site serves as a neutral space where users may communicate and create culture without technical or functional impediments. For instance, Huffman has noted that "Reddit is very much a reflection of humanity,"[73] a statement that both praises reddit as a site for community-making and shields it from criticism when a community provokes, offends, or astounds. Recent events—including the 2016 election—suggest that Huffman's claim about the "reflective" status of reddit is empirically true, insofar as trends, debates, and even movements that occur "IRL" and off the forums eventually end up on forums such as reddit. From this perspective, the website, which at times functions as a revealing mirror for society, cannot remain immune to larger culture wars. In the early '10s, a number of ultra-conservative interests resulted in the formation of new forums. Alongside the rise of the manosphere, a growing network of men's rights users and sites, the growth of the Tea Party, and, perhaps goaded by the Great Recession, far right extremists began organizing around a new brand: the Alt-right, a loose collection of digital communities, components of which have a home on reddit. In 2012, the now (in)famous "red pill" subreddit was formed, structured around a counter-culture that believed men had ceded their sexual and political power to women (and, in particular, feminists).[74] The red pill subreddit and counter-culture did not exist alone; other communities developed in response to what they saw as the precipitous rise of PC (political correctness) culture; feminists, racial justice activists, and SJWs (social justice warriors), all of whom have been the targets of such subreddits as KotakuIn-Action (KIA), which ultimately became a home to the now infamous Gamer Gate scandal.

In contrast to Huffman's claims, reddit is not only a mirror to society. Nor is reddit as technically or ideologically neutral as reddit's design aesthetic or administration might suggest. Rather, reddit's technical infrastructure, its design features, and communication from leadership collectively make a clear, if subtle, argument in favor of a libertarian approach to the creation of culture on the site. In other words, the exaltation of "community" as central to the proper functioning of the site shields against accusations that reddit harbors racist, sexist, and homophobic trolls. By foregrounding the positively-valenced term "community" in its mission statement, reddit leaves ample room for the site to expand, profit, and reach more publics while dodging criticism.

Reddit influences public culture via its technological and ideological capacities, namely, the ability to fashion content and disseminate it rapidly across a multitude of sites. One of the affordances of networked publicity on sites such as reddit and 4chan is that information moves quickly across each sites' nodes—oftentimes more quickly than on other media channels. *The Atlantic* noted that the 2012 movie theatre shooting in Aurora, Colorado, like so many tragedies in recent past, "was not just a documented massacre, but one that is being documented across the web, and across the web's media outlets: on Twitter, on Facebook, on news sites....But one of the most effective sources of information about the massacre has been Reddit."[75] In this instance, large amounts of information, often factual, was revealed on reddit faster than traditional news outlets could obtain, verify, and report it. The *New York Times* admitted that reddit had "Scooped the Press on the Aurora Shootings," including disclosing information that "news outlets seemed to have missed."[76] With the assistance of other redditors who crowd-sourced information, a Denver-based redditor operating under the pseudonym "integ3r" (IRL name: Morgan Jones) developed a minute by minute timeline of the Aurora massacre, updated in real time, with external links to news sources, "realtime Google coverage," an IRC (internet relay chat), maps, police scanners, and ways to crowdfund for victims of the attack. The comments on the timeline show redditors mining victims' social media sites for information. In that moment, reddit experienced a kind of mission inversion. In an interview reported in the *Times*, integ3r noted, "It was sort of a strange feeling, like Reddit's supposed to be this aggregate news site, but we're actually breaking news to the media right now."[77] Furthermore, while the information found on reddit eventually proliferated to major news networks, the role of redditors was obfuscated in several of the early reports.[78]

Although reddit served as an important source of information during and after the Aurora shooting, not every fact-finding mission led by redditors proceeded as smoothly. In 2013, reddit users and leadership learned the dangers of the crowdsourcing method after an attack at the April 2013 Boston Marathon, where two homemade bombs fashioned out of pressure cookers detonated near the race's finish line. While two brothers, Dzhokhar Tsarnaev and Tamerlan Tsarnaev, were ultimately found responsible for the attack, redditors networked to decipher images of the two suspects. In part because the images were low quality, redditors began a misdirected search for an innocent (and in fact, deceased) Sunil Tripathi. Tripathi, who had gone missing, was the leading focus because of his supposed resemblance to the bombers. In response, Tripathi's family received death threats. The media correctly called the crowdsourced search a "witch hunt" that was racially motivated.[79]

As a networked site, reddit both draws upon and creates public culture alongside other content producers and disseminators. In the case of the Aurora shooting, reddit's role in a broader network suggests that the site was not alone in prompting a misguided search, although the site certainly played a central role in propagating misinformation. Twitter was an additional source of misinformation.[80] On it, certain media wings of Anonymous sent its followers on a goose chase for the wrong suspect. Ultimately, leaders of the site posted an apology on "upvoted," reddit's blog, for their contribution to misinformed efforts. "[T]hough started with noble intentions," the announcement read, "some of the activity fueled online witch hunts and dangerous speculation which spiraled into very negative consequences for innocent parties. The reddit staff and the millions of people on reddit around the world deeply regret that this happened."[81] Thus, reddit participates in broader networks that situate the importance and influence of how this site interacts with others to produce shared, sometimes controversial, cultural influences.

The technological affordances of the site shape the ways that publics form both on and off the site. Indeed, the speed at which reddit can propagate all modes of content and facilitate mob actions plays into its controversial status. Aided by others on adjacent websites, in 2014, some reddit users leveraged the affordances of the platform to proliferate images, videos, and memes related to The Fappening and Gamer Gate. Each were complex events generally indicative of how mobs coalesced and caused significant upheaval on reddit and elsewhere. Adrienne Massanari deems these events indicative of a larger "toxic technoculture" on sites such as reddit, which function at the intersection of misogynist geek culture and platform politics that "implicitly encourage [sexist or extremist]…pattern[s]."[82] The platform itself is structured to amplify both these and other patterns, propagating violent content beyond the bounds of reddit proper. In particular, those who participated in The Fappening and Gamer Gate used reddit's capacity to quickly spread specific content within reddit and beyond it. Ultimately, the same structural characteristics of reddit make possible the rapid spread of vicious content and facilitated, as we will show, the memes that influenced the 2016 presidential election.

The Fappening named an event when nude (or almost nude) images of celebrities leaked on the internet, captured as a result of a vulnerability in Apple's iCloud settings.[83] A portmanteau, "The Fappening" is the merging of the words "The Happening" and "Fap," the latter of which is geek speak for the sound one makes masturbating with a penis. Starting on 4chan, and moving to reddit, hackers (and their helpers) began posting selfies of celebrities posing in the nude.[84] At least for 4chan's /b/, events of this type are not unusual, as explicit images circulate freely, likely without the consent of those portrayed. What was unique about "The Fappening" was the number of images released, as well as the people portrayed. Hundreds of illegally acquired images emerged on 4chan, and later, on reddit, before making their way to more mainstream platforms such as Twitter. Celebrities who otherwise maintained privacy were subject to the prying eyes of thousands. As Alice Marwick notes, the cache of stolen images exposed primarily female celebrities, prompting significant debate over whether "The Fappening" ought to be considered sexual assault, since the images were both acquired and shared without consent.[85] Although they denied responsibility, Apple took heat for a security liability in its iCloud service that allowed hackers access.[86] In 2016, Ryan Collins and Edward Majerczyk were convicted of "phishing," a common way for hackers and scammers to obtain personal information by posing as others, and what allowed the pilfering of celebrity photos.[87]

The networked relationship between 4chan, reddit, and more mainstream social media platforms ensured the quick distribution of these illegally acquired images. Massanari states that "After the stolen photographs were scrubbed from 4chan, they continued to propagate across the web."[88] The Fappening led to the development of several new subreddits, including r/theFappening/, dedicated to the discussion and dissemination of the leaked images. The subreddit grew exponentially in a short time, amassing 100,000 followers in the first day.[89] So popular was the subreddit (and related subreddits) that reddit became the *de facto* locale for those wishing to view the images, with *Wired* reporting that "If you saw Kate Upton or Jennifer Lawrence naked last week, there's a good chance that you saw them on the social news site reddit."[90] Though reddit did not technically "host" the images (instead requiring users to link to the images), it became a centralized node for users to access or share the photographs. The continuation of r/TheFappening/ undoubtedly influenced the wider circulation of the images, despite not being hosted on the site itself.[91]

For its part, reddit did little to curb the release and spread of imagery and the toxic posts encouraging these actions. Such structural choices indicate how the site abets particular forms of extremism. John Menese, the creator and one of the moderators for r/TheFappening/, noted reddit's complicity in keeping the leaked content public. In an interview for *Wired*, Menese notes that "If Reddit had wanted to, they could have banned us on Sunday when our traffic broke their servers. Instead, they chose to milk a week of publicity and a month of server time in Reddit gold before they stepped in."[92] As Massanari notes, reddit allowed the subreddit to exist despite "numerous Digital Millennium Copyright Act (DMCA) infringement notices," which were "filed on behalf of those who were impacted by the attack."[93] Eventually, administrators banned the subreddit after images of McKayla Maroney, who was a minor, appeared on the site, in effect making reddit a host of child pornography. Importantly, suggests Marwick, reddit "did not remove the Fappening due to ethical issues, or concern for the privacy of the women in the pictures. The Fappening community was instead removed due to legal pressure, child pornography laws and DMCA complaints—in other words, implications that might hurt reddit the company."[94] Although reddit may choose to extract itself from legal issues through rhetorical pivots identifying itself as a "community" forum and "platform" rather than "publisher," the site nevertheless becomes an early distributor of particularly controversial content and often sets the tone for other networked sites.

Following a chain reaction that is part and parcel of these networked connections, 4chan and reddit are early stops on the lifecycle of viral content (including memes), both of which amplify material by privileging user engagement via algorithmic sorting. In the case of 4chan, The Fappening rose to the top of various boards. In the case of reddit, the amount of upvotes and other activity on The Fappening material drove discussion (and links) of the nude images to the top of the front page. In both cases, the amplification of content ultimately helped disseminate that content outwards, to less enclaved and more mainstream sites such as Facebook and Twitter. The lifecycle of this viral content is not—and need not be—*teleological*. Rather, amplification cycles are recurrent and imperfect, with offshoots of memetic culture landing in various places across the internet as they are taken back up or slightly modified in their original hotbeds.

Even as reddit responded and assessed the site's role in The Fappening, yet another controversy would ensure that the features of the network once again benefitted mob-based extremism. Not long after the ambivalent frenzy of The Fappening, the Gamer Gate controversy erupted. Defining and describing Gamer Gate is necessarily to take a position on the event, which has been subject to great debate over its meaning. Reddit users conceive of #GamerGate (sometimes known as GG), as a movement in at least two parts. In the first part, they assert that basic journalistic integrity and ethics were broached when "a game developer and game journalist were having sex," and as a result, "developers of the game had received favorable coverage in the journalists [*sic*] publication. That set off alarm bells and upset a few peoplr [*sic*]."[95] Although there was no evidence to indicate that the game developer (Zoë Quinn) had slept with the journalist (Nathan Grayson) for favorable reviews, and although Quinn's spurned ex-boyfriend initiated the allegations in an online missive, GG participants organized against this perceived injustice. Gamers suggested that they were victim to a biased system that took advantage of their love for video games, and lashed out against the "quinnspiracy," leveraging the networked affordances of 4chan, Twitter, reddit, and related websites to attack. The second component of the movement, according to KIA, arose from the backlash to Gamer Gate by numerous parties who decried the sexism of GG, pointing out the GG participants who issued violent rape and death threats to Quinn and her family.[96] Quinn was ultimately forced to go into hiding after several of her personal accounts were hacked and private information leaked. Other prominent women in the gaming ecosphere, including feminist media critic Anita Sarkeesian and game developer Brianna Wu, were subject to doxing (releasing of personal information) and subsequent threats on their bodies and lives.[97]

From a rhetorical perspective, one of the most interesting and unsettling aspects of Gamer Gate as a cultural phenomenon is how well GG participants harnessed the memetic tools of the digital sphere, not only to unleash hell on their foes, but to rebrand their efforts as a "movement" for justice on behalf of victims who just wanted to play their video games in peace. The use of powerful networked sites such as reddit and 4chan was central to the "success" of the movement, here measured in terms of its ability to organize masses, unsettle "the establishment," and maintain longevity. This movement did not need a leader, although it at times borrowed social capital of some of its followers (including Adam Baldwin, who receives credit for the moniker "GamerGate").

Both Gamer Gate and The Fappening demonstrate the interconnectedness of the two primary websites under investigation in this book. These controversial events suggest the myriad ways 4chan and reddit contribute to the creation of public culture through networked sites. In each case, controversial content moved rather fluidly between the porous borders of 4chan and reddit. In fact, at various points, each of these enclaved websites served as a site of retreat for the other. That is, on occasion, some reddit users would turn to 4chan, either as a space of refuge, or as a rallying point, or as a reference point, a place where important content was held and discussed. Similarly, 4chan remained explicitly linked to reddit, which sometimes became an important "stop" on the way to the mainstream. Overall, GG and The Fappening evidence the interconnectedness of both sites, as nodes for promulgating content and as sites where publics and public culture form. These events also indicate how the structural features of these sites facilitate the work of those who seek harm or are driven by a mission. The formulaic and algorithmic affordances of the platforms paired with the volatility of the human condition create a tidal wave of both content and controversy that abound on nearly every internet shoreline.

New leadership for the site has attempted, unsuccessfully, to combat the structural mechanisms facilitating abuse. In 2014, CEO Yishan Wong was replaced by Ellen Pao, who endeavored to address the systemic abuse and harassment made possible by the website. For this and other reasons, Pao was not always a popular leader, receiving hate mail that, she later wrote in a resignation letter posted to reddit, "made me doubt humanity."[98] As the *Daily Dot* reports, Pao was a "controversial figure whom some redditors have taken to calling Chairman Pao."[99] As her tenure progressed, Pao was both the victim of and a one-woman army against one of reddit's most disconcerting elements: what she called "the troll hivemind" who at times "moved against me."[100] In the letter announcing her resignation, she praised the "off-the-wall inspiring" good parts of reddit while critiquing the culture that not only harassed her, but made users "afraid to post supportive messages openly."[101]

Users responded to attempts to curb toxic behavior just as they responded to the site's corporate sale and leadership changes.[102] In mid 2015, a number of "harassing subreddits" were banned, including r/fatpeoplehate/, r/hamplanethatred/ (similar to r/fatepeoplehate/), r/neofag/, and others. The move was met with varied reaction. One thread, in r/againsthatesubreddits/ celebrated the "Good news—Reddit admins remove a number of harassing subreddits, including r/FatPeopleHate. Nothing of value was lost."[103] r/freespeech/ responded with a thread noting that "Reddit increases censorship."[104] Other subreddits expressed their agitation more explicitly: r/circlefuckers/ linked to the announcement with a thread titled "RETARDED CRIMINAL CUNT PAO AND HE [*sic*] CUCK SQUAD ARE BANNING SUBS THAT HURT THEIR FATTY FEELINGS."[105] Administration banning subreddits signaled a major shift in how the site was run; rather than allowing moderators to regulate content, reddit's leadership attempted to take over the reins. For a site that both depends on moderators for free labor and prides itself on allowing communities to self-define and self-regulate, the change was seismic.[106]

Despite best attempts, these changes were not permanent. Journalistic assessment of the changes fueled the perception that the administration was undermining reddit's treasured and hard-won culture. The *Daily Dot* wrote that "Reddit devolved into a civil war Thursday night that has left dozens of its most popular communities inaccessible and uncounted refugee users fleeing for higher ground."[107] *Fortune* published an article proclaiming "Reddit is at war with itself."[108] Elsewhere, the blackout was called a "rebellion,"[109] a "revolt,"[110] and a "meltdown."[111] On July 6, CEO Ellen Pao issued an apology, noting that "We screwed up. Not just on July 2, but also over the past several years. We haven't communicated well, and we have surprised moderators and the community with big changes….The mods and the community have lost trust in me and in us, the administrators of reddit."[112] Four days later, Pao resigned and Huffman became CEO.

Huffman, who remains CEO at the time of this writing, would see his own share of controversy, although perhaps not at the level of Pao. After a year with Huffman at the helm, reddit announced significant changes to its content policy. These content changes included "restrictions on what people can say on Reddit—or at least on our public pages—in the spirit of our mission."[113] In it, CEO Huffman suggested that what reddit required was a "very clear line" about what content was appropriate and what was not.[114] Despite this pronouncement, that clear line has not materialized.

In the lead-up to the 2016 presidential election, reddit found itself in hot water once more. The development and subsequent rapid populating of subreddits such as r/the_donald/, the space on reddit valorizing Trump, demonstrated that prior attempts to regulate the site were insufficient at best. In addition to posting volatile content, r/the_donald/ gained a reputation for "brigading," that is, inciting others to collectively upvote or downvote material on the site. On a site where user engagement determines what is seen, brigading effectively games the algorithm so that some content is privileged over others. As such, it undermines the purported democratic, egalitarian ethos of reddit. Brigading (or "vote manipulation") is against the reddit terms of service for this reason.[115] Although r/the_donald/ was not the first subreddit to manipulate votes (and therefore the production and circulation content) on the site, it was among the most successful at using it to promote favored material.

So effective was r/the_donald/ that reddit administrators introduced "technological and process changes" including a change to the algorithm responsible for r/all/, the page that displays the most popular content across reddit.[116] In a *Gizmodo* essay, a moderator noted that the subreddit "used to make up 30%–40% [of r/all] in the past."[117] Taking up more than one third of r/all/'s prime real estate has a powerful effect on the millions of reddit users, and reddit administration noticed. Although CEO Huffman was clear to state that the algorithm change was not directly the result of brigading on r/the_donald/, he also noted "I cannot deny their behavior hastened its deployment."[118] Huffman suggested that as a community, r/the_donald/ "attempt[ed] to dominate the conversation on Reddit at the expense of everyone else. This undermines Reddit, and we are not going to allow it."[119] However, the algorithm changes described by Huffman did not hamper r/the_donald/ or other Trump-affiliated subreddits. On election night, r/the_donald/ users bragged about their successful gaming of the system. As *Gizmodo* reports, users mocked redditors with a thread entitled "HEY LOSER SJWS OF REDDIT HOW DOES OUR DICK TASTE? GO FUCK YOURSELVES. WE ARE THE FUTURE AND YOU ARE A BUNCH OF 100 % LOSERS. I OPENLY LAUGH IN YOUR FACE…."[120] Once more, efforts by reddit admins to recalibrate neutrality fell short.

The alteration of reddit's algorithm and the subsequent announcement linking the change to "The Donald" demonstrates the significant influence the structure of the site and the processes of users possess. On the site, r/the_donald/ effectively gamed reddit's algorithm while simultaneously operating under the democratic ethos central to the branding of the site. Off the site, r/the_donald/ and related subreddits used the networked nature of reddit to amplify pro-Trump content, including memes central to the election. Given the response of reddit administrators, it is clear that users exerted considerable influence on the discourse of reddit and aimed to sway outsiders using the affordances of the digital sphere. To wit, memes were both the medium and the message for redditors looking to influence the election. Memes generated within these digital enclaves afforded users sophisticated firepower.

Weaponized Memes: From Enclave to Public

Memes, at least as most internet users know them today, were formed in the enclaves of 4chan. As Dale Beran explains, "4chan invented the meme as we use it today. At the time, one of the few places you saw memes was there."[121] As a visual form, the combination of text and popular imagery was crafted by the anonymous users of 4chan. Beran continues,

> The white Impact font with the black outlines, that was them (via S.A.). Terms like 'win' and 'epic' and 'fail' were all created or popularized on 4chan, used there for years before they became a ubiquitous part of the culture. The very method of how gifs and images are interspersed with dialogue in Slack or now iMessage or wherever is deeply 4chanian. In other words, the site left a profound impression on how we as a culture behave and interact.[122]

4chan, given its relationship to the meme-hub Something Awful, became a veritable factory for memes almost immediately after launch. These early memetic creations on 4chan and SA were likely developed solely for internal use. Yet, as a networked site, 4chan's internal memes propagated beyond its walls to the mainstream. For instance, as we mentioned, LOLCats leaked to the masses, distributing the public meme grammar indelibly forged in rarefied sites. This transition from counterpublic enclave to a broader public certainly altered the generic code of the meme, in part because broad circulation of a meme required uptake by different sorts of audiences. Yet, importantly, the basic vernacular of the meme persisted beyond 4chan and reddit, coloring the memes that are created and spread today.

Given ongoing cross pollinations, memes are a communicative media familiar to many audiences. The growth of meme literacy is tied to the way internet culture has been mainstreamed, including so-called geek and troll culture on enclaved sites. The rise of "meme hubs" such as 4chan and reddit certainly contributed to the popularization and increased circulation of the modern meme. As these sites expanded, so did their cultural influence. Shifman, for instance, notes an upsurge in the popularity of memes since at least 2011, evidenced by a sharp uptick in internet users searching for the term.[123] Not coincidentally, 2011 was the year where reddit first celebrated a billion pageviews per month. Reddit serves dual roles as an aggregator and creator of content, both of which shape public culture. That is, although reddit is technically a "news aggregator site" where users post content from elsewhere on the internet, like 4chan, its communities also create and distribute content. As reddit gained influence and notoriety, so did the cultural content that leaked beyond its borders, including memes.

Memes are powerful rhetorical images insofar as they help fashion a discursive reality. At the same time, memes are forged from discursive spaces, including platforms. The co-constitutive nature of rhetoric and the environment from which it is uttered (or typed) is evidenced by the indelible mark memes make on platforms (and platforms make on memes). As constitutive artifacts, memes themselves can be understood as a form of symbolic exchange brought forth from and embedded into the platform logics where they are created and propagated outward. From this perspective, memes are a significant modality of user-expression and influence platform cultures. Consequently, platform culture prompts users to refer to and value replicability, iteration, collectivity, and interconnection, and synthesize these values in the making of memes. In turn, these platform cultures create, and continually recreate, a digital or networked public sphere.[124] The formation of a new, digital public correspondingly generates a new form of public discourse that invites user participation and content creation within these cultural parameters. Importantly, 4chan and reddit are central locales for the creation and recreation of the memetically networked, digital public sphere. As platforms (rather than static pages), both 4chan and reddit offer memes, and those who would make them, raw cultural material to use as rhetorical resources, a medium for symbolic exchange, and networks for memes to spread.

In the culture of Web 2.0, users are more engaged in the present ecosystem, which is interconnected, flexible, and accessible in more and different ways.[125] Web 2.0 users are afforded the opportunity and encouraged to create and/or share content across their social networks, another key component in the logic of the platform.[126] Memes are a natural extension of this logic, insofar as they are collective, creative, constitutive, and capable of influencing others. Web 2.0 platforms encourage invention and invite users to share across networks as they participate in the shaping of the digital sphere, facilitating the proliferation of memes.[127] Meme culture offers a way of communicating and crafting experiences on these participatory sites. A theoretically "democratic" or a-hierarchical model of content production and dissemination is crucial to the formation and circulation of a meme, in part because memes often function as expressions of the individual on digital networks. That is, users who fashion and share a meme participate in culture creation at multiple levels: through the self and through the other. As Shifman describes, "sharing…has emerged as a central cultural logic, encompassing realms such as 'sharing economies' and sharing emotions in intimate relationships. When I post a funny clip on Facebook, I distribute a cultural item and at the same time express my feelings about it."[128] The affordances of Web 2.0 as a set of networked platforms for sharing content ushered in the widespread uptake of the meme as a way of communicating and as a mode of deliberation. In this way, it is important to study the rhetorical elements of memes that play a part in democratic modes of discourse.

In part, memes are significant rhetorical devices that seek to change circumstances, often relying on object-oriented models of persuasive action. For memetic theorists—who study memes as any replicable phenomenon—memes garner their power by spreading much as a virus would. Richard Dawkins first refers to memes as a virus, noting that they infect users who are hosts for its spread. The human is not a fully aware subject for Dawkins, but rather the medium through which memes infect and move. As he writes,

> When you plant a fertile meme in my mind you literally parasitize my brain, turning it into a vehicle for the meme's propagation in just the way that a virus may parasitize the genetic mechanism of a host cell. And this isn't just a way of talking—the meme for, say, 'belief in life after death' is actually realized physically, millions of times over, as a structure in the nervous systems of individual men the world over.[129]

In this way, the goal of the meme is to spread, to take an idea or trend and make it sticky. The users of 4chan and reddit have long understood this principle, much as the term meme became used to identify a visual phenomenon that operated on the ideas of memetic theory. Dawkins' approach to memetics connects theories of evolutionary biology to those of cultural evolution. Dawkins seems to describe—at least partially—the ways that macro image memes become cultural agents via their circulation and proliferation in the digital sphere.

Yet, visual memes work somewhat differently than theories of evolutionary biology, a situatedness that impacts the nature of rhetorical analysis. Dawkins' theories about memetics have not always aligned with the ways that memes—as contemporary, visual phenomena—work. Shifman notes two major criticisms of Dawkins' work as it applies to internet memes. First, importing key descriptive characteristics of memes from genetics is deeply reductive, and fails to take into consideration (1) how culture is different from biology and (2) how memes are unique from genes. Second, and perhaps more importantly for Shifman, memes are not only agents of communication that infect a passive host who serve as "*vectors* of cultural transmission."[130] Rather, for Shifman, humans matter. She notes that "the depiction of people as active agents is essential for understanding Internet memes, particularly when meaning is dramatically altered in the course of memetic diffusion."[131] For our purposes, memes are rhetorical in the hands of agential rhetors, who contribute to the creation and flow of memetic content on platforms that lubricate persuasive possibilities.

Our rhetorical analysis proceeds with the idea that humans *do* matter to the spread of memes. With Shifman, we contend that humans are central to the creation, negotiation, and movement of memetic content. Humans who fashion memes can use them as vessels to launch content (e.g., Alt-right propaganda) far and wide. But as critical rhetoricians, we are drawn to consider the communicative effect of memetic travels. This approach allows us to theorize both the weaponization of memes, but also the rearticulation of memes in ways that humans neither intended nor predicted. We understand memes serve as an agential and communicative medium operating within a network of both human and non-human agents, including language, platforms, code, hardware, and wetware (e.g., humans). That is, memes interact with humans who interact with memes within a networked system that affords certain forms of action while limiting others. This co-constitutive process is simultaneously replicative and productive of difference, within an ecosystem that produces any isolated memetic image and in so doing, constitutes (partial and evolving) systems of meaning. From this perspective, it matters that humans and non-humans (e.g., bots) generate and propagate memes before, during, and after the 2016 election from reddit and 4chan, as interconnected nodal points on this vast network of content generation and replication. These sites, which algorithmically amplify content shared by anonymous or pseudonymous agents, have distinct infrastructures and cultures that privilege memetic propagation. The 2016 election shows that tech-savvy rhetors on reddit and 4chan understood the complex, intermingled relationship between the medium and the message and used both to their political advantage.

One of the principal powers of memes, of course, is their ability to communicate novel messages expeditiously with relatively little effort spent on their creation. Memes transmit information quickly often because they "infect" would-be participants to engage in the creative process of composing and circulating memes in exchange for social capital, including likes and retweets. Memes fashion the conditions of possibility for their own diffusion on social media sites where creative communication and original content is valued. At the same time, engagement with memes reify and amplify both memetic form and content. When (re)making a meme, users both contribute to a conversation and legitimate that conversation by drawing on a meme's communicative history and redeploying it.[132] Some of the most effective memes are powerful because they are self-referential or rely on already popular content. By "mimicking" and "remixing" imagery, texts, inside jokes, and other elements, memes use pastiche to fashion something new.[133]

Memes use rhetorical invention, the creation of discourse, to move an audience by wedding action and invention. As participatory media, memes require and encourage participation in their creation. That is, effective memes suture the rhetorical processes of creation and delivery; dissemination of memetic content necessitates audience engagement. Before such an engagement may occur, memes must offer an enticing proposition to would-be participants, who may not be determined in advance. Of course, it is not remarkable for a rhetorician to say that effective symbolic exchange relies on invention given one's available means. What's different about memes—what's new—is two-fold. First, successful memes speak to a contingent audience of strangers who may number in the millions. Memes—and those who make them—must deftly utilize the rhetorical canons of invention and delivery to form a public from these potentially fragmented individuals. Second, and relatedly, memes amplify the scale at which both *inventio* and *actio* might occur. For example, memes specific to the 2016 election relied on partisan tropes as well as common symbols to generate both broad interest and shape specific publics according to their interests. After constituting a shared community along partisan allegiances, related memes invited users to propagate divisive content outward, constituting polarizing but relatively coherent publics. In so doing, memes turned passive audience members into active participants manufacturing and sharing political content primed to activate even more would-be participants. In other words, the rapidity with which memes are constructed, circulated, recreated, and rearticulated primes this rhetorical artifact for viral uptake. In turn, the virality of the meme continually constitutes cultural context—and political messages—as it moves. At least for the 2016 election, memes evolved into tactical propaganda.

Memes are persuasive artifacts that can enact political work in myriad modes. At the most basic level, they can be used to broadcast persuasive messages quickly and succinctly. Because they propagate quickly without much effort, memes can carry persuasive arguments to vast audiences, often more effectively than traditional message forms. However, their utility in persuasive campaigns is not limited to their use as messages. Memes also invite user participation in argument creation during several stages of a meme's life cycle, including periods of creation, negotiation, and diffusion. For instance, users interested in participating in a digital persuasive campaign may fashion or otherwise alter an existing meme for the purpose of influencing others. From there, memes may undergo a period of argumentative negotiation, where users or collectives contest the meaning of a meme and how a message might be best expressed. Memes may then be altered or remain more or less the same. At this point, the argument may or may not be disseminated further, as users share the meme to their networks. Sharing may or may not lead to uptake, actual persuasion, or other changes.

The battle over the meaning of memetic content can sometimes lead to the weaponization of memes as part of larger political campaigns. For instance, James Alexander McVey and Heather Suzanne Woods have shown how a memetic hashtag campaign related to the Black Lives Matter Movement—#handsupdontshoot—became a centralized battleground in public conversations about extrajudicial police killings. Studying the politicized transmogrification of images bearing or otherwise tagged with #handsupdontshoot, the authors note that "a powerful rhetorical element of #HandsUpDontShoot was its mimetic capacity—its ability to function simultaneously as a Twitter hashtag and a visual meme."[134] In response to visual memes identified with the anti-racist #handsupdontshoot and #blacklivesmatter campaigns, oppositional parties questioned the aggrieved status of Michael Brown and other victims of police brutality. The deployed memes marked the dereliction of the black body and circulated the hashtag #pantsupdontloot, corralling a debate over the meaning of police violence in the US. These visual memes are contested and appropriated by competing campaigns partially because of their rhetorical force. The power of memes as constitutive of meaning but also as means of persuasion cannot be understated. The production, negotiation, and dissemination of memes is not a neutral process. Rather, as this example shows, memes can be tactical instruments used by competing parties for the purposes of challenging or reifying power structures.

The 2016 campaign saw a precipitous rise in the use of social media for political campaigns. To be clear, social media has long been integral to national political campaigns. President Obama, for instance, famously harnessed the affordances of social media to reach young voters.[135] Yet, the 2016 presidential campaign threw into stark relief the centrality of social media—and of memes—in electoral politics. The campaign was punctuated by candidates sparring on social media, many instances of which ultimately became fodder for memes. Hillary Clinton's campaign, for instance, tweeted "Delete your account" in response to then-candidate Trump's tweet calling her "crooked." Bernie Sanders had a "dank meme stash" on Facebook. Donald Trump emerged the meme master, turning "Crooked Hillary" into a rallying cry for his populist movement, retweeting Pepe memes, and flipping Clinton's "deplorable" comment into a badge of honor. The rhetorical function of these memetic moments receives significant attention in the chapters that follow.

During and after the election, memes became tools for transmitting propaganda produced by the masses as well as institutional actors such as political campaigns. The campaigns of Trump and Clinton recognized the utility of memes to influence potential voters and tried to wield them to their advantage. Technology journalist Dawn Chmielewski noted that "Both camps have embraced certain memes as a shorthand way to share inside jokes with supporters, spread campaign messages or deliver rhetorical gut punches to their opponent, while distancing themselves from the most hateful."[136] Yet, then-candidate Trump was the clear victor in the meme war, in part because of his (and his followers') deft usage of platform cultures to circulate memes and influence processes of deliberation.

Platforms contribute to the weaponization of memes as propaganda both implicitly and explicitly. Daniel Kreiss and Shannon C. McGregor outline the extent to which technology firms such as Facebook, Twitter, and Google seek to shape both institutional and political structures. Coming into the 2016 election, for instance, these platforms donated considerable monies to partisan political conferences.[137] They also advised campaign staffers, including social media managers, on how to best reach would-be voters. Given that these platforms monetize user data, it is not remarkable to learn that their representatives coached campaigns to purchase advertising space on their sites and applications. However, the attempt to influence electoral politics was not limited to increasing revenue streams. As Kreiss and McGregor note, "Alongside growing advertising sales, these firms also sought out the visibility that came with the uptake of their products in the political space…as well as the opportunity to create relationships with legislators that would further their government relations efforts."[138] Social networking firms imbricated themselves within the deliberative process and their primary focus on advertising ensured that memes and other memetic imagery found a ready audience. In addition to supplying valuable user data and other services to political candidates, these platforms organized entire corporate structures to interlink platform economies with larger systems of governance. As we will show in chapter four, these platforms facilitated the use of algorithmically amplified ads and memes from Russia's Internet Research Agency.

Memes were also weaponized by individual users on these platforms, who employed these images to circulate messages about political issues. Some of these agents may have been motivated by an ideological desire to influence electoral politics. Others may have simply done it "for the lulz." Still others might have transformed memes into tactical propaganda to take the memetic form to its (ir)rational consequence, just to see what that consequence might be. Some of these savvy internet users—which mounting evidence suggests operated from enclaves in 4chan and reddit—gleefully proclaimed "We actually elected a meme as president."[139] Regardless of intent, the 2016 presidential election has shown us that the meme as a rhetorical genre has become persuasive, tactical propaganda.

Memes are useful distributors of propaganda insofar as they can spread widely and quickly. Those who design memes on 4chan and reddit understand the spread of memes and aim to infect users in that they seek to create memes that will become heavily trafficked either within enclaved sites themselves or more broadly via social media. The memes with the most widespread rhetorical force are those that extend beyond reddit and 4chan to other networked sites. Sometimes, these memes become fodder for journalistic coverage of digital sites or the election proper. Although 4chan and reddit have a documented antagonistic relationship with both mainstream media and more popular social media such as Facebook and Twitter, from a memetic perspective, these enclaved sites actually benefit from a symbiotic relationship with non-enclaved sites. One of the key characteristics of a meme is its ability to propagate across multiple bounded contexts. Drawing from each of these bounded communities, a meme succeeds when it draws more and different types of users into an active, engaged relationship with it. Put simply: a meme is most effective when it reaches the eyes and minds of many people.

Virality can often mark a meme's effectiveness, though memes that are not viral images can also be effective. As a visual form, the benefits of virality for the meme are multiple. First and foremost, virality ensures a wider variety of audiences encounter a meme. An individual sharing a funny photo with a small, bounded group of people does not an effective meme make. Rather, memes benefit from increased sharing that occurs at the level of the exponent, wherein the rapid circulation of a meme increases precipitously. Second, and relatedly, viral memes become part of the cultural *zeitgeist*. When memes go viral, they become cultural touchstones subject to exponential memetic proliferation through self-referential remixing. On a social level, knowing, or better, remixing a viral meme becomes a marker of cultural belonging. Those who witness the viral phenomenon garner social capital as those "in the know" whereas those who miss the viral expression are out of the loop.[140] Sharing a viral meme demonstrates that a person is savvy enough to have a finger on the digital cultural pulse; being among the first to share a meme might indicate superiority.[141] Importantly, networked circulation of memes need not only be the result of intentional sharing by those who support the message. Sometimes, users will unintentionally propagate a meme by critiquing it, or expressing their intent to not participate in the type of culture proposed by the meme. At that moment, people who experience a positive association with the meme or its message may lead to its proliferation at the very same time as people experience a negative association with it. In sum, memes create culture by becoming part of it.

Toward a Rhetorical Analysis of Memes

Memes are important rhetorical artifacts because they are an increasingly primary mode of public address in the networked digital sphere. Like emoji text-speak, internet slang, and LOLspeak, memes have been understood as a distraction from the democratic deliberation process rather than a constitutive part of it. As this book will show, public culture is shaped by and constitutive of memetic images and discourse. And, because memes are both products of culture and produce culture, memes may be as constitutive as other forms of rhetoric. We reject the premise that content transmitted by memes does not contribute to democratic deliberation and argumentation. We also reject the objection that memetic communication is not an important avenue of persuasive public address. In fact, given the rapidity of a 24-hour news cycle and an attention economy dictated by rapidly-updating media, we believe succinct and humorous memes are potentially more likely than well-reasoned, lengthy debates to circulate rapidly and broadly. In that way, memes may infect (or at least influence) others. Memes also draw together several modalities of rhetoric—visual, affective, material—and propagate as an ever-adapting, constantly-updating rhetorical form. On the internet, memes may trump conventional discourse. No longer cordoned off to the "underbelly of the internet," memes have become a common language for persuasive communication. Their persuasive capacity is worth investigation, especially as they focus and form public discourse and conversation.

At every turn during the 2016 election, memes were the communicative media used by the American electorate, candidates, and elected officials to communicate key values about the republic. Supplementing, and at times overcoming, other forms of public address, memetic content overwhelmed traditional norms of presidential speechmaking proper. Memes also served as the means through which candidates could bypass institutional media such as television, print, and even digital press formats and the gatekeeping (or fact checking) measures endemic to them. Memes offered a way to speak directly to the electorate with very little interference. They also propagated quickly, with little cost and wider reach than traditional ad buys. Presidential candidates could—and did—wield memes as methods of reaching audiences more efficiently than ever before. In this sense, memes have become the latest communicative iteration of public address.

The rhetorical architecture of memes fashioned during the 2016 election and after offers substantial clues to understanding the radicalization of the American electorate. For the very same reason memes excel at addressing the public, they are also an imperfect vessel for democratic, deliberative dialogue. Suited well to rapid rearticulation, memes are fickle, fecund artifacts. They are ideologically ambivalent in their creation of public culture, favoring no singular partisan side or political perspective. Rather, memes are agnostic media subject to the whims of those who (re)create them. In the 2016 election, memes were effectively weaponized by both the Alt-right and foreign agents, benefitting Donald Trump's presidential candidacy and contributing to the downfall of Hillary Clinton's campaign. Certainly Clinton's loss was overdetermined by numerous factors, including the rise of democratic, erstwhile socialist Bernie Sanders, misogyny, xenophobia, anti-blackness, and a devolving political party system. Yet, memes played a powerful role in Donald Trump's populist renaissance, in part because memes appear to be populist in their orientation. Memes—and the algorithmically-mediated platforms that facilitate their widespread distribution—contributed to the polarizing division of the American electorate. In the ringing echo-chambers of the Alt-right, memes spoke volumes. Whether it was for "the lulz," to sow discontent, or to influence the political system, memes became a crucial tool for communicating increasingly divisive messages about what society ought to look like.

The 2016 election saw a precipitous uptick in the use of memes to communicate about politics. The Alt-right was one of the most important contingents to harness the rhetorical affordances of memes. The Alt-right deftly deployed memes on networked sites such as 4chan, reddit, Facebook, and Twitter. As we will show in chapter four, members of the Alt-right created the conditions of possibility for the meme to be weaponized—not just against a political candidate or ideology, but against public deliberation and democracy proper. With this in mind, in the next chapter we perform a critical reading of one of the memes most central to the 2016 Trump campaign, Pepe the Frog. Perhaps unlike any other meme during the 2016 election, Pepe's steadfast dominance in the digital sphere was unmatched by anything other than his flexibility and subsequent circulation.

Notes

1. Ben Schreckinger, "World War Meme," *Politico*, March 3, 2017, http://politi.co/2mPM37L.
2. Schreckinger, "World War Meme."
3. Other scholars often note that enclaves have the potential to be radical spaces that build coalitions. The spaces under study in this volume sadly do not actualize those possibilities. See Karma R. Chavez, "Counter-Public Enclaves and Understanding the Function of Rhetoric in Social Movement Coalition-Building," *Communication Quarterly* 59, no. 1 (2011): 1–18; Lisa A. Flores, "Creating Discursive Space through a Rhetoric of Difference: Chicana Feminists Craft a Homeland," *Quarterly Journal of Speech* 82, no. 2 (1996): 142–156.
4. "4Chan: The Rude, Raunchy Underbelly of the Internet," *Fox News*, April 8, 2009, http://www.foxnews.com/story/2009/04/08/4chan-rude-raunchy-underbelly-internet.html.
5. Asaf Nissenbaum and Limor Shifman, "Internet Memes as Contested Cultural Capital: The Case of 4chan's /b/ Board," *New Media & Society* 19, no. 4 (2017): 483–501.
6. Lee Knuttila, "User Unknown: 4chan, Anonymity and Contingency," *First Monday* 16, no. 10 (2011).
7. Nissenbaum and Shifman, "Internet Memes as Contested Cultural Capital," 484; Gabriella Coleman, *Hacker, Hoaxer, Whistleblower, Spy: The Many Faces of Anonymous* (Brooklyn, NY: Verso Books, 2014), 43. Coleman, for instance, notes "All this occurs with the knowledge of impermanence. In contrast to mailing lists or many other kinds of online boards, there is no official archive. If a thread is not 'bumped' back to the top by a time reply, it dies and evaporates. On an active channel, like /b/, this entire life cycle occurs in just minutes."
8. Michael S. Bernstein *et al.*, "4chan and /b/: An Analysis of Anonymity and Ephemerality in a Large Online Community," *Proceedings of the Fifth International AAAI Conference on Weblogs and Social Media*, 2011, https://www.aaai.org/ocs/index.php/ICWSM/ICWSM11/paper/viewFile/2873/4398.
9. Phillips uses "user-generated content" on similar sites to approximate /b/'s historical development. Whitney Phillips, "The House that Fox Built: Anonymous, Spectacle, and Cycles of Amplification," *Television & New Media* 14, no. 6 (2012): 494–509.
10. Bernstein *et al.*, "4chan and /b/: An Analysis of Anonymity and Ephemerality in a Large Online Community."
11. Phillips, "The House that Fox Built," 494–509.
12. "4chan," *Know Your* Meme, n.d., accessed June 6, 2018, http://knowyourmeme.com/memes/sites/4chan; "4chan," *Wikipedia*, June 4, 2018, https://en.wikipedia.org/w/index.php?title=4chan&oldid=844323810.
13. Bernstein *et al.*, "4chan and /b/."
14. Phillips, "The House that Fox Built," 498.

15. "Something Awful," *Know Your Meme*, n.d., accessed November 6, 2017, http://knowyourmeme.com/memes/sites/something-awful.
16. Phillips, "The House that Fox Built," 498.
17. "All Your Base Are Belong to Us," *Know Your Meme*, n.d. accessed June 6, 2018, http://knowyourmeme.com/memes/all-your-base-are-belong-to-us.
18. Phillips, "The House that Fox Built," 498.
19. Zachary "Spokker Jones" Gutierrez, "The Awful Forums," *Something Awful*, August 15, 2004, http://www.somethingawful.com/news/the-awful-forums/.
20. Gutierrez, "The Awful Forums."
21. Whitney Phillips, *This Is Why We Can't Have Nice Things: Mapping the Relationship between Online Trolling and Mainstream Culture* (Cambridge, MA: MIT Press, 2015), 57.
22. Knuttila, "User Unknown."
23. Phillips, "The House That Fox Built."
24. Tim Bavlnka, "/Co/Operation and /Co/mmunity in /Co/Mics: 4chan's Hypercrisis," *Transformative Works and Cultures* 13 (2013).
25. Bavlnka, "Co/Operation and Co/mmunity."
26. "FAQ—4chan," *4Chan*, n.d., accessed June 20, 2018, http://www.4chan.org/faq.
27. Limor Shifman, *Memes in Digital Culture* (Cambridge, MA: MIT Press, 2014), 58.
28. "LOLcats," *Know Your Meme*, n.d., accessed January 5, 2018, http://knowyourmeme.com/memes/lolcats.
29. "LOLcats," *Know Your Meme*.
30. Phillips, *This is Why We Can Have Nice Things*, 137.
31. Shifman, *Memes in Digital Culture*, 111.
32. Phillips, *This is Why We Can Have Nice Things*, 140.
33. Ryan M. Milner, *The World Made Meme: Public Conversations and Participatory Media* (Cambridge, MA: MIT Press, 2016); Kate M. Miltner, "'There's No Place for Lulz on LOLCats': The Role of Genre, Gender, and Group Identity in the Interpretation and Enjoyment of an Internet Meme," *First Monday* 19, no. 8 (2014).
34. Miltner, "There's No Place for Lulz."
35. Quinn Norton, "How Anonymous Picks Targets, Launches Attacks, and Takes Powerful Organizations Down," *Wired*, July 3, 2012, https://www.wired.com/2012/07/ff_anonymous/.
36. Gabriella Coleman, "Anonymous: From the Lulz to Collective Action," *The New Everyday: A Media Commons Project*, April 6, 2011, http://mediacommons.futureofthebook.org/tne/pieces/anonymous-lulz-collective-action.
37. For a more robust treatment of Project Chanology, please see Coleman, *Hacker, Hoaxer, Whistleblower, Spy*.
38. Heather Suzanne Woods, "The Rhetorical Construction of Hacktivism: Analyzing the Anonymous Care Package" (master's thesis, Baylor University, 2013).
39. Julian Dibbell, "The Assclown Offensive: How to Enrage the Church of Scientology," *Wired*, September 21, 2009, https://www.wired.com/2009/09/mf-chanology/.
40. Coleman, *Hacker, Hoaxer, Whistleblower, Spy*, 5, 54–66.
41. Quinn Norton, "Anonymous 101 Part Deux: Morals Triumph Over Lulz," *Wired*, December 30, 2011, https://www.wired.com/2011/12/anonymous-101-part-deux/.

42. Dibbell, "The Assclown Offensive."
43. Dibbell, "The Assclown Offensive."
44. Woods, "The Rhetorical Construction of Hacktivism"; Coleman, *Hacker, Hoaxer, Whistleblower, Spy*, 6. As Coleman describes it, during and after Project Chanology, "Trolling had given way to an earnest activist endeavor, as if Anonymous had emerged from its online sanctuary and set out to improve the world. Over the next two years, some Anonymous members would hatch unrelated activist subgroups, and many participants came to identify themselves as bona fide activists, albeit with a transgressive twist."
45. Coleman, *Hacker, Hoaxer, Whistleblower, Spy*, 63, 68, 73.
46. Coleman, *Hacker, Hoaxer, Whistleblower, Spy*, 72–3.
47. Coleman, *Hacker, Hoaxer, Whistleblower, Spy*, 72–3.
48. Coleman, *Hacker, Hoaxer, Whistleblower, Spy*, 3.
49. Coleman, *Hacker, Hoaxer, Whistleblower, Spy*, 3.
50. Phillips, "The House that Fox Built."
51. "About Reddit," *Reddit*, n.d., https://about.reddit.com/press/.
52. "The Evolution and Future of Reddit's Business Model," *Bloomberg*, August 24, 2016, https://www.bloomberg.com/news/videos/2016-08-24/the-evolution-and-future-of-reddit-s-business-model.
53. Bryan Menegus, "Reddit Is Tearing Itself Apart," *Gizmodo*, November 29, 2016, https://gizmodo.com/reddit-is-tearing-itself-apart-1789406294.
54. Andrew Couts, "Reddit Is in Open Revolt with Itself," *Daily Dot*, July 3, 2015, https://www.dailydot.com/news/reddit-revolt-blackout-2015-ama-victoria/.
55. "Frequently Asked Questions," *Reddit*, n.d., https://www.reddit.com/wiki/faq#wiki_why_should_i_try_to_accumulate_karma.3F.
56. David Carr, "Reddit Thrives Under Hands-Off Policy of Advance Publications," *New York Times*, September 2, 2012, https://www.nytimes.com/2012/09/03/business/media/reddit-thrives-after-advance-publications-let-it-sink-or-swim.html.
57. "The Evolution and Future of Reddit's Business Model," *Bloomberg*.
58. Julia Greenberg, "For the Record: The Relationship Between WIRED and Reddit," *Wired*, July 28, 2015, https://www.wired.com/2015/07/wired-conde-nast-reddit/.
59. Carr, "Reddit Thrives Under Hands-Off Policy of Advance Publications."
60. Greenberg, "For the Record."
61. Randal Olson, "Retracing the Evolution of Reddit through Post Data," *Dr. Randal S. Olson*, March 12, 2013, http://www.randalolson.com/2013/03/12/retracing-the-evolution-of-reddit-through-post-data/.
62. hueypriest, "Global Reddit Meetup Day Is Happening on Saturday, June 19th," *Reddit*, April 21, 2010, https://www.reddit.com/r/blog/comments/bu9d6/global_reddit_meetup_day_is_happening_on_saturday/.
63. "Reddit: Billions Served," *Upvoted*, February 2, 2011, https://redditblog.com/2011/02/02/reddit-billions-served/.
64. "Reddit: Billions Served."
65. Matt Lynley, "Reddit Had 1.8 BILLION Pageviews This Month," *Business Insider*, October 31, 2011, http://www.businessinsider.com/ignore-the-jailbait-reddits-users-doubled-in-eight-months-2011-10.

66. Carr, "Reddit Thrives."
67. Carr, "Reddit Thrives."
68. Anne Soellner in Alex LaCasse, "Reddit Director Talks Social Media's Impact on 2016 Election," *seacoastonline.com*, October 3, 2017, http://www.seacoastonline.com/news/20171003/reddit-director-talks-social-medias-impact-on-2016-election.
69. Soellner, "Reddit Director Talks Social Media's Impact on 2016 Election."
70. Christine Lagorio-Chafkin, "Reddit Is a 'Reflection of Humanity,' Says CEO," *Inc*, November 17, 2016, https://www.inc.com/christine-lagorio/reddit-and-the-platform-argument.html. Interestingly, Facebook's Mark Zuckerberg would mount a similar defense in front of Congress during a voluntary hearing in Spring 2018.
71. LaCasse, "Reddit Director Talks Social Media's Impact on 2016 Election."
72. "The Evolution and Future of Reddit's Business Model," *Bloomberg*.
73. Lagorio-Chafkin, "Reddit Is a 'Reflection of Humanity.'"
74. "Red Pill," *Know Your Meme*, n.d., accessed June 7, 2018, http://knowyourmeme.com/memes/red-pill.
75. Megan Garber, "Denver Resident Here. Reddit, I'm Doing My Best to Update This," *The Atlantic*, July 20, 2012, https://www.theatlantic.com/technology/archive/2012/07/denver-resident-here-reddit-im-doing-my-best-to-update-this/260115/.
76. Brian X. Chen, "How Reddit Scooped the Press on the Aurora Shootings," *New York Times*, July 23, 2012, https://bits.blogs.nytimes.com/2012/07/23/reddit-aurora-shooter-aff/.
77. Chen, "How Reddit Scooped the Press."
78. Chen, "How Reddit Scooped the Press."
79. Alyson Shontell, "What It's Like When Reddit Wrongly Accuses Your Loved One of Murder," *Business Insider*, July 26, 2013, http://www.businessinsider.com/reddit-falsely-accuses-sunil-tripathi-of-boston-bombing-2013-7.
80. Shontell, "What It's Like When Reddit Wrongly Accuses."
81. "Reflections on the Recent Boston Crisis," *Upvoted*, April 22, 2013, https://redditblog.com/2013/04/22/reflections-on-the-recent-boston-crisis/.
82. Adrienne Massanari, "#Gamergate and The Fappening: How Reddit's Algorithm, Governance, and Culture Support Toxic Technocultures," *New Media & Society* 19, no. 3 (2017): 330.
83. "The Fappening/Celebgate," *Know Your Meme*, n.d., accessed June 7, 2018, http://knowyourmeme.com/memes/events/the-fappening-celebgate.
84. Caitlin Dewey, "Meet the Unashamed 33-Year-Old Who Brought the Stolen Celebrity Nudes to the Masses," *Washington Post*, September 5, 2014, https://www.washingtonpost.com/news/the-intersect/wp/2014/09/05/meet-the-unashamed-33-year-old-who-brought-the-stolen-celebrity-nudes-to-the-masses/?noredirect=on&utm_term=.a94af958349d.
85. Alice Marwick, "Scandal or Sex Crime? Ethical Implications of the Celebrity Nude Photo Leaks," *AoIR 2016: The 17th Annual Conference of the Association of Internet Researchers* (Berlin, Germany: AoIR, 2016).
86. Quora Contributor, "Is Apple Responsible for the Hacked Leak of Private Celebrity Photos Via iCloud?," *Forbes*, September 3, 2014, https://www.forbes.com/sites/quora/2014/09/03/is-apple-responsible-for-the-hacked-leak-of-private-celebrity-photos-via-icloud/; Luke Dormehl, "Apple Was Aware of iCloud Security Flaw 6 Months before

The Fappening," *Cult of Mac*, September 25, 2014, https://www.cultofmac.com/297709/apple-aware-icloud-security-flaw-6-months-fappening; Brett Molina, "Apple: iCloud Not Breached in Celebrity Photo Leak," *USA Today*, September 2, 2014, https://www.usatoday.com/story/tech/personal/2014/09/02/apple-icloud-leak/14979323/.

87. Selena Larson, "Another Hacker Pleads Guilty for His Role in the 'Fappening,'" *Daily Dot*, July 2, 2016, https://www.dailydot.com/layer8/majerczyk-fappening-hacker-guilty-icloud/.
88. Massanari, "#Gamergate and The Fappening," 335.
89. Massanari, "#Gamergate and The Fappening," 335.
90. Andy Greenberg, "Hacked Celeb Pics Made Reddit Enough Cash to Run Its Servers for a Month," *Wired*, September 10, 2014, https://www.wired.com/2014/09/celeb-pics-reddit-gold/.
91. Reddit received harsh criticism that it happily used "The Fappening" to make money. This argument, from both internet critics and scholars, suggested that reddit had not only continued its "hands off" moderating policy in the case of the leak, but had perhaps actively waited to remove the illegal content because it was a boon for both traffic and the purchase of reddit "gold," which is a giftable "premium membership program" that "grants you access to extra features to improve your reddit experience." Later, systems admin moderator Jason Harvey (reddit pseudonym: alienth) released a thousand-word missive calling The Fappening "a very shitty thing."
92. Greenberg, "Hacked Celeb Pics."
93. Massanari, "#Gamergate and The Fappening," 336.
94. Marwick, "Scandal or Sex Crime?"
95. CloudyPikachu, "What Is Gamergate?" *Reddit*, July 20, 2017, https://www.reddit.com/r/KotakuInAction/comments/6og7ak/what_is_gamergate/.
96. CloudyPikachu, "What Is Gamergate?"
97. Wu, no stranger to harassment from trolls, received the following threat: "Guess What bitch? I now know where you live....your mutilated corpse will be on the front page of [feminist website] Jezebel tomorrow....nobody will care when you die." David Whitford, "Brianna Wu vs. the Gamergate Troll Army," *Inc*, April 2015, https://www.inc.com/magazine/201504/david-whitford/gamergate-why-would-anyone-want-to-kill-brianna-wu.html.
98. Ellen "ekjp" Pao, "Resignation, Thank You," *Reddit*, July 10, 2015, https://www.reddit.com/r/self/comments/3cudi0/resignation_thank_you/.
99. Andrew Couts, "Reddit Is in Open Revolt with Itself," *Daily Dot*, July 3, 2015, https://www.dailydot.com/news/reddit-revolt-blackout-2015-ama-victoria/.
100. Pao, "Resignation, Thank You."
101. Pao, "Resignation, Thank You."
102. The 2015 reddit blackout was not only precipitated by collective anger at the CEO, who was described by some users as aloof at best and an antagonistic, hypocritical feminazi, at worst. Rather, long-time reddit users critiqued changes made to corporatize the website, including changes to its content policy and how communication between unpaid moderators and administration functioned. David Auerbach, "What the Reddit Rebellion Is Really About," *Slate*, July 6, 2015, http://www.slate.com/articles/technology/bitwise/2015/07/reddit_amageddon_what_it_s_really_about.html.

103. "Good News—Reddit Admins Remove a Number of Harassing Hate Subreddits, Including /r/FatPeopleHate. Nothing of Value Was Lost," *Reddit*, June 10, 2015, https://www.reddit.com/r/AgainstHateSubreddits/comments/39bz4e/good_news_reddit_admins_remove_a_number_of/.
104. PostNationalism, "Reddit Increases Censorship," *Reddit*, June 10, 2015, https://np.reddit.com/r/FreeSpeech/comments/39bw25/reddit_increases_censorship/.
105. Dr_Wiggsel_Maarten, "Retarded Criminal Cunt Pao and He Cuck Squad Are Banning Subs That Hurt Their Fatty Feelings," *Reddit*, June 10, 2015, https://www.reddit.com/r/CIRCLEFUCKERS/comments/39c9jd/retarded_criminal_cunt_pao_and_he_cuck_squad_are/.
106. Auerbach summarizes this phenomenon: "Normally, it's the mods who clamp down on the uprisings of the hoi polloi and stamp out profane comments, inappropriate images, and mass cross-subreddit invasions ('brigades'), a mostly thankless task for which they also receive zilch. This time, however, the mods themselves revolted, and their powers let them do far more damage to Reddit than annoyed haters of fat people. The result makes evident the cracks in Reddit's business model—and raises questions about how long the site can survive in its present structure." Auerbach, "What the Reddit Rebellion Is Really About."
107. Couts, "Reddit Is in Open Revolt with Itself."
108. Mathew Ingram, "Reddit is at War with Itself: Is It a Community or a Business?" *Fortune*, July 6, 2015, http://fortune.com/2015/07/06/reddit-community-business/.
109. Auerbach, "What the Reddit Rebellion Is Really About."
110. Hayley Tsukayama, "Who Is Victoria Taylor, the Woman at the Heart of the Reddit Revolt?," *Washington Post*, July 6, 2015, https://www.washingtonpost.com/news/the-switch/wp/2015/07/06/who-is-victoria-taylor-the-woman-at-the-heart-of-the-reddit-revolt/.
111. Davey Alba, "Reddit's Meltdown Exposes Its Huge Conundrum," *Wired*, July 7, 2015, https://www.wired.com/2015/07/reddits-meltdown-exposes-huge-conundrum/.
112. Ellen "ekjp" Pao, "We Apologize," *Reddit*, July 6, 2015, https://www.reddit.com/r/announcements/comments/3cbo4m/we_apologize/.
113. Steve "spez" Huffman, "Let's Talk Content. AMA," *Reddit*, July 16, 2015, https://www.reddit.com/r/announcements/comments/3djjxw/lets_talk_content_ama/.
114. Huffman, "Let's Talk Content. AMA."
115. "Reddit Content Policy," *Reddit*, n.d., https://www.reddit.com/help/contentpolicy/#section_prohibited_behavior.
116. Steve "spez" Huffman, "Let's All Have a Town Hall about R/All," *Reddit*, July 16, 2016, https://www.reddit.com/r/announcements/comments/4oedco/lets_all_have_a_town_hall_about_rall/.
117. Menegus, "Reddit is Tearing Itself Apart."
118. Huffman, "Let's All Have a Town Hall about R/All."
119. Huffman, "Let's All Have a Town Hall about R/All."
120. Menegus, "Reddit is Tearing Itself Apart."
121. Dale Beran, "4chan: The Skeleton Key to the Rise of Trump," *Medium*, February 14, 2017, https://medium.com/@DaleBeran/4chan-the-skeleton-key-to-the-rise-of-trump-624e7cb798cb.
122. Beran, "4chan: The Skeleton Key to the Rise of Trump."
123. Shifman, *Memes in Digital Culture*, 13.

124. danah boyd, "Social Network Sites as Networked Publics: Affordances, Dynamics, and Implications," in *A Networked Self: Identity, Community, and Culture on Social Network Sites*, ed. Zizi Papacharissi (New York: Routledge, 2010), 39–58.
125. Graham Cormode and Balachander Krishnamurthy, "Key Differences between Web 1.0 and Web 2.0," *First Monday* 13, no. 6 (2008).
126. Tarleton Gillespie, "The Politics of 'Platforms,'" *New Media & Society* 12, no. 3 (2010): 347–64.
127. Shifman, *Memes in Digital Culture*, 19.
128. Shifman, *Memes in Digital Culture*, 19.
129. Richard Dawkins, *The Selfish Gene: 30th Anniversary Edition* (New York: Oxford University Press, 2006), 192.
130. Shifman, *Memes in Digital Culture*, 12.
131. Shifman, *Memes in Digital Culture*, 12.
132. As Milner notes, "Internet memes depend on collective creation, circulation, and transformation. They're multimodal texts that facilitate participation by reappropriation, by balancing a fixed premise with novel expression." See Milner, *The World Made Meme*, 14.
133. Shifman, *Memes in Digital Culture*, 22.
134. James Alexander McVey and Heather Suzanne Woods, "Anti-racist Activism and the Transformational Principles of Hashtag Publics: From #HandsUpDontShoot to #PantsUpDontLoot," *Present Tense: A Journal of Rhetoric in Society* 5, no. 3 (2016).
135. Derrick L. Cogburn and Fatima K. Espinoza-Vasquez, "From Networked Nominee to Networked Nation: Examining the Impact of Web 2.0 and Social Media on Political Participation and Civic Engagement in the 2008 Obama Campaign," *Journal of Political Marketing* 10, no. 1–2 (2011): 189–213.
136. Dawn Chmielewski, "Internet Memes Emerge as 2016 Election's Political Dog Whistle," *USA Today*, September 30, 2016, https://www.usatoday.com/story/tech/news/2016/09/30/internet-memes-white-house-election-president/91272490/.
137. Daniel Kreiss and Shannon C. McGregor, "Technology Firms Shape Political Communication: The Work of Microsoft, Facebook, Twitter, and Google With Campaigns During the 2016 U.S. Presidential Cycle," *Political Communication* 35, no. 2 (2018): 155–177.
138. Kreiss and McGregor, "Technology Firms Shape Political Communication," 161.
139. Abby Ohlheiser, "'We Actually Elected a Meme as President': How 4chan Celebrated Trump's Victory," *Washington Post*, November 9, 2016, https://www.washingtonpost.com/news/the-intersect/wp/2016/11/09/we-actually-elected-a-meme-as-president-how-4chan-celebrated-trumps-victory/?utm_term=.37abacf78b6e.
140. Nissenbaum and Shifman, "Internet Memes as Contested Cultural Capital."
141. Ryan Holiday, "A Fingertip Feel for the Internet: An Interview With Professional Meme Creator Ka5sh," *Observer*, August 8, 2017, http://observer.com/2017/08/a-fingertip-feel-for-the-internet-an-interview-with-professional-meme-creator-ka5sh-virality-influencers-meme-accounts/.

· 2 ·

PEPE THE FROG AND ICONIC ASSEMBLAGES

On October 13, 2015, a new meme appeared on Donald J. Trump's Twitter feed. It was a cartoon depiction of Trump as president of the United States, but in place of his tanned face was the visage of a green frog (See Fig. 2.1). The caption referenced the Drudge Report and Brietbart News—far right content and news sites—and @codyave, a Trump supporter. The retweet also linked to a video entitled, "You Can't Stump the Trump," a montage with scenes of Trump exerting his dominance over other presidential candidates and ending with a series of references to the Illuminati and other conspiracy theories. Despite this robust and complex message, what proved most significant about this tweet for the larger public was the candidate's green face. For those who recognized Trump's mask, they understood that Trump had retweeted an image of himself as Pepe the Frog. Although a cartoon frog might appear to the uninitiated as a rather curious association, the image was far from benign. Instead, the meme was a dog whistle to the Alt-right. It conveyed a secondary meaning only understood by those able to decode its significance. As marked by the accompanying conspiracy theory video, Trump's juxtaposition with Pepe enmeshed his candidacy with a particular group of would-be conspirators.

Figure 2.1: Can't Stump the Trump.

The use of Pepe aligned Trump with Alt-right members of 4chan and reddit. By October of 2015, Pepe the Frog had already become an iconic symbol of the Alt-right, particularly those associated with 4chan's /pol/ and reddit's r/the_donald/. Here, the juxtaposition of Pepe and Trump explicitly related his candidacy to a growing number of supporters in these forums. Reports indicate that 4chan users rejoiced at this tweet, calling him the "first meme president" and heralding their own prowess at meme invention.[1] The move, then, was strategic. The use of Pepe was a nod to those users who had already begun using memes to bolster Trump's candidacy. Indeed, Trump had a swath of meme creators who worked outside of the campaign but nevertheless helped shape a winning strategy. As stated by Matt Braynard, Trump's data team leader, "Whenever he would retweet something that was funny, or perhaps pretty cutting or a critical attack or anything like that—those were the holy moments."[2] As Braynard points out, such retweets were strategic, a wink to those 4chan and reddit members attempting to meme Trump into the presidency. By circulating memes of his supporters, Trump demonstrated his investment in their values and ideals. Moreover, these retweets emboldened the work of meme innovators, who were affirmed by Trump and continued to make memes on his behalf. "You Can't Stump the Trump" was a video meme designed by YouTuber "Comrade Stump," a montage of footage from Trump's campaign appearances used to depict him as an unassailable candidate.[3] Volume Four of Comrade Stump's series became memetic once the video link appeared on Twitter with the Pepe meme as the clickable connection. When Trump retweeted the meme and link, such investment validated and animated the efforts of 4chan and reddit members.

Some denounced Trump Pepe as emblematic of Donald Trump's racism and biases. However, despite their contestations, Trump's critics could not outstrip the candidate's Alt-right support. That is, efforts to demonize Trump for his alignment with white nationalists failed to undermine the support of his base, and may have invigorated supporters. On September 9, 2016, Hillary Clinton delivered a speech in which she called Trump's supporters "racist, sexist, homophobic, xenophobic, Islamaphobic."[4] She continued by saying that Trump voters were a "basket of deplorables"[5] (See Fig. 2.2). Her campaign website issued a statement directly implicating Pepe as a symbol of white supremacy and condemning Trump's refusal to disavow these constituencies.[6] For Clinton, these claims were an attempt to call out Trump's prejudice, his politics of fear and resentment. Yet, the statement had a boomerang effect.[7] Immediately, the meme army generated images that showed Trump, his potential cabinet, and Pepe the Frog as "The Deplorables." Instead of dissuading folks from supporting Trump, Clinton's speech facilitated the connection between Trump and his Alt-right supporters. David Auerbach, a tech culture writer, contends that this public moment forced the left to talk about Trump's memes, but to the benefit of Trump and the Alt-right. "You've got all these fear-mongering articles talking about how Pepe is frightening and the new Nazi symbol," he observed, "but it was just free advertising [….] Because it didn't do anything to decrease usage of it, it just made people say, 'wow, we're getting through.'"[8] The Pepe image drove attention, including both positive and negative responses. Attempts to denounce Pepe did not dispel the tide. Admonishments fueled investment in the image as an iconic symbol for Alt-right Trump supporters.

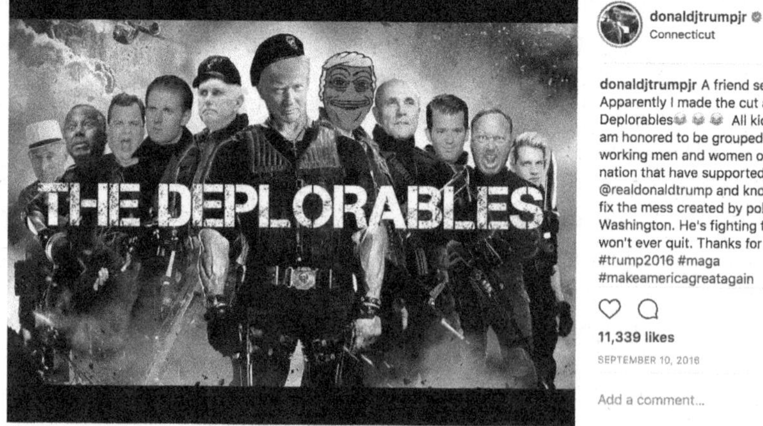

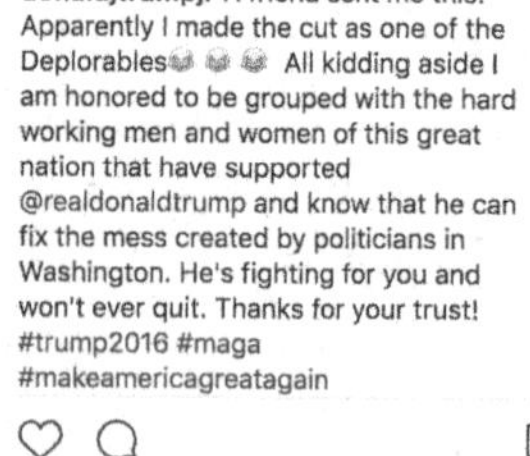

Figure 2.2: The Deplorables.

Pepe as an iconic symbol is key to explaining how the Alt-right became a publicly identifiable whole. For insiders, Pepe enabled meme generators on 4chan and reddit to find authorization for their work given the rapid replication of the image across social media platforms. Pepe was an alternative to the swastika, the Klan's blood drop cross, or other symbols of extremist groups. The frog image proved palpable because it was not easy to detect initially. The cute, and seemingly harmless, frog traveled quickly and allowed individuals to visually locate compatriots. For the mainstream public, Pepe offered a symbol of identification for the Alt-right—an image to mark who was spreading hatred and ought to be muted. Yet, even after Pepe had become identified as an Alt-right symbol, his replication persisted. The image was entrenched as an icon precisely because he was so reviled by the left. To understand how the Alt-right congealed in the public imagination and began to propagate its messages, it is necessary to interrogate the circulation of Pepe and the role of iconicity in identification and replication. By grasping how Pepe aggrandized the Alt-right for insiders and outsiders, scholars gain a stronger sense of how the Alt-right garnered a significant platform in public culture.

The Travels of Pepe the Frog

Pepe the Frog was not always a hate symbol. He first emerged in 2005 in a comic by Matt Furie entitled *Boy's Club*. The comics depicted Pepe as the typical college "bro," "playing video games, eating pizza, smoking pot and being harmlessly gross."[9] Pepe's use as a meme is said to have originated once the comic showed him urinating with his pants laying at his ankles. As articulated by Dani Di Placido, "When Pepe is questioned over his unusual choice, he responds with, 'feels good, man' (See Fig. 2.3). In that one simple statement, Pepe proved that he didn't give a toss about societal expectation, and simply does, well, whatever feels good."[10] By 2006, Pepe was a "sensation" who emerged on 4chan's /r9k/ board.[11] In early 2008, 4chan's /b/ board uploaded the comic strip of his urinating antics, which prompted users to create memes of Pepe's face and proliferate the phrase, "Feels Good, Man."[12] Pepe's irreverence to orthodoxy earned him legions of fans who adopted his catchphrase, "Feels Good Man," and scored him an entry on Know Your Meme.[13] Pepe remained an irreverent, fairly innocuous meme for over a decade. By 2015, he was one of the most popular memes on a number of social media outlets, with his own Tumblr feed, subreddit, and Facebook page.[14]

Figure 2.3: Feels Good, Man.

At the height of Pepe's popularity, he began to emerge as something else: a symbol for the Alt-right. By late 2015, 4chan and reddit boards mashed up Nazi Pepe with images of Donald Trump.[15] As Jason Koebler for *Motherboard* notes, "Pepe gained traction on the 'normal' internet and eventually became very, very popular on r/the_donald/, alt-right Twitter, and other online hangouts that generally support Donald Trump."[16] Generally, insiders to 4chan and other boards insist that when a meme becomes overly used by mainstream actors, that meme loses its cache. Pepe lost 4chan and reddit cultural capital given his overuse. In response, some users of 4chan and reddit began to deploy Pepe with Nazi imagery. The *Daily Beast* interviewed @JaredTSwift,[17] an avowed white nationalist, who asserted there was a concerted effort to "reclaim Pepe from normies."[18] While @JaredTSwift later admitted that he trolled the *Daily Beast* reporter into believing an Alt-right conspiracist plot (his posturing is something we will pursue in chapter three), public response to the *Daily Beast* story fueled Pepe's Nazism.[19] Pepe had already appeared regularly with Nazi symbolism. Yet, once the *Daily Beast* published the claimed association between Pepe and neo-Nazis, the coupling spread like wildfire.[20] Pepe appeared on 4chan, reddit, and other social media sites with Nazi imagery—swastikas, Hitler's mustache, etc. The image quickly became a symbol for the Alt-right with Twitter users who identified as such tweeting Nazi Pepe imagery and using a frog emoji in their descriptions.[21] Pepe became a new kind of white supremacist symbol, one that allowed like-minded folks to mark themselves without using necessarily explicit references. In this way, one of the most popular memes of the last decade became a brand symbol for the Alt-right.

Pepe's reclamation from unorthodox bro to renegade white nationalist enunciated the self-avowed outsider positionality of many Trump supporters. By many accounts, Trump was a laughable candidate who did not have mainstream media credit. Given this claimed underdog status, he appealed to those who sought to link him to Pepe. Trump embodied the ethos Pepe came to represent. Trump's failings—as understood by the left—were overlooked by those who brandished Trump memes, and even offered added value. As articulated by Dale Beran, "But, what the left doesn't realize is, this is not a problem for Trump's supporters, rather, the reason why they support him."[22] Trump's earlier defeats lubricated his connection with Pepe. The underdog character of each warranted such symbolic displacement and, indeed, incorporation. This rhetorical imagery bolstered those who found hope when a laughable candidate could aim, ultimately successfully, for the White House.

For users of 4chan and reddit, there was considerable momentum surrounding the idea that they could meme Donald Trump—an absurd nominee—into the presidency.

The articulation of Trump to Pepe came from a rough assemblage of board and social media users who deployed Pepe to promote Trump. As Parker Atkinson writes, from a "motley crew of censorship-hating internet refugees, libertarians, trolls, traditional conservatives and, in some cases, white supremacists, an uneasy alliance formed around a central figure who seemed to represent their shared interests: businessman and reality TV star Donald Trump, who was then running for president."[23] Trump had an army of meme makers who would come to dominate many social media fronts. None of these meme makers were officially connected to the campaign *per se*, but meme generators likely found sanction from Trump's and other's retweets. Other meme makers were freelance agents, creating content on their own. Memes of Trump proliferated on Twitter, spurred on by a huge fan base that participated in locations where meme-making was rewarded and revered—such as r/the_donald/. Take, for instance, a reddit discussion with the self-proclaimed creator of "You Can't Stump the Trump." Respondents throughout the forum heaped accolades on him (e.g., "We're not worthy") while they simultaneously explained how they became Trump supporters precisely because of his memes and videos.[24] Here, effective meme work, especially images of Trump as Pepe encourage the meme army working on Trump's behalf.

Memes became the mechanism the Alt-right used to generate media coverage and a stronger public presence. Indeed, in July of 2016, one tweet was able to shift the terms of engagement between the Trump and Clinton campaigns. This tweet did not involve Pepe, but nevertheless facilitated counter responses by the left and thereby created the grounds for identifying the Alt-right as a collective. On July 2, Trump retweeted an image of Hillary Clinton superimposed over a background of money, with the headline "History Made," and a Star of David textbox reading "Most Corrupt Candidate Ever."[25] While he later replaced the original image with a reboot—an identical image with a circle textbox instead of the Star of David (See Fig. 2.4)—reporters quickly learned that the anti-Semitic image emerged from 8chan and a group of far right Trump supporters.[26] In August, Clinton delivered a speech in Reno where she called out the "emerging racist ideology known as the alt-right" supporting Donald Trump's candidacy.[27] By the end of September 2016, the Anti-Defamation League deemed the Alt-right a hate group and designated Pepe a hate symbol.[28] In these key moments, the Alt-right began to make headlines and activated considerable interest. Memes and Pepe had expedited the group's appearance in the mainstream. Even if press coverage demeaned the Alt-right, these appearances provided more press for the group and piqued public interest.

Figure 2.4: History Made.

While for most, these condemnations of the Alt-right as white supremacists or neo-Nazis would weaken Trump's legitimacy as a presidential candidate, such reproaches did not diminish the resolve of many supporters. Instead, the knowledge that Clinton and the media were forced to respond to their memes, and that Pepe had found renewed life as a hate symbol, energized the work of meme creators. Attempts by the left to indicate Pepe's newfound white supremacist symbolism became fodder for more memes. Within hours, Clinton's comment that Trump supporters were a "basket of deplorables" invited a host of memes embracing the titular role. Several days later, even Donald Trump Jr. retweeted an image of the Trump campaign staff and possible cabinet members as black ops-style para-military (See Fig. 2.3).[29] Pepe was featured as the right-hand soldier to Trump's leadership. In these visuals, Pepe is the iconic symbol that stands up for deplorables. Pepe marks the victory of the underdog over political orthodoxy. These tweets demonstrate both the breadth of mainstream legitimization and the speed of the memes' virality. In drawing on conventions of political decorum, condemnations of Pepe could not appeal to the very audiences the Alt-right courted.

Quite the reverse, these denouncements spurred the invention of new flavors of Trump Pepe and enhanced the circulation of the message. The Clinton campaign spoke to its own supporters, calling out white supremacy to galvanize the Democratic base.[30] Yet, such actions assumed that this group of neo-Nazis could be curbed through rebuke. Instead, rebuke resulted in further attention to the Alt-right through the eruption of Trump Pepe memes. Little tactical ground remained to effectively combat the Alt-right. More audiences adopted the title of "deplorable" through bumper stickers, t-shirts, buttons, and the like.[31] The persona embraced a politics of victimhood and indicated an overdetermined investment in an outsider status—a status memetically and discursively sutured to white supremacy.[32] Given the way users discussed their outsider status on 4chan and reddit, this result makes sense. Memetic redeployment on sites like Twitter and Facebook re-created a similar politics of victimhood. Victimhood of this sort could not be combatted through political attack. In fact, attacks against this group only degraded Clinton's position with broader audiences, especially the white working class.[33] The repeated appearances of Pepe and the deplorables label widened the audience for Alt-right messaging and constrained Clinton's argumentative ground.

The absence of effective memes for Clinton and the mainstream left further exacerbated the situation. While Clinton and her supporters tried to bolster her campaign, such efforts were often ineffective and criticized for creating the false appearance of grassroots activism.[34] Angela Nagle argues that liberals pursued call-out arguments and memes to their own detriment—they were unable to gain social traction against the Alt-right. Leftist social media users became "ultra" puritans, too circumspect of their own language and practices.[35] Moreover, Alt-right harassment dissuaded internet users to create or share their own pro-Clinton memes. As Angelo Carusone, president of Media Matters for America, told *Politico*, "'raids' of other social media platforms and comment sections—discouraged expressions of pro-Clinton sentiment from people caught off guard by the vitriol."[36] Similarly, social media users who voiced opposition were silenced. As early as January 2016, Republican consultant Cheri Jacobus tweeted that Pepe was a symbol of white supremacists—a statement that earned her harassment and condemnation.[37] Others had similar experiences.[38] Taken together, these conditions established a ripe battleground for Alt-right memes with Pepe images leading the charge.

Nazi Pepe memes and similar images were rather shocking in orientation and content. This was by design. Atkinson explains that Alt-right memes seek to shock; they are "gleefully offensive."[39] The goal is to offend because it is enjoyable to do so—a concept we address in the next chapter—but also because outrageous images are more likely to garner news coverage and public outrage. For many users on /pol/ and r/the_donald/, these responses will only further enhance the positionality of the Alt-right in its ongoing tactical work. Nazi Pepe images show a laughing frog standing in front of a concentration camp smokestack, a dabbing frog with a Nazi-emblem t-shirt placed adjacent to bodies being burned in an oven, a masked Pepe with an AR-15 and a collection of nooses, Pepe holding a gun at the head of a woman marked with the symbol for Twitter wearing a blindfold reading "slut."[40] Each of these images targets Jewish folks, black folks, women, and more. They are designed to be vicious imagery—playful with the most morally depraved acts including genocide, lynchings, murder, and more. All of these images circulated broadly outside of 4chan and reddit, suggesting that these were not images speaking to insider audiences, but rather provocations to external audiences. These were "gleefully offensive" images, crafted to shock so as to gain a rhetorical advantage. That is, these images were made to be outrageous such that shock might enable public attention and enhance recognition of the Alt-right.

By occupying digital spaces in this manner, Pepe memes and the like intensified mainstream media coverage of white nationalists. The heightened coverage of such groups was, in part, generated by those publicity events that were made to signal their significance. Even when those stories contained falsehoods, the media was left scrambling to respond to these extreme pronouncements. Given his own trolling success, comments by @JaredTSwift, the individual who falsely created a story that garnered massive attention, are relevant:

> In a sense, we've managed to push white nationalism into a very mainstream position…Trump's online support has been crucial to his success, I believe, and the fact is that his biggest and most devoted online supporters are white nationalists. Now, we've pushed the Overton window. People have adopted our rhetoric, sometimes without even realizing it. We're setting up for a massive cultural shift.[41]

The Overton Window is the range of ideas that are acceptable to the mainstream. The concept was initially theorized by Joseph P. Overton and later fictionalized by Glenn Beck.[42] Radical or extremist ideas can be brought into the mainstream by arguing for a previously "unthinkable" idea.[43] Though there are limitations to the theory of the Overton Window, the concept of normalizing the extreme is especially relevant to Pepe as an icon.[44] In this instance, particularly through @JaredTSwift's trolling, Pepe facilitates radical ideas. Instead of arguing for something unthinkable, Pepe fuels the spread of tongue-in-cheek, proto-ironic images. Social media users can disseminate messages of hate while maintaining a certain amount of distance to them. After all, how serious can a cartoon frog be? Nevertheless, the range of ideas discussed in the mainstream is modified. Satire enhances the legitimacy of radical claims. Amber Day argues that claims made through a "satiric frame" have a greater impact on "broader discourses" and enhance the authority of pranksters.[45] Indeed, journalism scholars have shown how radically conservative news sources such as Breitbart shifted news coverage to the right during the election.[46] With Pepe, the Alt-right was able to create media spectacles that altered the political landscape.[47] At a minimum, politicians and the media were induced to report on a cartoon frog as an emblem of extremism.

Additionally, Pepe's transformation into a mainstream hate-symbol created an injunction to which both the media and other presidential candidates must respond. Clinton was compelled to describe who Pepe was to her supporters and as such, added a page on her website that detailed why Pepe was a white supremacist symbol. Alongside extensive policy platforms regarding disability rights, a fair tax system, voting rights, racial injustice, immigration reform, and more, it behooved Clinton to label a set of Trump supporters and clarify how white supremacists operate in the digital era. As Hanna Kozlowska wrote of the Pepe page on Clinton's website, "When one presidential candidate loves to communicate with his voters through 140-character bursts on Twitter, and a hasty tweet can cause an international scandal, the other side has to be quick to respond in similar fashion."[48] Pepe forged a demand to respond given that the 2016 election was often a campaign of warring memes.[49] If previous elections were changed based on the strategic use of media—the social media election of Obama, the television election of Kennedy, etc.—this election saw these images as "more than just gags," but "campaign opportunities."[50] The proliferation of memes often shifted public focus from extensive policy platforms to the image wars of memes. As Alana Levinson writes, "The sad truth is that it's a lot easier to get an easily distracted, information-overwhelmed public to grasp a meme than a policy proposal."[51] Of course, voters have long been easy to distract, but the novelty of Pepe is that his tactical proliferation as a hate-symbol hatched an immediate demand to rebuke this symbol and those it represented.

The rapid travels of Pepe, including his reclamation and rebranding, as well as flaccid responses by media pundits and the left, indicate that memes have the ability to garner considerable public presence and manage, at least functionally, the grounds of public debate. Pepe's replication enabled the Alt-right to continually assert itself as a potent brand. The frog's coupling with Trump earned the collective media coverage that would not have existed otherwise. Such coverage emboldened memetic efforts and ensured even more reports. Ultimately, the circulation of Pepe confirmed the publicity efforts of the Alt-right. As an image, Pepe became positioned as the symbol that galvanized the rhetorical potency of the Alt-right.

Memes and the Juxtaposition of Iconophilia and Iconophobia

Memes of the Alt-right are flashpoints for wildly dichotomous views—expressed both dismissively and hyperbolically. For many, Alt-right memes are either extraordinarily successful propaganda mechanisms or pithy banalities compared to other aspects of the group's ideology. For some, Alt-right memes and similar modes of communication explain the rise of the group's considerable power. Sophia A. McClennen of *Salon* writes that Alt-right memes and other aggressive propaganda images are "damaging to democracy."[52] Similarly, Jason Wilson argues that the Alt-right deploys memes such that it has "stormed mainstream consciousness."[53] For others, memes are simply one part of the Alt-right arsenal that are overshadowed by other aspects of the group. Nicholas O'Shaughnessy asserts that the Alt-right is a cult that seduces disciples through a secret language and other rituals.[54] The Southern Poverty Law Center likewise discusses the memes of the Alt-right as part of a "whole cultural mythology," that while potentially ironic, nevertheless deploys powerful, sacred symbols.[55]

These debates revolve around the question of iconicity: what role do images play in the development and proliferation of ideology? As a symbol, Pepe points to the struggle between a traditionalist understanding of public culture and the iconicity present in memes. For many viewers, there is a tight correspondence between a symbol and what it represents. A swastika is tightly tethered, for these viewers, to Nazis or neo-Nazis (even though there are other meanings available to the symbol). Images are often understood through the lens of iconicity, which foregrounds resemblance. Icons looks like what they represent. Yet, images are frequently not static such that they hold only one meaning. Rather, they are overdetermined with meaning. For some, there is an attempt to define Pepe as an image with one specific meaning. Yet, the multiplicity of Pepe's connotations, the meme's ability to both shock and retool irony, indicate that this particular icon represents the Alt-right insofar as this group congeals through an assemblage of meanings, not a rarefied or direct set of claims. Thus, it is important to grasp the nature of the icon and iconicity by using Pepe to unearth how the Alt-right forms as a recognizable collective. The issue is one that can be considered more productively by delving into the relationship between rhetoric and icons. It is within this relationship that we discover how memes can persuade heterogeneous audiences.

Icons generally are concrete images that have rhetorical sway given their recognizability and circulation. Lester C. Olson argues that the icon is "a visual representation so as to designate a type of image that is palpable in manifest form and denotative in function."[56] Janis L. Edwards and Carol K. Winkler point out that icons are denotative in their function, such that the image must evoke resonance to be persuasive.[57] Eric S. Jenkins elaborates that icons are often defined as both "signifiers that resemble their signifieds" as well as "culturally potent imagery."[58] For a number of scholars, the icon is compelling precisely because it is well-recognized and therefore seen as a significant image by virtue of its popularity or circulation.[59] Attending to the composition of particular icons, these scholars suggest that the denotation of the image—what it points to or resembles—is part of its recognitional sway. As Jenkins correctly contends, historically, these views of the icon position images as particularly influential.[60]

Powerful icons often vacillate between the dialectic of iconophilia and iconophobia. Depending on the audience using the image, icons are adored or denounced. Those who worship images engage in iconophilia while those who fear them are iconophobic. Yet, both positions stem from a certain reverence for the symbol and its potential impact on an audience. As W.J.T. Mitchell maintains, "iconophobia and iconophilia make sense primarily to people who think that *other people* think that images are alive."[61] Here, the life of an image is principally social—its ability to strike fear into individuals or its capacity to galvanize the chorus is premised on a collective social imagination that personifies the image as acting on others. Images that tread the juxtaposition between iconophilia and iconophobia are especially important images. Specifically, these kinds of images "produce new arrangements and perceptions of the world."[62] That is, iconic images are most salient when there is ample debate regarding their meaning and function. When social conflict revolves around the sacredness of an image, its ritualistic uses, or its meanings, much can be learned about its role in the sociopolitical arena.

Pepe the Frog is positioned as a conspicuously powerful symbol given ongoing contestation about the image's meaning. For those who designate Pepe as a symbol invoking a cultural mythology or as a badge of the Alt-right, there is an attempt to shore up Pepe as a uniquely powerful symbol—either as a religious icon or as an effective branding logo. For those who argue that Pepe has infiltrated consciousness as insidious propaganda, that mode of iconophobic argument concedes this symbol works as proxy for the Alt-right. Pepe thus becomes a way to spread a particular worldview by virtue of his public circulation. Both claims revolve around the idea that Pepe is a forceful symbol given the social power invested in him. Debates over what Pepe means or how Pepe ought to be deployed reify his status as a supreme rhetorical figure. Consequently, there are concerted efforts to control this symbol.

Iconoclasm names how Pepe demarcates public culture's boundaries. Historically, iconoclasm refers to the attempt to destroy images, or a distrust of images.[63] Iconoclasm, or "the will to control images," manifests as individuals pontificate on what Pepe is and his power as a persuasive icon.[64] For instance, when 4chan and reddit users attempted to reclaim Pepe away from hate mongers, those actions evidence an impulse toward iconoclasm. Reclamation highlights the role of the image in the formation of publics—who is allowed to use Pepe and what are they allowed to say? In this instance, Pepe was to be employed by a distinct set of individuals who could understand his "true" significance as alienated from outsiders. Similarly, in September 2017, the artist who originally sketched Pepe, Matt Furie, served a series of cease and desist orders to Alt-right public figures.[65] This mode of iconoclasm aims to once again redeem Pepe. The lawsuits endeavor to circumscribe the availability of this image and thereby what modes of discourse are publicly acceptable. Altogether, these efforts engage in a robust debate regarding what should be communicated publicly and who may participate in that exchange. The image becomes a lightning rod for the creation and re-creation of public culture.

Yet, most importantly, Pepe helps shape public culture by defining what the Alt-right is and how it can be identified. The image enables the creation of the Alt-right as a singularity. As Nagle argues, the Alt-right is not a monolithic group, but instead a series of diffuse actors, contradictory claims, and often wildly-divergent perspectives.[66] The use of the icon enables the Alt-right to become publicly and collectively marked. Pepe stands in place of a complex and inconsistent set of actors. Journalists can easily refer to Pepe as a symbol of the Alt-right and thereby delineate the group, without necessarily engaging in the set of antagonistic, ironic, and incongruous statements comprising the collective. Similarly, those who proclaim to be Alt-right can employ Pepe to prove predominance. Pepe works in a rhetorically complex way to produce the Alt-right as a monolith, a singularity out of heterogeneous elements.

To be sure, the Alt-right is more aptly understood as an assemblage, a permeable constellation of components that are related, yet likely engage in distinct activities. Gilles Deleuze and Felix Guattari originally coined the term assemblage to convey phenomena with less deterministic explanations. This perspective suggests the study of particular bodies account for the relational dynamics at play, as well as the heterogeneous aspects of the ever-changing system and its processes. An assemblage identifies the ways an individual enunciation becomes connected to certain modes of discourse. Ideology cannot explain group membership fully, as the distinction between in-group and out-group is less valuable in understanding the movement of discourse. Instead, there are only relations articulated such that particular statements seem joined. As Deleuze and Guattari write: "The distinction to be made is not at all between exterior and interior, which are always relative, changing, and reversible, but between different types of multiplicities that coexist, interpenetrate, and change places—machines, cogs, motors, and elements that are set in motion at a given moment, forming an assemblage productive of statements."[67] The goal is therefore to analyze the production of statements so as to grasp the relations of discourse at play.

Manuel DeLanda has smartly operationalized assemblage theory in the study of social groups and organisms. He insists that social relations are predicated on exteriority, that which is constituted as the outside against which the inside is stabilized. Relations of exteriority hold several implications for De-

Landa. First, "a component part of an assemblage may be detached from it and plugged into a different assemblage in which its interactions are different."[68] Second, these connections can "never explain the relations which constitute a whole."[69] There is not a causal linkage between the parts and the whole or vice versa. Yet, there is a mutually productive relationship among the constituent elements. DeLanda distinguishes the first articulation of components to a larger whole (what he calls territorialization) from a second process (coding) that consolidates "the effects of the first and further stabiliz[es] the identity of assemblages."[70] The example he cites is modern bureaucracy. While there are a number of ways bureaucracies create statements that attempt to manage the populace (e.g., laws, disciplinary force, regulations), overarching "narratives establishing the sacred nature of authority" codify the dominion and identity of the assemblage.[71] In other words, the identity of a whole comes about not from an essence or determining feature, but rather through modes of discourse that establish the functions of the assemblage and its presumed identity as a whole.

In this way, the Alt-right is best considered as an assemblage—a group that only exists in terms of the rhetorical articulations of its public statements. Take, for instance, the multiplicity of channels used to proliferate Alt-right messaging: YouTube, Twitter, Facebook, 4chan, reddit, and even public protests. There is little official coordination between these media—no integrated marketing campaign *per se*. Yet, the content is usually similar regardless of the platform. The messages are articulated to one another by virtue of their circulation and pronounced similarities. Even when popular messaging strategies change or veer in dramatic new directions—what assemblage theory would deem heterogeneous and contingent components—there is a resemblance entailed by the configuration of the messages themselves. In other words: the Alt-right is not simply a group that can be explained by a central or deterministic ideology. Nor is the Alt-right a system with its own coordinated rules that, if discovered, will reveal its full goals and impacts. Instead, the Alt-right is a constellation of mediated discourses that share a logic and a loose structure—one that must be investigated in its heterogeneity, in its rhetorical responses to changing on-the-ground conditions. The meme becomes a genre of public discourse that helps the Alt-right use enclaved invention and media publicity to structure those connections, while providing effective responses to changing conditions.

Employing Pepe as the poster-child for the Alt-right circumnavigates this heterogeneity by using iconicity to shore up the Alt-right as a fully coherent group or system. There are several implications to this line of thought. First, Pepe becomes the coding discourse that materializes the strength and identity of the Alt-right as a singularity. Second, and relatedly, Pepe forecloses Alt-right ideology by becoming a symptomatic image—he represents the poisonous ideology of an assumed core. The problem is that the Alt-right is neither singular, nor organized around a simple ideological perspective as its essence. A more nuanced, rhetorical analysis of Pepe can reposition this figure not as a singular icon that represents a specific group or its essence, but rather as a figure of the Alt-right's multiplicity. In this sense, rhetorical scholars are able to study the resonances among the different circulations of Pepe and how they enunciate the various modes of Alt-right messages. A rhetorical approach considers how, although Pepe is an icon that *seems* to create the group as a monolith, he is more productively used to mark the constellation of discourses at play. Indeed, it is the multiplicity of Alt-right discourses that prefigures its current success—flexibility abets effective adaptation.

For those who work under the moniker of the Alt-right, Pepe allows the group identity to form a well-recognized set of discourses and images that ostensibly cohere. Pepe memes are often diverse in terms of form and messaging. One image of Pepe can look quite different from another. And yet, Pepe is still recognizable—he displays the denotative functions of iconicity. This recognizability is a result of articulation. Heterogeneous images can be seen as related to one another and categorized into varieties of a visual form based on the way they are socially and materially connected.[72] Pepe travels frequently with Alt-right messaging and as such his image becomes designated as a symbol representative of the group. It is this representational slippage that also makes Pepe stand in for the Alt-right as though the group is a consistent whole. Once Pepe becomes a pronounced symbol of the Alt-right, his denotative function fashions a particularized reference: The Alt-right is concretized. The image stands in for the group as though it were a monolithic or singular entity. As Ernesto Laclau suggests of group psychology, the image becomes a point of cathexis—it is the "common object of identification which establishes equivalentially the unity of the group members."[73] It is this relationship of equivalence that structures how both members and outsiders understand what the Alt-right is.

In terms of public presence, the Alt-right emerges as a formidable identity through an icon that helps establish its authority. Icons are typically worshiped images, images that mark dominion or conviction. Pepe's transformation into a denotative symbol for the Alt-right facilitates this status as a sacred image.

Icons are devotional, often religious, symbols that help to convey God's presence in the material plane.[74] Yet, as Martin Kemp suggests, religious icons are not the only worshipped images; often corporate imagery and pedestrian symbols are afforded the same reverence.[75] Once Pepe became a symbol for the Alt-right and his likeness merged with Trump and Nazi imagery, the meme nevertheless gained a certain kind of esteem. Many 4chan users tied Pepe to the Egyptian diety Kek, reportedly a frog-headed man.[76] By early March 2016, Pepe's cult status and divine ordination provided a surrogate, albeit ironic, religion for some 4chan and reddit users.[77] Adherents pontificated on meme magic, or the ability for certain rituals and memetic images (Pepe foremost among them) to usher in massive social change.[78] In these discourses, Pepe becomes a powerful symbol by virtue of these cultish maneuvers. But, in terms of Pepe's rhetorical resonance, his significance continues to grow by virtue of his amplified recognizability. Pepe is powerful both because of cult-like rituals but also, and primarily, because of his continued circulation. His repeated public appearances engender a broad awareness of the Alt-right and publicity for its power.

The work of Pepe, then, is to create a shared manner of perception: to inspire fear of the Alt-right as a powerful collective. The icon acquires a kind of deification by virtue of Pepe's status as a denotative term. Pepe becomes something to identify the Alt-right and as such performs a secular deification—the symbol materializes the divine status of the group as a purportedly sacred whole. Jenkins writes that the Byzantinian understanding of icons materialized the deity, giving form to that which lacked an earthly substance.[79] Likewise, Pepe's designation as a symbol of the Alt-right supplies material presence to an amorphous group whose actions are not always visible to the broader public. The image becomes denotative by virtue of this representative slippage—he creates presence in a broader sense for the Alt-right. For Jenkins, icons are not best understood as an image that concretely resembles its referent.[80] Instead, the icon is a "shared manner of perception," in particular "a manner of engagement."[81] Pepe is thus a significant image because he ostensibly designates a particular worldview. In other words, Pepe is an icon because he comes to be worshipped as a stand in for the Alt-right, an image anchoring public perception. The Alt-right becomes something to be feared given such effective branding.

Moreover, the denotative labeling of Pepe as a symbol of the Alt-right fashions a fundamental identity for the collective. Jenkins suggests that to see an image as iconic "drives image circulation by orienting audiences to see and photojournalists to look for images hypostatizing events or values."[82] Pepe is understood as a representation of a palpable ideology, even when a coherent one is not present. In this way, Pepe is made to hypostasize, to narrow and codify a plethora of battling perspectives into a singular hate-group—able to be attacked as such by political opponents. These attacks also affirm Pepe's status as an icon, by labeling the image as solely an expression of hate. As Amelia Tate writes in the *New Republic*, "racists embraced Pepe after the Anti-Defamation League chimed in and officially declared the meme a hate symbol."[83] Broadly speaking, then, the rhetorical function of Pepe as icon is to generate a singularity from a multiplicity—to deify an image as that which represents an influential whole. Pepe becomes the synecdochal figure of an assumed core.

Thus, journalists used Pepe to diagnose the group and create a singular ideology from a multiplicity of users. Here, Pepe aids community-building and identification, coalescing the values of many different users on boards. As Dale Beran writes from his extensive interviews:

> The grotesque, frowning, sleepy eyed, out of shape, swamp dweller, peeing with his pants pulled down because-it-feels-good-man frog *is an ideology*, one which steers into the skid of its own patheticness. Pepe symbolizes embracing your loserdom, and owning it. It is what all the millions of forum-goers of 4chan met to commune about. It is, in other words, a value system, one reveling in deplorableness and being pridefully dispossessed. It is a culture of hopelessness, of knowing "the system is rigged." But instead of fight, the response is flight, knowing you're trapped in your circumstances is cause to celebrate. For these young men, voting Trump is not a solution, but a new spiteful prank.[84]

Here, Beran deploys the term ideology to understand collective identification with Pepe—what the image expresses as an icon of worship. Pepe becomes the embodiment of the struggle against a system that does not support you. In this passage, Pepe exposes the value system of the board. In relationship to assemblage theory, though, Beran uses Pepe to hypostasize or code nearly any expression by the Alt-right. Pepe is not a representative for a diffuse set of actors who modify their values and approaches given changing circumstances; instead, he is a singular reference. The description shores up what Pepe means or does for the Alt-right as a whole.

Yet, even for internal users who understand the divergent viewpoints and contestation inherent to participation in any board, Pepe presents a useful public relations instrument. Interviewing Alice Marwick, journalist Emma Grey Ellis notes that "extremists are using memes for recruitment," and according to Marwick, the technique 'is not that different from Islamic radicalization.'"[85] Ellis continues: "People come for the edgy aesthetic; some stay for the ideology."[86] Pepe's recognizability aids recruitment of those who might participate in the meme war or at least share these images. Pepe as a branding mechanism has helped position the Alt-right as cutting edge, at the forefront of cultural innovation. To recruit and change the status quo (which they want to do), Alt-right enthusiasts require modes of publicity that attract new users and create novel modes of identification. Pepe does so by fashioning a brand identity, one that can envelop differences. Indeed, it is his flexibility that enables his persuasive role.

Pepe as Flexible Icon

While Pepe as icon is designated as a symbol marking a singularity, the image sustains a multitude of audiences. That is, a multiplicity of users can identify with Pepe given that he is an image that can be remade in a plethora of forms that remain recognizable despite differences. Limor Shifman and Ryan M. Milner both highlight how memes can re-appropriate and adapt imagery for a new context.[87] Pepe's capacious form speaks to different users who can thereby represent their differences within this iconic symbol. Frequently, discussion centers on how the Alt-right creates Nazi-esque memes driven by a singular ideology. Presenting 4chan or reddit boards as singular ideologically disavows both the heterogeneity of their users as well as how users respond variously to social landscapes. In so doing, the meme battle between board users and others becomes overly simplified. In other words, this debate fails to grasp how memes of the Alt-right enable a malleable form of identification and investment. Pepe is a key example of this elasticity. If the Alt-right is an assemblage, then it is crucial to illuminate the mechanisms of Alt-right rhetorical efforts beyond simplistic identification. Pepe helps to form the group not because he is a denotative term—a term that represents the group as a singularity—but because he is an elastic term—a term that both represents the group but enables productive ambiguity.

Pepe as a rhetorical symbol highlights the importance of iconicity and the way imagaic multiplicity resists public representation. Namely, the icon encourages a plethora of viewpoints to proliferate even as the image seems to designate a rarefied worldview. The icon is a malleable image, able to envelop and represent a wide array of beliefs.[88] For instance, Christians—of diverse denominations—can see themselves in the icon of the cross. Yet, the icon also travels with a whole host of specialized discourse, these articulations branding both the icon and Christianity writ large.[89] Moreover, many Christians use the cross to enunciate a particularized understanding of their faith. Their actions also transform what the cross means or does. In this way, the cross represents multiplicity and singularity. The icon of Pepe functions similarly for the Alt-right. Pepe's cartoon form generates flexibility for the image. It is precisely because Pepe can be drawn and redrawn endlessly that the image is a vehicle for a whole host of viewpoints. For some meme scholars, the radical possibilities of Pepe should facilitate innovation and a disarticulation from the Alt-right.[90] Yet, Pepe's flexibility abets the travels of numerous extremist views all under the guise of a singular icon.

To be sure, Pepe has long been a relatively moldable image. Early images of Pepe look quite different than those now circulating. In Matt Furie's original comic strip, wherein Pepe declares his catchphrase, "Feels Good Man," the character is a lanky, anthropomorphized, near-human creature garbed in traditional college attire.[91] Alongside frog-like hands and feet, the head of Furie's Pepe is the primary indicator of his amphibian status. Although the original comic was a simple black and white line drawing, Pepe's head was clearly frog-like with wide eyes, several eyelid folds, and a broad mouth. In other editions of the comic, Furie colored Pepe in a mid-tone green with dark green lips and a red mouth sporting a pink tongue. As Pepe became the memetic "Feels Good Man," his head was separated from his body and often circulated on its own with a voice bubble illustrating his catchphrase.[92] His green skin tone darkened and his lips became a brownish-red. It was this image that catalyzed his iconic status and the one that is now most readily understood as Pepe.

Over time, Pepe evolved into a number of different images that all played off of the "Feels Good Man" disembodied head. Sad Pepe depicted the frog with a frown. Smug Pepe included a smirk. Angry Pepe overlaid the color red on top of a seemingly screaming face. Well Meme'd Pepe translated Pepe into a near game-show host figure with a debonair grin. Yet, for the most part, all of these images bore some obvious resemblance to the original. The face was clearly one of a frog. The color green was usually retained as was the wide mouth and general characterological features of the "Feels Good Man." These variations all re-worked the Pepe theme and built the image into an icon. Recognizability is key to iconicity. As Kemp writes, an icon is an image that "has achieved wholly exceptional levels of widespread recognizability and has come to carry a rich series of varied associations for very large numbers of people across time and cultures, such that it has to a greater or lesser degree transgressed the parameters of its initial making, function, context, and meaning."[93] As Pepe moved from comic character to prolific meme, he began to function as an icon. He was the most widely recognized meme on the internet, and his variations suggested a broad set of meanings and associations for users. At just over a decade old, Pepe may not yet operate as a memetic icon for the ages, yet he has certainly transgressed his original context to work in some rather novel ways. It is, in fact, the flexibility of Pepe as meme that set the stage for his far right makeover.

Pepe's recognizability despite dozens of variations made him an easy figure to couple with Trump. Know Your Meme explains that on July 22, 2015, a user on 4chan's /pol/ created an image from Smug Pepe illustrating him as "Donald Trump overlooking a fence at the U.S.-Mexican border holding back sad Mexicans."[94] Because Pepe could be adapted with the simple addition of a cartoonish comb over, his combination with the likeness of Trump was easily accomplishable. By 2016, meme campaign posters of Trump and Pepe appeared. A more stylized image of Trump as Pepe with the caption "Build It" emerged on Twitter. Pepe popped up wearing a "Make America Great Again" red hat. Other images with Pepe showed Jesus wearing the same hat. Later, Pepe was mashed with Nazi swastikas, Hitler's mustache, and more. All of these memes were easy to fashion with available technology. The flexibility of the cartoon—Pepe's ability to be reworked and re-used with other imagery—nourished his iconicity.

Each of these images demonstrates that heterogeneous audiences can identify with Pepe. Meme enthusiasts, Trump supporters, proto- or current Nazis, and more, all positioned Pepe as representative. This broad identification created a relationship among such audiences. It is this capacity for a number of identifications that speaks to how Pepe enables the multiplicity to function. With numerous images and forms, Pepe is deployed, in part, to constitute an assemblage named the Alt-right. Out of diverse elements, the Alt-right becomes a singularity joined together by the figure of a frog. This frog can be reworked to inflect different aspects of the Alt-right and thereby invite broad sets of audiences to find affinity and kinship through their shared use of the image. Here, the icon is not powerful because it is a denotative image. Pepe as an icon is powerful because he stitches together audiences in and through the travels of the image.

This mode of identification is premised on the mobility of symbolism. Identification here allows divergent audiences with conflicting sets of goals and beliefs to come together in the icon as symbol. In *On Symbols and Society*, Kenneth Burke argues that "in considering the wavering line between identification and division, we shall always be coming upon manifestations of the logomachy, avowed as in invective, unavowed as in stylistic subterfuges for presenting real divisions in terms that deny division."[95] For Burke, the word (logomachy) or the symbol can shore up divisions or reproduce divisions depending on its deployment. The symbol is a flexible tool for the constitutive process of group development. Pepe as an icon diminishes how differences are represented among self-identified members of the Alt-right and allows them to come together in the symbol. Yet, that mode of identification simultaneously enables individuals to maintain separate perspectives given the adaptability of the image. In this sense, this mode of iconic identification sustains shared identity and difference.

An additional aspect of Pepe's flexibility is the ironic distanciation that birthed his memetic replication. While we address irony fully in chapter three, to be sure, both Nazi Pepe and Trump Pepe were created by those who were sometimes earnest in their efforts but at other times enthralled with the ability to rail against established norms. The culture of imageboards is often one of ironic playfulness. For instance, Amelia Tait explains one brand of ironic Nazism in which furries (people who typically appreciate anthropomorphic or animal character play) embrace Nazi iconography. As she explains, this performance is not often earnest:

> Alt furries are furries who have embraced far-right messages and Nazi iconography on the social network. Some wear armbands, others write erotic Nazi literature, some tweet anti-Semitic jokes. When I spoke to some last month, I was shocked when only one of them actually admitted to holding Nazi views. Many claimed they were being "ironic" or fighting back at what they consider to be left-wing intolerance.[96]

Memes of Pepe and Trump Pepe function similarly. Attempts to reclaim Pepe by infusing him with hate symbols were not necessarily explicit expressions of a felt ideology. Rather, the use of hate symbols had the effect of alienating outsiders and reveling in such duplicity. As a corollary, consider the way Trash Dove was used as a direct foil. Trash Dove was a Facebook sticker of a purple bird later mashed with Nazi imagery and replicated across social media sites to troll those who assumed it was akin to Pepe.[97] Tait notes that Trash Dove was positioned as an Alt-right symbol in a satirical post and similarly ironic memes. Yet, when "people began to fall for this, 4chan won."[98] Thus, the meaning of Pepe is not nearly as important as his rhetorical function. Pepe does not offer a singular meaning, but instead becomes a flexible icon that prompts a whole host of responses. Pepe invites divergent modes of investment even as the symbol works as an ostensibly unifying image. Meanwhile, meme creators can use Pepe to perform irony, find like-minded folks, and troll the left.

Pepe's flexibility is, in part, directly related to his ironic posturing. Spreading Pepe as a potentially ironic white supremacist symbol facilitated his replication and broader audience impacts. For meme generators, Pepe was attractive precisely because his visage could traffic in the caustic through a humorous, specifically cartoonish façade. Yet, despite such jovial assertions, the action itself affirms a distinction that disavows the very racism fueling such actions. Leslie A. Hahner and Scott J. Varda argue that individuals may understand certain "acts as racist when practiced by others, but rationalize their own racist performances through a presumed exceptionalism."[99] The impact of these exceptionalist actions is explained by Olivia Nuzzi of the *Daily Beast*, who asserts that combining Pepe with extremist imagery "also had the effect of desensitizing swaths of the Internet to racist, but mostly anti-Semitic, ideas supported by the so-called alt-right movement."[100] Pepe's purported ironic symbolism in no way makes such humor any less significant or hateful. In a broader sense, once the image becomes circulated with hate speech or symbols of hate, the ironic intention matters little. Instead, the symbol nevertheless impacts public discourse by legitimizing and spreading hate speech. The icon is flexible and Pepe's adaptability is precisely what offers the Alt-right a broad invitation to identification. One can use and see Pepe in a number of ways, but these identifications often fuel racist, anti-Semitic discourse.

The broad flexibility of Pepe lies at the core of his iconicity. The novel rhetorical function of Pepe is that he can be used to create a singular identity, even as that identification can speak differently to sets of audiences. Generally speaking, then, Pepe encourages a variety of audiences to understand themselves as Alt-right while simultaneously prompting the public to see the Alt-right as a cohesive group. Significantly, the public may misperceive the Alt-right given the representative slippage Pepe performs. Yet, Pepe as an iconic figure is able to delimit the terms of the conversation. What is said, by whom, and the broader available responses to these utterances, can be productively explored by considering how iconic memes punctuate public culture.

Pepe as Icon in Circulation

Pepe's iconicity is predicated on his robust and fast-paced circulation—a status that punctuates the public's attention to the Alt-right. Generally, one of the most notable rhetorical features of visual internet memes is the speed at which they can replicate. On 4chan and reddit, memes move quickly because of user engagement and because the best are algorithmically amplified. Social media such as Facebook and Twitter hasten the pace at which memetic images and ideas can take hold and reproduce in the mainstream. Many Pepe memes move at a particularly rapid pace. For instance, Trump's retweet of "You Can't Stump the Trump" occurred within twenty-four hours of the original tweet. Over the next day, the tweet gathered "3,000 favorites and 2,800 retweets."[101] The very same day, published articles on the meaning and significance of Pepe and the tweet appeared online.[102] To understand how Pepe helps to shape publics, then, it is imperative to interrogate both the circulation of the image and the movements of actors and discourses that articulate the Alt-right. It is this continuous movement and the points of articulation that develop in those travels that impact the temporal attention of public culture. Ultimately, Pepe is a unique icon in that he is an elastic figure that nevertheless becomes overcoded with a particularized set of ideas via his persistent deployments by the Alt-right.

Given that the Alt-right is best understood as an assemblage wherein discourses are articulated to create and stabilize the identity of the whole, it is crucial to grasp how Pepe and these discourses move. Bruno Latour argues that too often, images are not considered in relationship to their travels. He encourages scholars to fight "*freeze-framing*," or "extracting images out of the flow, and becoming fascinated by it, as if it were sufficient, as if all movement had stopped."[103] Freeze-framing is one way to consider how shallow responses to Pepe prefigure him as a monolithic representative of the Alt-right. For instance, Abby Ohlheiser engages with the ways Pepe has changed meaning over time. She writes that "Pepe is now a part of right-wing online culture, protected from earnest analysis by layers of irony. Pepe's face is used both by genuine white supremacists and by anti-PC conservatives and Trump supporters who think it's funny to freak out liberals and the media by using 'racist' symbols."[104] Here, Pepe is only a hate symbol protected by the irony that fuels his deployment. Pepe, for her, is "dead" because he is only a hate symbol. Ohlheiser's freeze-framing does not consider the travels of the image and the group to which he corresponds. On our view, the movement of the image and other discourses are all part of a constitutive process shaping public culture. To grasp how icons impact public culture, scholars must consider how iconic movement structures broader response. How do the journeys of Pepe interact with the machinations of the Alt-right—and subsequently, how do these travels influence public discourse? Pepe is not an Alt-right symbol simply because he is identified as such by those like Ohlheiser, but rather through repeated articulations that suture Pepe to the group. Thus, Pepe is used to mold public understanding of the Alt-right as he is continually recirculated.

In the simplest sense, Pepe memes direct public attention. As with the classical model of agenda setting, Pepe memes don't tell the public what to think, but what to think about.[105] When Trump retweets Pepe, he creates a rhetorical injunctive to respond to what this symbol represents. The response need not be any particular argument, but will nevertheless grapple with the representative work of the icon. As Emma Balfour and Rodney Taveira wrote regarding Clinton's deplorables comment: "Clinton engaged with the memetic idea of Pepe rather than the political narrative of reclamation that Pepe represented. Trump spoke loudly and endlessly to this desire to reclaim that which had been taken—whether this was jobs, racial and gendered power, or memes."[106] For the larger public culture, this simple tweet set the tone for what was to be publicly addressed. Major news networks, smaller outlets, social media streams, and more all then focused on what Pepe is or does in terms of his representative status. There was little discussion of broader themes or resonances. Instead, the discourse became routed through the icon as a figure of singularity. As Braynard, Trump's campaign data manager stated, "The memes were such a tremendous distraction during the campaign…They'd get enough traction, and so than [*sic*] rather than focusing on policy issues, Clinton would be forced to give a speech attacking a cartoon frog instead."[107] News networks and even Clinton herself treated Pepe as an image frozen in time—he represented a narrow, seemingly ideologically driven group: the Alt-right. In effect, the focus of discussion became Pepe himself. What the public paid attention to was narrowed by virtue of iconicity.

The icon, then, plays a role in the temporality of public attention. The short attention span of social media is rendered merely a blip by the ways memes circulate. A key aspect of the formation of publics is a reflexive understanding of the temporality of circulation. In his work on publics and counterpublics, Michael Warner writes that "The temporality of circulation is not continuous or indefinite; it is punctual. There are distinct moments and rhythms, from which distance in time can be measured."[108] Warner references the ebb and flow of publication cycles and the expectations of readers and viewers. That is, the public is shaped by those who understand that these punctuated discourses create a public of which they are members, and an investment in how information and ideas travel through culture. With memes, the flow of that public is unique. For instance, members of the public often turn to Twitter and other social news sources to grasp the issues of the day. The brevity of Twitter posts (140 characters, now 280 characters) and the incredibly short propagation of Twitter posts (the majority of hashtags reach their peak use at around two hours after origination) demarcate the temporality of this public.[109] Users on Twitter, at least, are accustomed to a rapid-fire mode of engagement, wherein one particular hashtag or image will offer intense scrutiny for a short time and then be discarded.

Pepe memes help to shift public culture through their prolific *and* expeditious propagation. In distinction to other memes, which come and go quickly, Pepe enjoys relative staying power. From "Feels Good Man" to Trump Pepe, he has circulated as a beloved image for well over a decade. Pepe's specific temporality is punctuated by momentous tweets, investigations, news stories, and the like. Pepe's proliferation turns on a boom and bust model of media, wherein individual events are bolstered through the algorithms of different circulatory networks. When pop star Katy Perry tweets Pepe, that incident grabs mass attention and incentivizes broad investment in Pepe as a significant image. When Pepe is tweeted multiple times with Nazi imagery, those discrete instances likewise change the nature of how that image moves, just as those same discourses create new space and time for white supremacy. When candidate Trump or his campaign staff retweet a Pepe image, both Pepe and Trump's candidacy move and are reshaped once again. Just as Pepe becomes tethered to Trump, Trump becomes sutured to the Alt-right. In all of these instances, the public's attention and interest is rhythmic relative to these discourses.

The reflexive circulation of Pepe constitutes an imagined investment in the Alt-right as a powerhouse political group. Warner claims that the reflexive circulation of discourse is key to the formation of publics. As he writes, the "imagined scene of circulation" generates the recognition that there are discourses and peoples which comprise a public.[110] Cara A. Finnegan and Ji-yeon Kang extend this insight to argue that the imagined scene of circulation is part of "sighting the public."[111] For them, the public comes into being by the circulation of images that invite and demarcate shared ways of seeing. In this sense, Pepe is a reflexive figure insofar as the battle over his meaning and status highlights the movements of public culture. To wit, if Pepe were to be understood less through the lens of iconoclasm—the will to control what images are—and more through the elastic work of icons, he is best considered a flashpoint. Pepe is not a signifier merely to be discarded as a hate symbol. Instead, he is a moment to interrogate the means through which assemblages begin to ostensibly cohere. Pepe functions a site through which a swath of individuals could territorialize, or make present, their own interests.

Moreover, the image of Pepe enables members of the Alt-right to respond quickly to public events. Given that the assemblage is comprised of diffuse actors, those very same actors can create memes, debate the construction of those memes, and ultimately revise memes as rhetorical images that address on-the-ground conditions. Most theories of public culture, Warner's among them, rely on traditional verbal discourse and tend to ignore the role of images.[112] Yet, in assemblages, the image or representations also function as points of articulation. The image is not merely the symbol of something "real," but instead another point in the broader constellation public culture. Put differently, the image is not an epiphenomenon of public culture but constitutive of public culture itself. For users, Pepe provides a quickly responsive discourse with flexible articulation. When a speedy response is needed, Pepe memes are fashioned and critiqued in terms of their persuasive resonance. The memes that rise to the top can then be rendered for particular purposes (e.g., deplorables memes). Memes are especially capable rhetorical tools for influencing public culture because they can so rapidly establish new lines of connection and seize novelty in the midst of ongoing social changes.

Memes are significant rhetorical images for visual culture, then, insofar as they can capture public attention and interest more swiftly and enduringly than verbal or written discourse.[113] Twitter and Facebook posts travel farther and quicker if they include easily spreadable content or emotionally charged images.[114] Through algorithmic amplification, memes are able to capture attention by virtue of their visuality and their ability to evoke emotional resonance. In this sense, the persuasive mechanism of the meme is less often its specific content (though the content is still relevant), and more often its ability to work with and through the circulation that constitutes the public as such. Pepe's numerous images are able to travel quickly given that meme makers can change the audiences addressed by this visage. Pepe can become a bro figure for comic book aficionados and meme enthusiasts. He can also become an image that speaks to and for Trump supporters. Pepe, much like the Alt-right itself, is an assemblage of meanings and functions all related to his iconicity. Pepe's frequent travels and modalities are not a detriment to his iconicity but the very fuel that generates his iconic status. As an icon, Pepe is flexible and can be remade endlessly while still seemingly bearing a direct, concrete reference to the Alt-right. This is what makes him a particularly powerful symbol, one that creates a great deal of persuasive resonance for a multiplicity of users.

As much as Pepe can be remade as a symbol, at present this icon remains imbued with meaning by the Alt-right, tainted by the association with extremists. Part of that recalcitrant coupling comes about from his heavy circulation by avowed members of the Alt-right and on Alt-right platforms. Any attempt to publicly move Pepe to new (or even old) associations is often responded to vehemently. That is not to suggest that Pepe does not circulate through his other modalities on particular sites. Smug Pepe, Feels Good Man, Sad Frog, Angry Pepe, and other iterations of Pepe still travel across different internet locales, especially within particular enclaves on 4chan and reddit. And yet, the public visage of Pepe as an icon is still tightly tethered to the Alt-right. Take recent efforts by Pepe's creator to stop Pepe's connection with the Alt-right. Furie initiated a campaign to "Save Pepe," by "flooding the internet with 'peaceful or nice depictions' of the character."[115] In response, members of the Alt-right amped up their efforts. When Furie tried to kill off Pepe in his comics, "the alt-right…brought him back to life as a zombie—a way of reminding Furie that you can't kill a meme."[116] Furie's 2017 copyright lawsuits similarly floundered in reclaiming Pepe, as news coverage of his cease and desist letters fashioned another opportunity to redeploy Alt-right images of Pepe and stitch this icon to the assemblage.

Rhetorically speaking, any event that generates news coverage for Pepe invents an exigence that Alt-right meme enthusiasts can use to their advantage. An exigence is "an imperfection marked by urgency," an obstacle that requires rhetoric to be addressed or overcome.[117] It matters not whether Pepe is reviewed positively or negatively, or by whom. For the Alt-right, Pepe is a useful meme to respond to such moments. Pepe can be redeployed quickly and easily whenever opportunity strikes. Moreover, Pepe's function as an icon suggests that to be rhetorically useful for the Alt-right—to create and engender this collective as a singularity while enabling a host of different viewpoints to identify with him—he must be retooled and reused repeatedly. This flexibility is demonstrated and enacted through these regular dispatches. Public responses that steal back Pepe for other uses forge the conditions for his capacious rhetorical connections in the future.

Thus, while generally memes are radical images that can move in heterogeneous ways, the rhetorical work of the Alt-right situates the figure of Pepe as a primary tool of its arsenal. Pepe becomes used again and again to maintain the public presence of the Alt-right and narrow the nature of discourse about that assemblage. That is, the figure of Pepe demarcates and stabilizes the Alt-right's identity. These efforts are rhetorical tactics, mechanisms of persuasion that bolster the agenda of the group. Pepe aggrandizes the influence of the Alt-right by opening up a pathway to mainstream coverage of its views.

Conclusion

The Pepe the frog meme reveals much about the role of the icon in the formation of the Alt-right for both insiders and outsiders. Pepe becomes the site of attachment for both those who proclaim themselves members of the Alt-right and those who denounce the group. Controlling Pepe—the work of iconoclasm—becomes the rhetorical means of generating news coverage, codifying insiders and outsiders, and solidifying Pepe's supposedly true meaning. While many journalists and scholars have pronounced Pepe as a rather simple symbol that represents the Alt-right, his rhetorical work belies such a claim. It is not his denotative status as a symbol for the Alt-right that is most illuminative. It is the fact that he can be remade endlessly while remaining tethered to a particular constellation of Alt-right discourse, evidencing his existence as more than merely a representative visual. Pepe is a symbol that influences public discourse by creating injunctions that demand public response, by limiting the nature of public conversation, and by rapidly redirecting the foci of those conversations. Pepe is not interesting as an icon because he was reborn as Alt-right. Pepe is fascinating rhetorically because of how he shapes public culture.

The rhetorical machinations of public culture are moved through and by the creation of new articulations and the happenings of particular assemblages. With Pepe, his connections to the Alt-right mark the need for a common point of identification to generate larger impacts. The Alt-right redeployed Pepe as an extremist symbol precisely because his new use would provoke outrage and immediate response. These uses founded the connections of the Alt-right assemblage. Throughout the life cycle of Pepe as icon, there have been contentious debates as to what Pepe is and what he means. Each time the media, politicians, or advocacy groups decries the association between

Pepe and the Alt-right, their contestations fail to resignify the image. Instead, the stubborn links between the Alt-right and Pepe are renewed by creating a rhetorical exigence for Alt-right meme work. Repeated appearances of Pepe as an Alt-right symbol against efforts of resignification display how Alt-right rhetors are able to generate their own publicity. At each of these moments, the Alt-right has been able to use the figure of Pepe to garner public attention and to occupy public discourse. Members of the Alt-right, then, have relied on Pepe to replicate their identity such that the public and social media users all focused on the impact of the Alt-right writ large.

Similarly, the travels of Pepe direct public attention to the Alt-right and its ongoing actions. In effect, the public is often focused on talking about the memes of the Alt-right. Each public response to its shocking memes creates an opportunity for more memes, and so on, and so on, *ad infinitum*. The media and the public end up jumping from one meme to the next. When reddit and 4chan users proclaim that they are winning the meme war, this might be what they portend. To win the meme war is not simply to generate effective memes but to control the flow and focus of public culture.

Pepe, then, is emblematic of the ways the Alt-right is able to pace and manage the nature of public discourse about the group. He is deployed repeatedly to answer criticisms, provoke outrage, and embolden fellow members of the Alt-right. Given efforts to move Pepe in particular ways, his circulation highlights how memes are deployed tactically. Memes are not simply singular responses invented by individual users. Instead, memes allow the Alt-right to create more devotees, organize activism, and broaden the resonance of extremism. Memes are key messages for the Alt-right that help it recruit new members via the resonance of their imagery. To grasp this expansion, we turn to how the Alt-right uses memes to radicalize in the digital age.

Notes

1. Jacob Steinblatt, "Donald Trump Embraces His 4Chan Fans," *Vocativ*, October 13, 2015, http://www.vocativ.com/239143/donald-trump-embraces-his-4chan-fans/.
2. Parker Atkinson, "There's a New Culture War, and It's Being Fought Online," *Deseret News*, September 6, 2017, http://www.deseretnews.com/article/900001520/meme-warfare-how-memes-and-the-internet-are-redrawing-the-lines-of-americas-cultural-conflict.html.
3. Brad, "Can't Stump the Trump," *Know Your Meme*, n.d., accessed October 3, 2017, http://knowyourmeme.com/memes/can-t-stump-the-trump.

4. Angie Drobnic Holan, "In Context: Hillary Clinton and the 'Basket of Deplorables,'" *PolitiFact*, September 11, 2016, http://www.politifact.com/truth-o-meter/article/2016/sep/11/context-hillary-clinton-basket-deplorables/.
5. Drobnic Holan, "In Context."
6. Elizabeth Chan, "Donald Trump, Pepe the Frog, and White Supremacists: An Explainer," *HillaryClinton.com*, September 12, 2016, https://web.archive.org/web/20160913043519/https://www.hillaryclinton.com/post/donald-trump-pepe-the-frog-and-white-supremacists-an-explainer/.
7. For an astute summary of the extant communication research and novel theoretical framework on the boomerang effect, see Sahara Byrne and Philip Solomon Hart, "The Boomerang Effect A Synthesis of Findings and a Preliminary Theoretical Framework," *Annals of the International Communication Association* 33, no. 1 (2009): 3–37.
8. Atkinson, "There's a New Culture War, and It's Being Fought Online."
9. Jessica Roy, "How 'Pepe the Frog' Went from Harmless to Hate Symbol," *Los Angeles Times*, October 11, 2017, http://www.latimes.com/politics/la-na-pol-pepe-the-frog-hate-symbol-20161011-snap-htmlstory.html.
10. Dani Di Placido, "How 'Pepe the Frog' Became A Symbol Of Hatred," *Forbes*, May 9, 2017, https://www.forbes.com/sites/danidiplacido/2017/05/09/how-pepe-the-frog-became-a-symbol-of-hatred/.
11. Imad Khan, "4Chan's Pepe the Frog is Bigger Than Ever—And His Creator Feels Good, Man," *Daily Dot*, April 12, 2015, https://www.dailydot.com/unclick/4chan-pepe-the-frog-renaissance/.
12. SabrinaTibbets, "Feels Good Man," *Know Your Meme*, n.d., accessed September 14, 2017, http://knowyourmeme.com/memes/feels-good-man.
13. SabrinaTibbets, "Feels Good Man."
14. Olivia Nuzzi, "How Pepe the Frog Became a Nazi Trump Supporter and Alt-Right Symbol," *The Daily Beast*, May 26, 2016, sec. politics, http://www.thedailybeast.com/articles/2016/05/26/how-pepe-the-frog-became-a-nazi-trump-supporter-and-alt-right-symbol; Triple Zed, "Pepe the Frog," *Know Your Meme*, n.d., accessed September 14, 2017, http://knowyourmeme.com/memes/pepe-the-frog.
15. Triple Zed, "Pepe the Frog."
16. Jason Koebler, "Hillary Clinton is Right: Pepe is a White Supremacist,'" *Motherboard*, September 14, 2016, https://motherboard.vice.com/en_us/article/aek4ge/hillary-clinton-is-right-pepe-is-a-white-supremacist.
17. TSwift in this handle likely refers to Taylor Swift, who is also an Alt-right darling as well as a topic used to troll others.
18. Nuzzi, "How Pepe the Frog Became a Nazi Trump Supporter and Alt-Right Symbol."
19. Jonah Bennett, "Journo Trolled into Believing Pepe White Nati," *The Daily Caller*, September 14, 2016, http://dailycaller.com/2016/09/14/heres-how-two-twitter-pranksters-convinced-the-world-that-pepe-the-frog-meme-is-just-a-front-for-white-nationalism/.
20. Amelia Tait, "First They Came for Pepe: How 'Ironic' Nazism Is Taking over the Internet," *New Statesman*, February 16, 2017, https://www.newstatesman.com/science-tech/internet/2017/02/first-they-came-pepe-how-ironic-nazism-taking-over-internet; Warrior-

Tang, "Nazi Pepe Controversy," *Know Your Meme*, n.d., accessed October 6, 2017, http://knowyourmeme.com/memes/events/nazi-pepe-controversy.

21. Roy, "How 'Pepe the Frog' Went from Harmless to Hate Symbol."
22. Dale Beran, "4chan: The Skeleton Key to the Rise of Trump," *Medium*, February 14, 2017, https://medium.com/@DaleBeran/4chan-the-skeleton-key-to-the-rise-of-trump-624e7cb798cb.
23. Atkinson, "There's a New Culture War, and It's Being Fought Online."
24. "I'm the Guy Behind the 'You Can't Stump the Trump' Series," Discussion, *reddit.com/r/the_donald*, February 15, 2016, https://www.reddit.com/r/the_donald/comments/45tguz/im_the_guy_behind_the_you_cant_stump_the_trump/.
25. Mike Wendling, "Trump's Shock Troops: Who Are the 'Alt-Right'?" *BBC News*, August 26, 2016, http://www.bbc.com/news/magazine-37021991.
26. Wendling, "Trump's Shock Troops."
27. Abby Ohlheiser and Caitlin Dewey, "Hillary Clinton's Alt-Right Speech, Annotated," *Washington Post*, August 25, 2016, https://www.washingtonpost.com/news/the-fix/wp/2016/08/25/hillary-clintons-alt-right-speech-annotated/?noredirect=on&utm_term=.9f05502f842e.
28. Roy, "How 'Pepe the Frog' Went from Harmless to Hate Symbol."
29. Roy, "How 'Pepe the Frog' Went from Harmless to Hate Symbol."
30. Asma Khalid, "To Some Democrats, Clinton's 'Deplorables' Comment Is Insensitive But 'Honest,'" *NPR*, September 15, 2016, https://www.npr.org/2016/09/15/493915186/how-does-basket-of-deplorables-play-in-the-real-world.
31. For example, the copy advertising a bumper sticker on a GOP merchandising site proclaims, "The woman who launched our 'Vast Right Wing Conspiracy' products 20 years ago, now attempts to insult us with 'Deplorable.' We are proud of this label as well!" See "Deplorable and Proud Sticker," *GOPStore.com*, https://www.gopstore.com/products/deplorable-and-proud-sticker.
32. Lee Bebout, *Whiteness on the Border: Mapping the U.S. Racial Imagination in Brown and White* (New York: New York University Press, 2016).
33. "Why the White Working Class Voted for Trump," *Harvard Business Review*, November 18, 2016, https://hbr.org/ideacast/2016/11/why-the-white-working-class-voted-for-trump.
34. Jack Smith IV, "This Pro-Clinton Super PAC Is Spending $1 Million to 'Correct' People Online—and Redditors Are Outraged," *Business Insider*, April 22, 2016, http://www.businessinsider.com/clinton-pac-spends-1-million-to-correct-people-online-2016-4.
35. Angela Nagle, *Kill All Normies: Online Culture Wars from 4chan and Tumblr to Trump and the Alt-Right* (Winchester, UK: Zero Books, 2017), 7–8.
36. Schreckinger, "World War Meme."
37. Nuzzi, "How Pepe the Frog Became a Nazi Trump Supporter and Alt-Right Symbol."
38. Aja Romano, "Reddit Shuts down 3 Major Alt-Right Forums Due to Harassment," *Vox*, February 3, 2017, https://www.vox.com/culture/2017/2/3/14486856/reddit-bans-alt-right-doxing-harassment; Sean Illing, "The Reality of Trump's Alt-Right Trolls: They'll Put Your 7-Year-Old's Face on a Gas Chamber," *Vox*, October 27, 2016, https://www.vox.com/conversations/2016/10/27/13428612/donald-trump-david-french-alt-right-trolls-republican-party; Julia Carrie Wong, Olivia Solon, and Sam Levin, "Google Cancels Staff

Meeting after Gamergate-Style Attack on Employees," *The Guardian*, August 11, 2017, http://www.theguardian.com/technology/2017/aug/10/google-cancels-meeting-james-damore-memo-alt-right-gamergate; David French, "The Price I've Paid for Opposing Donald Trump," *National Review*, October 21, 2016, http://www.nationalreview.com/article/441319/donald-trumps-alt-right-supporters-internet-abuse-must-end.

39. Atkinson, "There's a New Culture War, and It's Being Fought Online."
40. These images cannot be reprinted given copyright restrictions but they can be found via Know Your Meme or a simple image search for Nazi Pepe. The simplicity of locating these images, in fact, bespeaks their broad circulation.
41. Nuzzi, "How Pepe the Frog Became a Nazi Trump Supporter and Alt-Right Symbol."
42. Glenn Beck, *The Overton Window* (New York: Pocket Books, 2010).
43. Laura Marsh, "The Flaws of the Overton Window Theory," *The New Republic*, October 27, 2016, https://newrepublic.com/article/138003/flaws-overton-window-theory.
44. Marsh, "The Flaws of the Overton Window Theory."
45. Amber Day, *Satire and Dissent* (Bloomington: Indiana University Press, 2011).
46. Yochai Benkler *et al.*, "Study: Breitbart-Led Right-Wing Media Ecosystem Altered Broader Media Agenda," *Columbia Journalism Review*, March 3, 2017, https://www.cjr.org/analysis/breitbart-media-trump-harvard-study.php.
47. Niko Heikkilä, "Online Antagonism of the Alt-Right in the 2016 Election," *European Journal of American Studies* 12, no. 2 (2017).
48. Hanna Kozlowska, "Hillary Clinton's Website Now Has an Explainer about a Frog That Recently Became a Nazi," *Quartz*, September 13, 2016, https://qz.com/780663/hillary-clintons-website-now-has-an-explainer-about-pepe-the-frog-a-white-supremacist-symbol/.
49. Alana Levinson, "Meet the 'Meme Scientists' Who Tracked This Election's Crazy Viral Phenomena," *Splinter*, November 8, 2016, https://splinternews.com/meet-the-meme-scientists-who-tracked-this-elections-cra-1793863563.
50. Amanda Hess, "Memes, Myself and I: The Internet Lets Us All Run the Campaign," *New York Times*, November 6, 2016, https://www.nytimes.com/2016/11/06/arts/memes-myself-and-i-the-internet-lets-us-all-run-the-campaign.html.
51. Levinson, "Meet the 'Meme Scientists' Who Tracked This Election's Crazy Viral Phenomena."
52. Sophia A. McClennan, "Forget Fake News—Alt-Right Memes Could Do More Damage to Democracy," *Salon*, July 8, 2017, http://www.salon.com/2017/07/08/forget-fake-news-alt-right-memes-could-do-more-damage-to-democracy/.
53. Jason Wilson, "Hiding in Plain Sight: How the 'Alt-Right' Is Weaponizing Irony to Spread Fascism," *The Guardian*, May 23, 2017, http://www.theguardian.com/technology/2017/may/23/alt-right-online-humor-as-a-weapon-facism.
54. Nicholas O'Shaughnessy, "Make No Mistake about It: The Alt-Right Is a Cult, and This Is How Its Members Lure People In," *The Independent*, September 10, 2017, http://www.independent.co.uk/voices/alt-right-neo-nazi-donald-trump-hitler-memes-pepe-the-frog-ubermensch-based-stickman-a7938911.html.
55. Southern Poverty Law Center, "Explaining the Alt-Right 'Deity' of Their 'Meme Magic,'" *Intelligence Report*, August 8, 2017, https://www.splcenter.org/fighting-hate/intelligence-

report/2017/explaining-alt-right-%E2%80%98deity%E2%80%99-their-%E2%80%98meme-magic%E2%80%99.

56. Lester C. Olson, "Benjamin Franklin's Pictorial Representations of the British Colonies in America: A Study in Rhetorical Iconology," *Quarterly Journal of Speech* 73, no. 1 (1987): 38.
57. Janis L. Edwards and Carol K. Winkler, "Representative Form and the Visual Ideograph: The Iwo Jima Image in Editorial Cartoons," *Quarterly Journal of Speech* 83, no. 3 (1997): 289.
58. Eric S. Jenkins, "My iPod, My iCon: How and Why Do Images Become Icons?" *Critical Studies in Media Communication* 25, no. 5 (2008): 467–68.
59. See, for example, Catherine H. Palczewski, "The Male Madonna and the Feminine Uncle Sam: Visual Argument, Icons, and Ideographs in 1909 Anti-Woman Suffrage Postcards," *Quarterly Journal of Speech* 91, no. 4 (2005): 365–94; Robert Hariman and John Louis Lucaites, *No Caption Needed: Iconic Photographs, Public Culture, and Liberal Democracy* (Chicago, IL: University of Chicago Press, 2007); Olson, "Benjamin Franklin's Pictorial Representations of the British Colonies in America."
60. Jenkins, "My iPod, My iCon," 471.
61. W.J.T. Mitchell, *What Do Pictures Want? The Lives and Loves of Images* (Chicago, IL: University of Chicago Press, 2013), 93.
62. Mitchell, *What Do Pictures Want?*, 93.
63. Kristine Kolrud and Marina Prusac, ed., *Iconoclasm from Antiquity to Modernity* (New York: Routledge, 2016).
64. Cara A. Finnegan and Jiyeon Kang, "'Sighting' the Public: Iconoclasm and Public Sphere Theory," *Quarterly Journal of Speech* 90, no. 4 (2004): 379.
65. Matthew Gault, "Pepe the Frog's Creator Goes Legally Nuclear Against the Alt-Right," *Motherboard*, September 18, 2017, https://motherboard.vice.com/en_us/article/8x8gaa/pepe-the-frogs-creator-lawsuits-dmca-matt-furie-alt-right.
66. Nagle, *Kill All Normies*, 13.
67. Gilles Deleuze and Felix Guattari, *A Thousand Plateaus: Capitalism and Schizophrenia*, trans. Brian Massumi (Minneapolis: University of Minnesota Press, 1987), 36.
68. Manuel DeLanda, *A New Philosophy of Society: Assemblage Theory and Social Complexity* (London: A&C Black, 2006), 10.
69. DeLanda, *A New Philosophy of Society*, 11.
70. DeLanda, *A New Philosophy of Society*, 15.
71. DeLanda, *A New Philosophy of Society*.
72. Torkild Thanem and Stephen Linstead, "The Trembling Organisation: Order, Change and the Philosophy of the Virtual," in *Deleuze and the Social*, ed. Martin Fuglsang (Edinburgh: Edinburgh University Press, 2006), 39–57.
73. Ernesto Laclau, *On Populist Reason* (New York: Verso, 2005), 52.
74. Natalie Carnes, *Image and Presence: A Christological Reflection on Iconoclasm and Iconophilia* (Redwood City, CA: Stanford University Press, 2017).
75. Martin Kemp, *Christ to Coke: How Image Becomes Icon* (New York: Oxford University Press, 2012).
76. Don, "Cult of Kek," *Know Your Meme*, n.d., accessed August 29, 2017, http://knowyourmeme.com/memes/cult-of-kek.
77. Don, "Cult of Kek."

78. Paul Spencer, "Trump's Occult Online Supporters Believe 'Meme Magic' Got Him Elected," *Motherboard*, November 8, 2016, https://motherboard.vice.com/en_us/article/pgkx7g/trumps-occult-online-supporters-believe-pepe-meme-magic-got-him-elected.
79. Jenkins, "My iPod, My iCon," 473.
80. Jenkins, "My iPod, My iCon," 469–70.
81. Eric S. Jenkins, "The Modes of Visual Rhetoric: Circulating Memes as Expressions," *Quarterly Journal of Speech* 100, no. 4 (2014): 455, 446.
82. Jenkins, "The Modes of Visual Rhetoric," 456.
83. Tait, "First They Came for Pepe."
84. Dale Beran, "How the 'Isolated Man-Boys' of 4chan Turned a Meme into the President of the United States," *Quartz*, February 17, 2017, https://qz.com/914142/how-the-isolated-man-boys-of-4chan-turned-a-meme-into-the-president-of-the-united-states/.
85. Emma Grey Ellis, "Red-Pilled: My Bizarre Week Using the Alt-Right's Vision of the Internet," *Wired*, September 27, 2017, https://www.wired.com/story/alt-tech-social-media/.
86. Ellis, "Red-Pilled."
87. Limor Shifman, *Memes in Digital Culture* (Cambridge, MA: MIT Press, 2014), 22; Ryan M. Milner, *The World Made Meme: Public Conversations and Participatory Media* (Cambridge, MA: MIT Press, 2016), 61.
88. Paroma Chatterjee, *The Living Icon in Byzantium and Italy: The Vita Image, Eleventh to Thirteenth Centuries* (New York: Cambridge University Press, 2014), 31; Clemena Antonova, *Space, Time, and Presence in the Icon: Seeing the World with the Eyes of God* (New York: Routledge, 2010), 164.
89. Crystal L. Downing, *Changing Signs of Truth: A Christian Introduction to the Semiotics of Communication* (Downers Grove, IL: InterVarsity Press, 2012).
90. W. Lance Bennett and Alexandra Segerberg, "The Logic of Connective Action," *Information, Communication & Society* 15, no. 5 (2012): 739–68 Limor Shifman, "The Cultural Logic of Photo-Based Meme Genres," *Journal of Visual Culture* 13, no. 3 (2014): 340–58; Bradley E. Wiggins and G. Bret Bowers, "Memes as Genre: A Structurational Analysis of the Memescape," *New Media & Society* 17, no. 11 (2015): 1886–1906.
91. SabrinaTibbets, "Feels Good Man."
92. SabrinaTibbets, "Feels Good Man."
93. Kemp, *Christ to Coke*, 3.
94. Triple Zed, "Pepe the Frog." *Know Your Meme*, n.d., http://knowyourmeme.com/memes/pepe-the-frog.
95. Kenneth Burke, *On Symbols and Society* (Chicago, IL: University of Chicago Press, 1989), 190.
96. Tait, "First They Came for Pepe."
97. Y F, "Trash Doves," *Know Your Meme*, n.d., accessed April 23, 2018, http://knowyourmeme.com/memes/trash-doves.
98. Tait, "First They Came for Pepe."
99. Leslie A. Hahner and Scott J. Varda, "Yarn Bombing and the Aesthetics of Exceptionalism," *Communication and Critical/Cultural Studies* 11, no. 4 (2014): 315.

100. Nuzzi, "How Pepe the Frog Became a Nazi Trump Supporter and Alt-Right Symbol."
101. Brad, "Can't Stump the Trump."
102. Brad, "Can't Stump the Trump."
103. Bruno Latour, "What Is Iconoclash? Or Is There a World beyond the Image Wars?," in *Iconoclash*, ed. Bruno Latour and Peter Weibel (Karlsruhe and Cambridge, MA: ZKM/MIT Press, 2002), 21.
104. Abby Ohlheiser, "Pepe the Frog Became a Hate Symbol. Now He's Just a Dead Hate Symbol," *Washington Post*, May 8, 2017, https://www.washingtonpost.com/news/the-intersect/wp/2017/05/08/pepe-the-frog-became-a-hate-symbol-now-hes-just-a-dead-hate-symbol/.
105. Maxwell E. McCombs and Donald Shaw, "The Agenda-Setting Function of Mass Media," *Public Opinion Quarterly* 36, no. 2 (1972): 176–87.
106. Rodney Taveira and Emma Balfour, "How Donald Trump Won the 2016 Meme Wars," *The Conversation*, November 30, 2016, http://theconversation.com/how-donald-trump-won-the-2016-meme-wars-68580.
107. Atkinson, "There's a New Culture War, and It's Being Fought Online."
108. Michael Warner, "Publics and Counterpublics," *Public Culture* 14, no. 1 (2002): 66.
109. Krishna Y. Kamath *et al.*, "Spatio-Temporal Dynamics of Online Memes: A Study of Geo-Tagged Tweets," in *Proceedings of the 22nd International Conference on World Wide Web* (New York: ACM, 2013), 667–78.
110. Warner, "Publics and Counterpublics," 63.
111. Finnegan and Kang, "'Sighting' the Public."
112. Finnegan and Kang, "'Sighting' the Public."
113. Larry Kim, "16 Eye-Popping Statistics You Need to Know About Visual Content Marketing," *Inc.com*, November 23, 2015, https://www.inc.com/larry-kim/visual-content-marketing-16-eye-popping-statistics-you-need-to-know.html; Lindsay Willott, "20 Stats That Will Change the Way You Survey Your Customers," My*Customer.com*, May 25, 2016, https://www.mycustomer.com/experience/voice-of-the-customer/20-stats-that-will-change-the-way-you-survey-your-customers; Amanda Sibley, "19 Reasons You Should Include Visual Content in Your Marketing [Data]," Blog, August 6, 2012, https://blog.hubspot.com/blog/tabid/6307/bid/33423/19-reasons-you-should-include-visual-content-in-your-marketing-data.aspx; Ritu Pant, "Visual Marketing: A Picture's Worth 60,000 Words," *Business 2 Community*, January 16, 2015, http://www.business2community.com/digital-marketing/visual-marketing-pictures-worth-60000-words-01126256#6JTK8OjBie7kyoLo.97; Cheryl Conner, "The New Era Of Media: Visual Public Relations," *Forbes*, October 28, 2016, https://www.forbes.com/sites/cherylsnappconner/2016/10/28/the-new-era-of-media-visual-public-relations/#d9e757f54275.
114. Leonardo Bruni, Chiara Francalanci, and Paolo Giacomazzi, "The Role of Multimedia Content in Determining the Virality of Social Media Information," *Information* 3, no. 3 (2012): 278–89; Saeideh Bakhshi, David A. Shamma, and Eric Gilbert, "Faces Engage Us: Photos with Faces Attract More Likes and Comments on Instagram," in *Proceedings of the SIGCHI Conference on Human Factors in Computing Systems* (New York: ACM, 2014), 965–974; Jennifer Aaker and Andy Smith, *The Dragonfly Effect* (New York: John Wiley & Sons, 2010).

115. Elle Hunt, "Pepe the Frog Creator Kills off Internet Meme Co-Opted by White Supremacists," *The Guardian*, May 8, 2017, http://www.theguardian.com/world/2017/may/08/pepe-the-frog-creator-kills-off-internet-meme-co-opted-by-white-supremacists.
116. Aja Romano, "Pepe the Frog's Creator Can't Save Him from the Alt-Right, but He Keeps Trying Anyway," *Vox*, June 28, 2017, https://www.vox.com/culture/2017/6/28/15879734/matt-furie-save-pepe-kickstarter-campaign.
117. Lloyd F. Bitzer, "The Rhetorical Situation," *Philosophy & Rhetoric* 25 (1992): 6.

· 3 ·

LULZ

White Nationalism for the Digital Age

In early 2017, a new Alt-right symbol began to occupy public consciousness. On February 7, users on /pol/ drafted a post entitled "Enter the Milk Zone" that showed, among other items, a meme marking areas of the world where lactose intolerance was high.[1] Comments indexed an odd combination of eugenics and genetics to show how lactose tolerance was related to "racial purity."[2] As one user pronounced, "Roses are red, Barack is half black, if you can't drink milk, you have to go back."[3] Within this thread, veganism was deemed a Jewish plot for world domination and racial intermixing justified as the reason one user (who identified as black) could digest milk.[4] After this thread gained traction in social media, a whole host of others began posting about milk tolerance. The president of the National Policy Institute, and an avowed white nationalist, Richard Spencer, placed a milk emoji in his Twitter profile and tweeted about his tolerance to milk.[5] Baked Alaska—aka Tim Gionet, a well-known troll—followed with his own milk emoji on Twitter.[6] Neo-Nazis popped up on YouTube drinking gallons of milk at Shia LaBeouf's latest performance art.[7] Soon, the mainstream media was covering milk as a symbol for neo-Nazis and the Alt-right.[8]

Except milk was not necessarily a symbol adopted by the Alt-right. Instead, this elaborate coupling of milk with racist claims about lactose digestion and the proliferation of milk imagery began as a prank, a large-scale troll initiated in 4chan and taken up by a whole series of actors. For their part, 4chan users suggested that the prank was ironic. As one user wrote, "Nobody actually takes these memes literally…Just as nobody thinks every black person on the planet is fatherless, or every Muslim on the planet is a terrorists [*sic*], nobody on 4chan actually believes that the ability to drink milk in [*sic*] genetic. It's just ironic meme shitposting."[9] The prank proved to be yet another successful troll for the Alt-right, who had floated a number of false symbols (e.g., Trash Dove) to garner media attention. This comment invoked irony as the lens justifying the patent racism of milk memes. Users insisted they did not "really" believe the hateful memes they created about other peoples, but participated in racism through ironic play. Milk memes were all in good fun for those users and outsiders were a pawn in their games. These memes were just for the lulz.

More generally, memes are often fashioned for the pursuit of lulz, a neologism wedded to irony via the work of subversion. Ryan Milner explains that lulz is based on a logic that "favours distanced irony and critique."[10] Memes play upon "dominant cultural assumptions" with a "bait and switch" that reverses the original assumption.[11] Deployments of this ironic critique may be directed toward outside audiences such that lulz operates via *schadenfreude*, pleasure derived from the misfortune of others. Whitney Phillips asserts that "In the trolling world, lulz may mean one basic thing—amusement at other people's distress—but can be deployed in any number of directions, for any number of reasons."[12] Gabriella Coleman contends that lulz can "encompass lighthearted jokes as well" but lulz are often "darker: acquired most often at someone's expense, prone to misfiring and, occasionally, bordering on disturbing or hateful speech (except, of course, when they cross the border entirely: thank you rape jokes)."[13] Lulz, for Coleman, "speak foremost to the pleasures of transgression."[14] Such transgression toys with messages to subvert mainstream ideals, often in ways that shock or purposefully offend. As it relates to the boards under study here, lulz is typically an attempt at trolling to create a social backlash. Shitposting, for instance, is an evolution of lulz—a strategy that replicates derivative images or floods a public forum to distract or annoy.[15] It is entertaining for those pursuing lulz to watch as "normies" are rattled or emboldened by their racist actions, even as users insist that these images do not reveal sincere beliefs. Altogether, lulz and shitposting bespeak an orientation to memes: namely, irony frames the way users commonly create and circulate memes to upset decorum and antagonize outsiders.

As a rhetorical form, irony rests on the ambiguity of figuration and that same ambiguity is at work in lulz. Irony is notoriously difficult to define given that it is diffuse in operation. Wayne Booth writes that the term typically is "seen as something that undermines clarities, opens up vistas of chaos, and either liberates by destroying all dogma or destroys by revealing the inescapable canker of negation at the heart of every affirmation."[16] The duplicity of irony is that, as Kenneth Burke intimates, it offers a "perspective of perspectives."[17] Irony is the master trope that reflects and undermines a number of tropological relations—or those ways of seeing marked by rhetorical forms. In this sense, irony is a mode or an orientation to discourse. It is an attempt to open up the field of signification. The bait and switch of lulz is ironic in that it represents some effort to resist dominant relations. While one part of lulz is predicated on trolling others, another component of this rhetorical tactic aims to upend the taken for granted. In this way, lulz recalibrates irony as a rhetorical form, an effort moved through memetic imagery.

For the Alt-right, the deployment of ironic images through lulz supplies rhetorical cover for hate-filled messages. As with the milk memes and events above, the use of lulz often participates in the disavowal of one's racist actions. Such disavowal recognizes the racism contained in far-right memes but refuses to accept responsibility for conveying racism.[18] This mode of engagement has long been central to trolling and lulz. As Phillips writes, "Although trolls are aware of and in fact are dependent upon the power of racist language, they are often outright dismissive of their role in replicating racist ideologies (the same racist ideologies, it must be noted, they gleefully and unapologetically seek to exploit)."[19] This iteration of white nationalism is predicated on both a possessive investment in whiteness and a privileged insistence that one can espouse such claims without personal consequence.[20] In other words, users proclaim they can make such memes and singularly determine whether or not the images are racist. Lulz as a mode of ironic engagement rhetorically deploys racism under the guise of humor or misread intentions. As with other forms of ironic racism such as minstrel shows, blackface, and more recently, hipster racism, the use of lulz to craft memes performatively enacts racism.[21] The distanced or meta-perspective manifest in some Alt-right images is itself a form of racism that reifies white supremacy.

To analyze the visual relationships of irony at stake, here, we use the concept of *détournement*. *Détournement* is a strategy first named by Guy Debord. Debord and the Situationists imagined *détournement* as the careful rearrangement of imagery to interrupt the spectacle of hegemony, to resist the workings of the dominant order.[22] Memes are often read through *détournement* given that, as Phillips notes, trolls use *détournement* to "challenge dominant ideals through creative and often absurdist appropriation."[23] *Détournement* is evident in Alt-right memes insofar as they use pastiche to rework and appropriate commonly accepted ideas. In this chapter, we use the phrase "memetic *détournement*" to explain the rhetorical work of lulz and the ways these subversive efforts ultimately entrench white supremacy in the digital age. Our approach here is novel in that we focus on the meme as a visual form of memetic *détournement*. While other scholars, such as Phillips, note how trolls use *détournement*, our analytical efforts return *détournement* to its imagaic origins. As we described in the previous chapter, the meme is an image uniquely suited to arrest attention and intervene in public culture. Alt-right memes commonly adopt a critical stance that not only appeals to some insiders on 4chan and reddit, but more importantly, creates a rhetorical strategy with traction for outside audiences. One can engage in vicious advocacies as though they are simply humorous spectacles, all the while those same advocacies fuel the larger adoption of white nationalism as though its material impacts were a side effect. In other words, lulz in Alt-right memes often manifests through the visual deployment of radical discourse that allows users to disavow their own complicity while nevertheless emboldening the hatred indexed by those images.

The Magic Land of Memes

Current scholarship and popular essays on 4chan and reddit suggest that the election of Donald Trump represents "meme magic." Meme magic identifies when desired outcomes are ostensibly brought into being by the calculated proliferation of internet memes and the apparent sorcery of particular images, rituals, and signs. In this scholarship, meme magic foregrounds ritualistic logic that suggests memes can actualize the impossible. According to Know Your Meme, meme magic first emerged as a term of art in 2015, when users on /pol/ claimed that meme magic had crashed the Germanwings Flight 9525 on its way to Düsseldorf.[24] Leading into the election, meme magic began to refer to the supernatural power of memes to elect Donald Trump, against polling data that indicated his likely loss to Hillary Clinton. As with the Germanwings flight crash, the meme magic that supposedly elected Trump turned on the symbolism of internet icons. Users invested in the occult power of certain images, most especially Pepe the Frog. Pepe the Frog was deemed to possess magical powers to elect Trump to the highest office. Meme magic demarcates what appears to be an occult or ritualistic understanding of memes as rarefied images able to usher in ordained consequences. Yet, despite the importance of meme magic for grasping the ritualistic behaviors of online group behavior, we argue that a focus on ritualism often obfuscates the work of irony as the primary rhetorical appeal of Alt-right memes.

Perhaps because they seem to have magical powers of actualization, a number of scholars and journalists have described Alt-right memes in ritualistic terms. For instance, Abby Ohlheiser reported the various instances when meme magic was celebrated on 4chan after the election of Donald Trump.[25] Yet, her article failed to remark on how those posts may have used an ironic posturing or engaged in lulz—either for direct enjoyment or with the understanding that the board was now being watched by journalists and liberals. This assessment highlights the frame many scholars use to understand memes: these images are understood as creating a cult-like superstition. Interviewing occult researcher Théodore Ferréol, Paul Spencer deems the proliferation of Pepe and other Alt-right imagery as ritualistic. He explains: "The technique involves charging a symbol, which will then act as a proxy for a clandestine plan. In occult tradition, this is known as chaos magic…This is a new era of chaos magic, fueled by viral sharing: enter the world of meme magic."[26] Here, meme magic names the cultic work of users who employ memes to enact their conspiratorial plans. For scholars such as Ferréol, meme magic is ritualistic—memes mystically attract latent audiences. The work of the meme ostensibly impacts the audience as though it were a magic bullet. As Spencer claims, "If you think this sounds a bit like hypnotism, you're right."[27] Memes, then, are important for these authors because they are the vehicles for evangelizing the populace, often unwittingly.

Still other writers maintain that memes indicate how 4chan and reddit users are a subculture wholly unlike the mainstream public. These readings solidify the Alt-right as outsiders—those who do not participate in the same cultural or rational logics as broader segments of society. Morgan Quaintance contends that the Alt-right, as it emerged through social media sites (e.g., YouTube, 4chan, reddit, etc.), used discourse that promoted cult-like behavior.[28] For him, these groups are part of the "cultic milieu, a 'cultural underground of society' that is composed of and conducive to the creation of cults: groups whose members are unified by adherence to a set of principles deviant from dominant cultural orthodoxies."[29] Milner and Phillips suggest that the magic of these memes is "opaque," but exhibit ideological patterns and beliefs.[30] Here, the work of memes is limited to a select set of users who have created their own subculture. Within this subculture, these authors maintain, memes take on a specific purpose such that they are seen as tools of chaos magic. Memes in this posturing are ritualistic symbols of a small group of individuals. These scholars insist that to grasp the work of these groups, we must demystify their habits and interrogate the cultic figurations of their practices.

To be sure, if you read the forums of /pol/ and r/the_donald/, users at least articulate the claim that they memed Donald Trump into the White House.[31] Despite these assertions, scholars cannot interpret meme magic simply as a ritual for cult-like internet users. Such a depiction minimizes how memes are dispatched to broader publics and the ways these images participate in the discursive patterns of public culture. As Phillips writes, memetic discourse, much like the Alt-right, cannot be treated as an aberration but rather as a reflection of contemporary culture and the peoples within it.[32] In this sense, memes are not simply a mode of persuasive discourse for a small number of individuals. Rather, memes reflect the contradictions of mainstream culture. Indeed, the meme's retooling of irony often resonates for a wider audience. To understand how memes persuade, then, scholars must engage with the tactical elements of meme creation and distribution. Memes are not necessarily magic images, even if their effects appear enchanted. They are visual and verbal appeals designed to hold sway in the world of social media.

Irony within Alt-right memes is often deployed as a rhetorical tactic that emboldens white nationalism in the digital age. As we briefly discussed in chapter two, in May 2016, @JaredTSwift trolled the *Daily Beast* into believing that Trash Dove—a Facebook sticker that was proclaimed the new Pepe, or the new symbol for the Alt-right—was a specific attempt to convert the masses.[33] During the interview, @JaredTSwift insisted that these memes pushed "white nationalism into a very mainstream position."[34] The reporter believed @JaredTSwift and published the story including his direct statements. Responses to the article were speedy, with a number of publications denouncing the continued vile efforts of /pol/. Yet, @JaredTSwift later recanted his story, indicating that he fabricated an organized propaganda effort to troll the reporter and the liberal readership of the *Daily Beast*. After this denial, the reporter and the publication—as well as many other reporters—lost credibility, especially for covering the inner workings of the far right. Here, the supposed veracity of this exchange is less significant than the overall framework of lulz that guides the actions of @JaredTSwift and a number of other memetic engagements. Lulz authorized both the initial story and the later recantation—@JaredTSwift trolled the reporter to see if the story would stick and then recanted his words to further her humiliation. With both the initial story and the later retractions, reporters aggrandized the growth of white nationalism because of the source's ironic engagement. Indeed, the irony of lulz advantaged the Alt-right by increasing media coverage and bolstering Alt-right actors who then felt able to manipulate the media further.

Reading memes solely as ritualistic images ignores the rhetorical ways that lulz emboldens and enacts white supremacy. For users, lulz creates the conditions in which racism is routed through an ironic distanciation—irony facilitates the creation of vicious memes without personal consequence to those who craft them. Nevertheless, these very actions perform racism goaded by the social capital of resistance to orthodoxy. As Nicole Hemmer writes, "Attitudes like white supremacy are about power, and they dress up in whatever way they need to in order to protect that power."[35] Here, white supremacy may be clothed in irony but that dressing does not change its impacts. Ultimately, lulz enables the proliferation of Alt-right discourse and reifies the attitudes of white supremacy. Therefore, to understand how lulz are rhetorically deployed by the Alt-right, we draw on a similar visual tactic from an earlier era: *détournement*.

Lulz as *Détournement*

As a tactical deployment of irony, *détournement* employs visual and performative pastiche. For Debord, humans lived in a spectacular society; they were bound to capitalism via those relations that fixated their focus and energy on the promises of imagery. The spectacle "inverts the real" and enables humans to mistake consumption and projections of material life as materiality itself.[36] *Détournement* subverts the spectacular imagery propping up investment in capitalism. The Situationists argued that when objects were placed into relation, especially in advertising or in other modes of publicity, two independent expressions or modes of feeling were brought to bear on one another.[37] The goal is to briefly resist the pleasures of consumption and capitalism with pleasure in opposing the regular order. *Détournement* uses bricolage and appropriation to mark the fault lines of the society of the spectacle, reworking oppressive imagery for radical aims. It does so on a formal level—in terms of visual and thematic contrast—but also in a performative sense—in terms of shaping the rhetorical orientation of the community. The imagaic work of *détournement* is key to its enactment. Images seize the spectacular means through which capitalism and the like are sustained. To study memetic *détournement* is to attend to the very foundation of how the Alt-right gains rhetorical advantages in public culture: through visual modes of ironic address.

Memes are a contemporary iteration of *détournement* insofar as these images use pastiche to bring contrasting ideas and concepts into relation. As we described in chapter one with LOLCats, the intertextuality of the meme produces a new way of seeing. These pastiche images regularly generate outside interest in the creativity of those participating on 4chan or reddit. For instance, 4chan often garners media coverage when members of its /b/ subgroup seek out lulz, through trolling or insulting others, staging elaborate real-life pranks, and other actions.[38] In these events, the ability to garner attention—even or especially through vicious advocacy—shows the originality of meme creators. Provocation and lulz justify any approach so long as those methods are oppositional to the mainstream. Some of these methods can become quite intimidating, even dangerous. Aja Romano explains,

> Sometimes, trolls will fake outrage online in order to drum up real outrage, like the time 4chan attempted to manufacture a dangerous fitness trend among teen girls called the "bikini bridge" (similar to the "thigh gap"), then fabricated fake outrage in response to the fake trend, in order to generate real outrage among feminists. Occasionally, trolling "events" can also spill over into real life, some of which, like swatting (using the internet to create fake threats and summon a real-life SWAT team to a target's house), are extremely dangerous.[39]

In this way, 4chan and reddit users have often created memes in keeping with this anarchic understanding of lulz, such that memes are diffuse in form and message yet typically counter to acceptable standards of decency. Here, lulz becomes a mode of *détournement* given that these images use pastiche and interrelationships to provoke others and introduce chaos to the status quo. Memes are a central mechanism of pursuing lulz given how they can visually contrast spectacular modes of relation. As with traditional understandings of *détournement*, it is the visual disparities of spectacular imagery that most enables an interruption to the given order.

Moreover, as we elaborated in chapter one, the creation of memes in enclaved sites (e.g., the /b/ board, r9k, etc.) shapes those communities by articulating the values and norms of those locales. In its traditional deployment, *détournement* shapes and forms groups such as the Situationists. As Vincent Kaufmann writes, "*Détournement* is a poetry produced by several individuals and theoretically by everyone…The situationist community is constituted by *détournement*, precisely because of its character as an act: It institutes a pragmatics at the heart of poetic language."[40] Alt-right memes are similarly poetic in that they shape community despite difference. As creators and users assessed the memes posted in enclaved sites, those images and interactions help constitute the community. Often discussions about memes or the memes themselves explicitly distinguished board membership from outsiders. These interactions suggest that the work done by memes was performative—these images are poetic enunciations of a radical departure from the mainstream. Kaufmann describes the work of *détournement* as a poetry that is theoretically accessible by everyone—the principles could be used by anyone who "diverts out of revolutionary conviction."[41] The creation of memes on /pol/ and r/the_donald/ are often born from that same revolutionary conviction. As texts created with lulz, some Alt-right memes aim to "implode" the present "politics of communication."[42] These individuals come together as actors given their shared framework for creation—resistance itself generates an orientation that organizes. Memes, then, are a type of *détournement*, such that they are tactical images as well as sites of invention that constitute a community of oppositional actors.

While quite often *détournement* is understood as resistant, the strategy can also be appropriated for conservatizing aims.[43] The Alt-right and others have long quoted Saul Alinsky's *Rules for Radicals* as a manual—a guidebook for tactics that can be turned back on the left. As surmised by George Michael, "Unlike old-school white nationalist movements, the alt-right has endeavored to create a self-sustaining counterculture, which includes a distinct vernacular, memes, symbols and a number of blogs and alternative media outlets."[44] This counterculture relies on polarization and antagonism to expand the Overton Window, or the range of acceptable public discourse. Memetic *détournement* works not as a leftist or rightist political strategy, but by seizing imagery that seems countercultural. This oppositional posturing emboldens a community to labor against institutions, events, and people understood as "establishment." Tim McDonough writes that the "bourgeoisie was as adept at *détournement* as the Situationists themselves, that, in fact, recuperation and *détournement* were one and the same, a shared cultural strategy."[45] While the Situationists and others have proclaimed the tactic as potentially revolutionary, it has been used effectively by the right. As Toby Heys and Andrew Hennlich write, "the right are assimilating the tools of the left, resulting in a re-territorialisation of one of Western culture's cherished notions of resistance."[46] The strategy of pastiche, of re-arranging modes of relation between commonplace imagery, need not reach toward revolution but can reify the very structures of domination the Situationists and Debord sought to resist. Moreover, the constitutive function of *détournement* can found a new community, one that may develop political strategies that foreclose the potential effectiveness of the left.

Building the Strategy

Meme designers in /pol/ and r/the_donald/ often labor to diminish liberal arguments and direct leftist agendas toward new political realities. Here, the deployment of *détournement* reroutes lulz for far right advocacies. Those who use message sites on 4chan or reddit steal imagery of the mainstream to use against the status quo, but the aims are quite opposed to those who birthed *détournement*. Memetic *détournement* is deployed to "introduce white nationalism to a new generation" and fuel regressive politics.[47] Heys and Hennlich assert that such appropriation "ultimately results in the stark realisation that the traditional leftist position can no longer count on its ideological weapons."[48] Now, the *détournement* of memes builds an Alt-right agenda. Some members of the Alt-right consider their memetic advocacy key to countering the hegemony of the left and the presumed liberal stronghold on public values and commitments. Here, the Alt-right aims to broaden acceptance of its advocacies by creating images that provoke thought and vilify opponents.

As it relates to /pol/ and r/the_donald/, the use of *détournement* is in keeping with the longstanding traditions of humor and trolling by its users. Trolling in pursuit of lulz is typically proclaimed to be ironic, even if the force or intent of those actions is not. For instance, Romano interviewed white nationalist Andrew Anglin who argued that while his blog uses humor and vulgar themes, he is "also very clear that the point of using irony is to mask something utterly straightforward: 'The true nature of the movement, however, is serious and idealistic.'"[49] In contemporary culture, Anglin claimed that "absolute idealism must be couched in irony in order to be taken seriously."[50] The work of irony lubricates the acceptance of sincere racism. As Milner argues, "The blur between irony and earnestness makes room for discourse otherwise impermissible."[51] Through irony, the Alt-right is able to rework and interrupt a given order, by using humor as a lure and mask for its agenda.

The Alt-right uses memetic *détournement* to craft a set of appeals that recreate found images and assert subversive claims. The ironic appeal is integral to this work, insofar as users of online forums and the broader public understand memes as predicated on irony. Milner writes that the memes developed on 4chan and other online discussion boards operate as a mode of "reappropriation," such that the "bricoleur becomes a staple of mediated public conversation."[52] Importantly, resonance is cardinal to the work of memes. As he claims, "the motives and meanings of this play are not always straightforward…memetic irony and humor can both forward racist and misogynistic perspectives and critique" those same perspectives.[53] In this way, the ironic mode of address can use pastiche to bend and twist the appeal. Nothing is straightforward, claims are oblique and may even undo the original assertion. It is the ironic posturing of the idea that is most crucial to rhetorical effectiveness. Oblique claims present a posturing that allows for the proliferation of toxic claims under the guise of ambiguity.

Because memes are built by collections of users, they help galvanize the political agenda of the group and bolster the role of *détournement* in creation. Milner identifies group work as essential to building memes—memes come together through collage and compilation.[54] Memes are self-referential and iterative by nature. Iterations rely upon a shared language and a collective history for collaboration. In this way, memes are infused with and propagate the cultures of those who manufacture or alter them. Memes are generated by and generative of specific communities. As communicative media, they also inspire and transmit messages important to those communities. Much as the Situationists came into being via the work of *détournement*, here, the work of constructing the meme likewise constitutes the people and specific claims of the Alt-right. Most importantly, the framework of memetic *détournement* generates even more images that adopt such a lens.

For instance, on a thread discussing new tactics of meme warfare, posters both critique the current trends and provide a template for future memes. As one poster wrote discussing the idea of meme warfare, "But going and showing normies that people can have different opinions is absolutely necessary. Get normies to be brave enough to start speaking out against antifa and blm by showing them that it's not uncommon or unacceptable and our work is done for us."[55] Here, Antifa and blm (Black Lives Matter)—leftist political movements—are to be critiqued by the Alt-right as well as by "normies." This post does triple rhetorical work. First, it bounds a particular community by its apparent antithesis (normies and non-, the Alt-right and Antifa). Second, it outlines imperatives for various communities; in this case, the Alt-right ought to be encouraging normies to act, and normies ought to act. Third, and finally, it foregrounds the procedure by which those imperatives should be carried out: through meme warfare. The post demonstrates significant faith that ironic memes can mediate deep divisions in America and align latent audiences with the Alt-right. For the poster, Antifa and BLM are problematic because they impede the march of white nationalism. In effect, this discussion codifies the Alt-right as a community and clearly articulates its goals and directives for the conversion of larger audiences.

The viral spread of some Alt-right memes engenders a community beyond the enclaves of an anonymous (or pseudonymous) digital forum. The proliferation of memetic *détournement* creates a trend, a way of seeing the world amplified and sustained by the spectacular work of ironic engagement. The meme warfare post encourages members to speak out against Antifa and BLM, to demarcate the boundaries of acceptability. If some Alt-right memes can suggest that a rejection of leftist political viewpoints is not "uncommon," then these efforts embolden others to reject the advocacies of at least BLM and Antifa. More generally, this form of critique suggests that if normies can see the counter-perspective presented by Alt-right, they too might adopt that perspective or at least an anti-leftist position. As Phillips writes, the creation of a meme precipitates additional "memetic creation and fortif[ies] a sense of community between participants."[56] While Phillips is focused on the in-group of 4chan, by the time of the 2016 election, that participatory generation of community is extended out to those who can adopt the same frame of viewing marked by the meme.[57] In this way, the Alt-right users of 4chan and reddit become the breeding ground for a larger community.

The nature of these online discussions suggests a significant investment in the use of *détournement*, especially spectacular intervention. In the discussion regarding the best course of action after Charlottesville, one user distinguished among different white nationalist groups through an analysis of various rhetorical tactics. As this user wrote, "White nationalism 1.0: Stormfront, Fail-Soc, Hitler, Duke, being edgy for the sake of being edgy[.] White nationalism 2.0: 4chan, frog memes, intellectual Millenials/Gen Z, Spencer, DS[.] We are WINNING and we are going to get the job done. The NSDAP will look like larping children compared to the shit we're pull [*sic*] with NPI. The UTR rally was just a preview to what's coming."[58] Here, this user articulates the strategies that will be most effective in terms of furthering white nationalism. On this user's view, memes, a supposedly intellectual understanding of the movement, and the arguments of Spencer will attract younger millennials and Generation Z members to the cause. In this statement, the user distinguishes white nationalism 1.0—demarcated by emphasis on Adolph Hitler, David Duke, and edgy statements—from the ironic white nationalism of 4chan. White nationalism 2.0 deploys the spectacle of memes as intellectual tools used in combination with other weaponry. The poster, for example, references the NPI headed by Richard Spencer.[59] The organization offers a corporate face to white nationalism, while memes become a different line of recruitment. Together, these two modes of approach—the visual and spectacular appeal of memes alongside the institutional work of the NPI and Richard Spencer play off of one another. The images capture attention while institutional discourse sutures that worldview to a particular politics. The work of memes, then, helps to articulate what this community aspires to accomplish. With this post, debating how memes and other forms of spectacle can address the masses founds a community who then seek ways to further the cause.

Memetic *détournement* continues to evolve alongside changing rhetorical exigencies and cultural conditions. Significantly, 4chan and reddit users on /pol/ and r/the_donald/ have turned to shitposting to rework the spectacular intervention of memes. These efforts refashion lulz from the idea of pleasure in the pain of others to that of distraction and control of public discourse. For example, in a discussion on the best way to convince others and avoid "dumb ass propaganda," the self-professed older members of the community bemoan shitposting as unoriginal.[60] While these writers lament the tactic, they nevertheless accurately assess the shift in lulz: "I don't disagree, if people are willing to put in the work to find an irrefutable source, but more often than not, that's just another opportunity for them to shitpost. When you post some article proving they're full of shit, they're just going to respond with some 'fake news' bait that gets them 6 more responses from the idiots on this board."[61] The comment regrets that shitposting does not invent original content, but instead, provokes by repeatedly posting derivative material. Even as they criticize the practice, though, participants recognize how shitposting derails the conversation and diverts attention. That same strategy is mirrored with other uses of shitposting.

Shitposting is often deployed through a flood of memes that circumvent the flow of rational discourse, preventing leftist arguments or even oppositional arguments from gaining traction within a particular public forum or comments section. If someone posts a series of memes that are nonsensical or even toxic, "normal" public discussion and debate is taken to a new arena of discourse. This strategy was used with Pepe. If Hillary Clinton was forced to respond to a cartoon frog given Pepe's proliferation, shitposting in general distracts broader publics from more significant issues. The distraction works if

Clinton seems rigid and conventional while the far right appears deft in their rhetorical footwork. This strategy comes together as a specific mode of *détournement* given that, often, community members on /pol/ and r/the_donald/ understand themselves as intervening in the problematic methods of debate—especially identity politics—of the left. The work of shitposting, then, is an attempt to underscore what they view as the absurdity of these modes of debate. For some users, debating on the ground the left provides is a dead end that does not forward their goals. Shitposting is a form of *détournement* by highlighting the absurdity of public discourse and the need for a counter-hegemonic intervention by the Alt-right. White nationalist memes are part of this impulse—an effort to bring about a dramatic change either in the status quo or as an actual politics. Ultimately, the spirit of memetic *détournement* is one of resistance to the status quo and a public proclamation embracing the absurdity of political life.

For many users, memes are part of a revolutionary perspective, one that adopts the affective resonance of lulz as pleasurable. In the fall of 2017, one poster on r/the_donald/ supplied an assessment of how such radical memes worked. He linked to an article describing how Saul Alinsky's *Rules for Radicals* could be deployed against the left. This user continued, "I'll be damned if we—as a domreddit—don't do every single one of these. It's crazy how good we are at it. One of the important rules mentioned in the book is that whoever is being 'radical' should have fun doing it. I have never in my 6 years in Reddit seen a more jovial group than the ones here in this dom. I'd also like to point out how great it is that we turn anything from the left into the 'xxx is Isis' meme. (Cnn, NFL, etc.). It's Saul alynski [*sic*] 101. Kudos to all of you. We really are writing history right now."[62] For this user, shocking, radical, or even mundane memes must be created and spread with pleasure, for the pursuit of lulz. The pleasure, or affective resonance, of meme creation is key to their revolutionary impact.

Here, lulz is part of a renegade status and an almost anarchic goal. The users of these forums often describe themselves as bringing about a cultural revolution. Chaos, subversion, and entropy are the goals of a set of users who commonly insist that such radical possibilities can upend the stalemate of the status quo. As Phillips writes, "caring about anything, including trolling itself, is regarded as…inherently cancerous."[63] That rejection of caring, or common values, is maintained by trolling or otherwise acting against anyone or anything who questions this goal. As we discussed in chapter one, even if not every (or most) 4chan and reddit user is toxic, forums such as these often generate a certain level of toxicity. Apparent in the Gamer Gate scandal and in The Fappening, there is often a ramping up of vitriol in response to those who attempt to curb or otherwise shift the momentum of these sites. Adrienne Massanari's critique of such "toxic technocultures," suggests that while there are outliers, the overall tenor of a particular forum is often focused on the "implicit or explicit harassment of others."[64] That harassment evidences an orientation toward radicality, toward the utter undoing of the status quo. The resulting chaos and humiliation that may be unearthed is part of what drives lulz. A momentary chaos engendered by lulz, then, marks memetic *détournement* as that which seeks to interrupt the spectacle of the status quo, through whatever methods might disrupt.

Users of /pol/ and r/the_donald/ do not usually imagine themselves as ideologues, but rather as individuals who deploy these toxic messages for spectacular ambitions. The gap between intention and outcome is coded into the process of rhetorical invention, into the act of making memes. Massanari argues that users on these sites often engage in toxic behavior while disavowing their complicity. Users are able to separate "themselves from what they perceive as the more ethically dubious (and illegal) actions of others, suggesting they are 'not really part' of whatever toxic technoculture under which they are acting."[65] This a mode of engagement might be properly called ironic distanciation, where the actions of users are separated from their intentions. Massanari marks this distanciation as part of this discursive process, wherein the goal is to maintain toxic patterns while allowing individuals some level of reprieve from their own responsibility. Much as with the pattern of meme creation we describe, users can often create toxic imagery while disavowing their own role in such an outcome. This mode of ironic distanciation situates the role of memes on an imagined battlefield.

More generally, meme conversations turn to the notion of the meme war—a sometimes humorous, sometimes earnest understanding of the role of memes in battles against the left, the mainstream media, and others. References to the meme war abound. Even when such comments are flippant, there is nevertheless the notion that memes are essential to countering the prevailing order. A meme posted in August 2017 depicted "the great meme war," with a Pepe general instructing a tadpole Pepe in the meme army to "shitpost" as if "your life depends on it."[66] The meme is a humorous take on the battle imagined between the Alt-right and the left (as symbolized by an Antifa flag). The image represents the role of memes in countering the mainstream media and the left. Here, using memes to shitpost on digital forums is an effort to recalibrate the nature of public discourse about particular topics or the Alt-right itself. Memes are posited as the key battlefront of the culture wars. As Kalle Lasn forewarned in 1999, "Meme warfare has become the geopolitical battle of our time. Whoever has the memes as the power."[67] Memes are posited as a cardinal form necessary to stop the flow of images from the mainstream media or the left. They are the primary weapon deployed in a manufactured battleground for the hearts and minds of the public.

Shitposting moves this weaponry in new directions insofar as it suggests a way for 4chan and reddit users to more heavily lean into the irony of memetic *détournement*. Once cat macro memes have become too pedestrian, aggressive shitposting of offensive or distracting spectacular material takes its place. As Whitney Phillips, Jessica Beyer, and Gabriella Coleman wrote for *Motherboard*, "the alt-right's pro-Trump 'shitposting'—the act of flooding social media with memes and commentary designed to bolster their 'God Emperor' Trump—raised the public visibility of the alt-right and its memetic handiwork. And it is also true that this uptick in public visibility forced people to focus on Trump more than they would have otherwise."[68] The absurdity of Trump supplied an interesting case for users to play with lulz. But, as these scholars maintain, these events did not "happen in a vacuum, and [were not] self-propelling."[69] Instead, these happenings were spurred from the idea that the mainstream media controlled the flow of information and that shitposting could garner journalistic coverage "that amplified their message."[70] In total, this form of shitposting grabbed attention and used the affordances of the mainstream media for Alt-right purposes.

Indeed, 4chan and reddit users often proclaim that they must resist the mainstream media and the false narratives provided by these outlets. In these instances, the mainstream media is painted as a monolith, a singular agency run by corporations and their cronies without countervailing information. The mainstream media is also understood as promoting a leftist agenda. For instance, after Charlottesville, a number of posters on r/the_donald/ were outraged that the media had connected a smaller group of neo-Nazis present at the rally to their board and to the Alt-right more generally. Board members responded by suggesting that artists needed to "meme the truth out."[71] They asked, "Can we get good artists to somehow create a barrage of memes connecting these actual Alt-Right neos to the smaller community they really are, and remove them from the general population of pedes. Shills."[72] To be sure, board members did not want to be connected to these "actual white supremacists" given that they believed "This is information that can actually damage the general public idea on racial issues actually being natural."[73] Nevertheless, users espoused the idea that racial differences were natural and sought to divorce themselves a broader white supremacist messaging and a larger media narrative. Members of r/the_donald/ did not consider themselves *actual* white supremacists, even if they espoused white supremacist arguments. Instead, the mainstream media was to blame for this understanding. Memes were key to shifting this narrative such that the "truth" of the board could be revealed.

Overall, for this far right collective, *détournement* helps theorize the ironic role of memes in revolutionary change. Memes are the perfect tool to twist and turn the imagery of the mainstream and highlight false logics. Users often develop this strategy by explicitly discussing lulz as a framework for their work. Such a nuanced understanding of meme creation generates an ironic investment in memes as rhetorical devices. From this perspective, memes are not simply images that persuade audiences. Instead, memes are ironic images crafted by users to invent new pathways to regressive cultural transformation. Being able to attract users who can grasp the wink of irony, who can understand the strategy of the meme, indicates how the Alt-right can metastasize as a community. That is, users and audiences who grasp the lulz of the meme provide cover for vile messages. Both users and audiences can maintain some level of distance from such memes so long as the lulz framework sustains a belief in an ulterior, ironic motive. Memes are not simply images that propagandize but rather help to normalize extreme claims under the guise of irony.

Translating the Spectacle for Normies

Much as the Situationists did, 4chan and reddit users often deploy ironic memes to interrupt the machinery of the status quo. The goal is not merely to subvert the spectacle for themselves but to strategize on how to do the same for others. Users of 4chan and reddit on /pol/ and r/the_donald/ often posit themselves as renegades who are uniquely able to see the prison of the status quo. Their goal is to craft memes that mark these shackles and indicate the contradictions of public culture. Memes are then dispatched to recruit others to the cause. The juxtaposition apparent within certain memes aims to radicalize the audience—to encourage them to see the spectacle as the Alt-right does.

As with historical uses of *détournement*, memes of the Alt-right regularly employ spectacular modes of address. Indeed, the notion of the spectacular as a key mode of persuasion is a hotly debated topic on the boards. While users generally agree that memes or other modes of spectacle must be used, they nevertheless argue about the most effective modes of deployment. For instance, after the Unite the Right rally in Charlottesville, and the massive media coverage of the Alt-right that followed, board users discussed the best use of this heightened attention. For some users on 4chan, the coverage indicated how inept massive public protest was at portraying the work of the Alt-right and recruiting potential devotees. As one anonymous user posted of the *Vice* coverage, "We missed an opportunity to spread propaganda on one of the biggest millenial [*sic*] channels (Vice) because 2 retards decided they were going to be the face of the rally and starter sperging about Jews in front of Vice cameras. Now instead of whites looking up more Jared/Spencer videos (which would naturally convert them after a few videos), now they think we're the villain because we look like the old white nationalists. They are destroying EVERYTHING we worked for and memed until now."[74] In this description, conversion required a positive media presence and villainous portrayals impeded their ambitions. Moreover, as we learn from this post, memes are central to the project of persuasion insofar as they direct users to other forms of influential media. Other users suggested that the optics of the rally were ideal. As one poster commented, "Our movement is BLOWING UP. Through the fucking roof! WE ARE IN FUCKING ORBIT! We are going to be everywhere, by the millions. Soon you will have no place to hide."[75] In both instances, the spectacle is key to persuasive efforts. The task is to control the narrative spun by those instances of spectacular attention.

Spectacular attention of this sort is a visual tactic that seeks to interrupt the flow of mainstream narratives. For Lasn, memes are both productive of the malaise prompting acceptance of consumer culture and the means through which individuals might resist. For him, the memes of marketing (e.g., "electronic ads, jingles, slogans, images, and sounds") must be interrupted by manipulating those messages with memes "contrary to their original intent."[76] Lasn highlights how visuality enables resistance to the flow of the status quo, in particular the titillation of consumerism. *Détournement* is an effort to arrest the stream of images that entrench a perverse understanding of the world. As Lasn writes, "Each time the flow of images and information is interrupted—by any spontaneous, individual act, or any act of mass media *detournement*," such disruptions add up to an understanding of how life can be different.[77] He continues, "If enough people saw the light and undertook spontaneous acts at once, the Situationists believed, the result would be a kind of mass awakening that would suddenly devalue the currency of the spectacle."[78] The goal then, of memetic imagery that twists and turns the visual logic of the mainstream, is to create a spark—one that can hopefully enable a revolution. For the Alt-right, memes are conceptualized as radical imagery, able to usher in a seismic shift.

In keeping with this theoretical proposition, Alt-right memes often display the subversive mode of engagement central to *détournement*, a strategy that aims to open up the revolutionary potential within viewers. The most rhetorically effective images for the Alt-right attempt to subvert standard assumptions. After the Charlottesville rally, a number of board users were off put by renewed public efforts to remove confederate monuments. Conversations turned to memes as interventionist tools. One meme highlights how this mode of *détournement* operated. The image is a still shot showing a confused black woman. The impact font caption reads, "Black people who were never slaves are fighting white people who were never Nazis over a confederate statue erected by Democrats, because Democrats can't stand their own history anymore and somehow it's Trumps fault?"[79] The caption twists the arguments supporting the removal of confederate monuments. In this caption, modern peoples—black people and white people—are fighting a historical battle of which they are not actually a part. That idea is simultaneously juxtaposed to the notion that the monuments belong to contemporary Democrats and it is the party's history that is being erased. As if those two contortions were not enough, the caption adds in the idea that Trump is not necessarily to blame for these ongoing disputes. The sentence, then, braids those ideas both together and against one another to create an interruptive image. Of course, the meme ignores the historical changes in the Democratic party and a number of other contextual factors. Yet, the meme touches on just enough information to seem historically situated while at the same time eliciting an alternative way of viewing the removal of confederate monuments. In this way, the meme takes on an important function. The meme is designed to stop, howsoever briefly, the flow of ideas and information emerging from the media about this issue by circumventing a more robust investigation of history and context. Simultaneously, the meme supplants historical fact for an Alt-right-associated fiction.

Other images work similarly but are far more simplistic examples of *détournement*. These memes speak to a broader audience and deploy memetic *détournement* for those who are less versed in the affordances of memes. On January 4, 2018, the Twitter feed of r/the_donald/ retweeted a meme from the feed of Fox radio host Mark Simone. The image showed plummeting winter temperatures with the caption, "Trump has been in office 1 year & has already fixed global warming."[80] While the retweet was later deleted, the image attempted to intervene in the scientific narrative on global warming. The image capitalized on popularized rejections of proven climate change. That is, despite the fact that scientists argue that climate change also results in lower winter temperatures, those frigid days and months have often provided ammunition for those seeking to disprove global warming.[81] These memes are rhetorically effective insofar as they shape public discourse about timely public issues. For instance, after backing out of the Paris climate accords, President Trump tweeted about the lowest New Year's temperatures in New York on record, boastfully joking that he saved the nation trillions.[82] Simone's retweeted meme builds on those commonplace, but incorrect, assessments of temperature to assert that belief in climate change is misguided. In this way, the image adopts a *topoi*, or regular topic, that often appears in popular culture.

While the image is not a perfect example of *détournement*, the meme mobilizes one of its cardinal expressions: the posturing of resistance to the mainstream as a key rhetorical intervention. It is this resistant posturing that affords the image rhetorical impact. The image posits resistance itself as valuable. Here, that oppositional stance cross-pollinates with those who view climate science as a myth. Oppositional rhetoric is a mainstay of enclaved sites such as 4chan and reddit. For a broader audience, such as those on Twitter or Facebook, it is this posturing that enables mass appeal and the potential for similar memes to further impact audiences. These individuals may find affinity with messages that suggest they are uniquely able to see through the myth of climate science. The image is all important in these meme endeavors, as it is a spreadable text capable of outstripping these larger (fact-based) discourses.

Overall, the use of spectacular imagery seeks to grab the attention of outsiders. Memes attract focus to certain issues in the hopes that "normies" can grasp the supposed prison of the status quo. What was birthed as a visual tactic aimed against capitalism is now used to battle the presumed scourge of liberalism. Of course, no minoritarian strategy is inherently leftist. Instead rhetorical strategies are protean by nature.[83] These deployments of *détournement* widen the bounds of acceptable conservative discourse. What was once extreme—racism, misogyny, anti-semitism, anti-queer, etc.—becomes emboldened by the power of memes. By deploying memes on both enclaved and mainstream sites, claims of the far right shift to become natural or at least neutral. Phillips writes that "these platforms [4chan and reddit] provide users with more efficient ways of doing the things they were already doing."[84] In this way, memes supply a reliable vehicle to translate the racism and hatred of the boards for outside audiences, to make Alt-right messaging palatable instead of abhorrent. Memes become the key imagery in radicalizing audiences in that 4chan and reddit rhetorically design these images as gateways to a particular politics. Memes are not simply one aspect of the Alt-right rhetorical strategy. They instead shape the broader contours of the movement by being the most accessible image for proselytization. Once founded, these memes may amplify Alt-right discourse. Memes that encapsulate Alt-right logics can attract new devotees and open the gateway to a more profound conversation.

Memes for Radicalization

Some of the memes created within /pol/ and r/the_donald/ ultimately aim to radicalize sympathetic audiences. One 4chan user describes the influence of memes on popular culture in graphic terms: "Memes cause chaos they, [*sic*] interfere with the status quo. This is why the elite can't use them because the elite need to build illusions, not destroy them. It's like asking why are terrorists better at IEDs than the government."[85] Here, the user describes memes in a way that shares remarkable affinity with Lasn's definition of *détournement*. Moreover, this user demonstrates the broader purpose of memetic *détournement*. In particular, the political utility of memes is revealed here. For this user, as for many others, memes generate chaos and break down commonplace systems. The metaphor of the IED (improvised explosive device) is revealing. Like IEDs, this user positions memes as improvised and explosive—a tool for the masses rather than the elites. The destruction of spellbinding illusions is key. Meme creators take on a radical subject position in this comment. The user compares meme makers to terrorists insofar as each seek to tear down prevailing orders. These rebels are willing and able to use memes to subvert the dominant order.

Such rhetoric is emphasized elsewhere on 4chan and reddit Alt-right enclaves. Indeed, conversations in these forums often focus on "red pilling normies," or more recently "following the white rabbit." Each phrase references a moral imperative to convert members of the mainstream public. Alt-right memes become a gateway to a new reality. As one member lamented, "A worthy concern, but look around you. Everything's fucked now. People are screaming nonsense all over. It's now a game of triggered vs triggered. May the best memery win, and may it provide the light to the normies about the red pill."[86] For this commentator, memes are fighting other memes—they are imagined as images attempting to restore or break the present system. 4chan and reddit users position themselves as uniquely able to subvert common logics and convert others through the suasory power of memes. Memes are not simply one part of this strategy. Rather, they are at the forefront of a politics that seeks to galvanize others. The meme war is not a metaphor for these users. It is the place where persuasion is most crucial if the Alt-right is to prevail in this contest. Advocacy and recruitment is key to winning, and memes are the main weapon.

To recruit, some memes entice "normies" by using tools of enemyship.[87] This tactic creates the left as enemy and the Alt-right as heroes. As one anonymous poster articulated on 4chan, "the idea is to use MAINSTREAM conservative/republican issues and try to float the narrative that conservatives are the oppressed/good guys and liberals are the oppressors."[88] Memes created with this mode of *détournement* highlight purported contradictions in liberal logic. One meme shows a confused Mike Pence with the following text: "HETEROSEXUALITY IS A SOCIAL CONSTRUCT BUT GAYS ARE BORN THIS WAY."[89] The meme twists a popularized understanding of sexuality (which could easily be shown as false and problematic) to lure mainstream users. Here, memetic *détournement* is once again made a bit more simplistic for a broader audience. That same outsider positioning—the Alt-right becomes anti-establishment just as those fighting for equal rights become positioned as fascists—similarly attracts audiences who like to imagine that they are anti-establishment. Here, the left is situated as the illogical establishment while the right crusade against such dogma. Altogether, the tactic positions those who enjoy or spread the meme as outsiders engaged in their own resistance.

Often meme images sustain this anti-establishment viewpoint by depicting white nationalists as heroes who are simply misunderstood by the media. In response to the homicide of one protestor in Charlottesville, a number of board users discussed the best way to present their ideas to the public and reclaim an assumed popularity. One 4chan user posted on August 13, 2017, that "We need to create a positive outcome from the Charlottesville rally. Whether it be online or real life, we need stand up and show that the MSM narrative is false. It's the only way of getting normies back onto our side. At this point, the alt right is about to be labelled as a terrorist group. Then there were will be no more rallies, no more movements…I say we have a peaceful rally – something like a park BBQ…Bring families. Show them what a peaceful white ethno state could be like and they'd want to join."[90] Here, images—either digital memes or coverage of live events—are explicit propaganda attempts, an outreach campaign for the Alt-right. The goal is to make a "white ethno state" look appealing, not hateful or potentially deadly. Without any acknowledgement of the idea that "white ethno states" are inherently violent and exclusionary, this poster seems to base the popularity of white nationalist ideas on the public relations instruments used to communicate them. Here, memes and other images control the nature of public understanding and invite potential adherents. In this instance, memetic *détournement* is stitched together with a drive to recruit others. These recruits are then prompted to recognize the artifice of the status quo and the purported desirability of a "white ethno state."

Recruitment often depends on creating memes that spread to large audiences, a possibility that increases in likelihood through the use of *détournement*. Images that can capitalize on the spectacle are potentially more spreadable. Phillips contends some memes are more successful "because [they] harnessed and exploited a particularly sensitive cultural trope, and in the process generated a great deal of lulz."[91] In these contexts, virality is driven by the exploitation of mainstream content and the pursuit of lulz may hold the key to converting outsiders or red pilling normies. Through this process, individual activities (memeing, trolling) are organized according to collective Alt-right principles. As Milner writes, "individual resonance spirals into collective participation. Memetic media are the result of folk and populist—if not always inclusive—practices that give mass perspective priority over individual expression."[92] Taken more generally, the resonance Milner suggests fuels collective participation becomes a potential generator of virality. Using well-known images supplies resonance to both users and outside audiences—popular images are selected because they are recognizable and beloved. That resonance principle—drawing on ideas that are already mimetic—and layering those recognizable images with new ideas fuels the possibility of replication. Such memes move because they are built to do so. By capturing the *zeitgeist* of the public while upturning the logics of the status quo, these memes seek to subvert what creators see as the spectacle of liberal hegemony and open the eyes of more normies.

The radicality of memetic *détournement* is key to grasping the absurdity at stake in the impact of memes on public culture. Goals for meme generation are diffuse and that ambiguity often allows the Alt-right a greater latitude in determining the success of its actions. To be sure, users may unleash memes on an unsuspecting public without regard for how audiences will read those images, given that outsiders are often unable to understand more complex memes and modes of *détournement*. Meme generators, then, are sandwiched between the pursuit of specific political outcomes and the anarchic lulz that often motivates their creations. One user questioned a meme strategy being discussed on the boards, writing "it will radicalize non political normies against us [*sic*] We can take it. Do it for the cause or do it for the lulz. Either way we win."[93] For this user, memes are the gateway to a radical opening up of the status quo. The cause was important but even if meme generators were not behind the cause, they should pursue the Alt-right agenda for the lulz. This is a sophisticated understanding of audience adaptation insofar as the frame for invention is doubled. Meme makers see these images as propaganda *and* as a pleasurable practice of invention. The intention matters little up against an image that can persuade *or* antagonize outsiders. Much as with @JaredTSwift's trolling, if the image is able to antagonize or persuade, meme makers have been successful with memetic *détournement*. Thus, the potentiality of rhetoric is opened up such that a number of outcomes are read as successful.

This expanded potential is evident in the way nihilism, even chaos, become situated as an instrumental good for some users. For instance, in early January 2018, one /pol/ member lamented his vote for Trump and the ensuing maelstrom of the political arena. One user responded with "trump is (and always was) the chaos candidate.../pol/ is an agent of chaos. Oh and you know the thing about chaos? Its [*sic*] bare."[94] For this user, the overall strategy must pursue a radical opening up of the status quo. The memes created for this process can be deployed by those who believe the message or can be used just for the fun of it. It matters not the end goal cannot be predicted. Instead chaos serves as the rejection of current governing systems of predictability. At times, the use of memetic *détournement* can move the Overton Window, or just provoke aggressive responses, or create chaos, or do nothing at all. But when chaos or subversion are the outcomes, the resulting disorder affects outsiders in monumental ways.

For many commenters on the boards, that disorder and chaos may be the most persuasive element of Alt-right memes. As a case in point, a r/the_donald/ post from mid-2017 describes one user's conversion to a Trump supporter as follows:

> Folks, let me be honest with you guys. I am someone who when Trump first announced thought "oh dear God, the egomaniac from The Apprentice is running for president. I wonder if this is a publicity stunt? Frankly I think this is pretty awesome just because politicians have been so corrupt that some crazy Loose Cannon jumping in and screwing everything up might be the only way to get the system fixed. Fine you know what, fuck it. I'm supporting Trump for the lulz. And hopefully whatever clean

> up the person who comes after him does will get this country on the right track." Initially I never took him seriously but put my support behind him simply to see The Establishment wiped.
> And initially I was drawn to his internet troll made real-life demeanor and the way he manhandled verbally all these soft and wimpy politicians.
> And slowly, over time, the man won me over. I started seeing him away from the media coverages. And frankly what was instrumental, was coming here to the_Donald. When I found you crazy fucks here, I said "oh wow, I finally found my people!" Here I was able to get unfiltered news about Trump and see the man for who he really was which was one I was truly one over and has been a supporter of his 100 % ever since. I proudly pushed that button for president Trump, I love all the memes and shit postings, and how we keep each other in the loop.[95]

This user situates lulz as the gateway to radicalization. In this comment, a Trump presidency would facilitate a fundamental shift. This user's support of Trump, then, was predicated on lulz, a haphazard pleasure wrought by that which might uproot the status quo. A love of memes and shitposts is part of this transformation. The commentator came to r/the_donald/ to find a community, "my people," and a new truth that the media ignored. The currency of the board—memes—is essential to that shift. Through the pursuit of lulz and by engaging with memes that countered narratives this user heard elsewhere, the transformation was complete. This user emblematizes the way meme images are conceptualized. Memes are designed to attract audiences by capitalizing on the absurdity of the status quo—a humorous take that opens the door to further oppositional appeals. Memes as tools of persuasion build on the drive toward absurdity and chaos and then move those impulses to constitute new ways of seeing the world.

The notion that memes are crucial to radicalization persists even when users are trying to resist the assumptions of enclaved sites. By January 2018, a number of 4chan users expressed disillusionment with the nature of board discussions. One user described "red pilling" as "bullshit meant to control potential dissidents by distracting them and offering a sense of novelty/reward at being clever enough to comprehend it/be in on the secret—a memetic Skinner box that spreads propaganda and disinformation as a fun bonus."[96] Memes are the operating force of a Skinner box that conditions users to think in particular patterns. But, memes are also capable of undoing rote conditioning. In response to another post asking about how to unswallow the "red pill," a user wrote that the original poster should "Shit post. Shitpost as hard as you can. Shit this board up as much as you can. This place is a hive mind at this point. Its [*sic*] a prison and we can't escape. So smear shit all over the walls. Burn it down."[97] Such shitposts, and the lulz that motivate them, would necessarily rely on memes as their communicative form. Thus, memes are both the mechanism of entrapment and the mechanism of release. In either instance, the power of memes is sustained given that these images are uniquely able to intervene in formulaic thinking and acting.

Ultimately, given the inventional possibilities of memes, users are continually adapting memes to radically changing circumstances. During the last few years, memetic invention has risen to an incredible level of adaptation such that Alt-right memes work with considerable finesse. Notice that memes can be deployed in a number of ways—from simplistic subversion and iconography to shitposting and absurdity. These shifts are not simply changes based on ideological affinity, or the magic culture of the sites where they are created. Instead, memes are rhetorical tools of the avant-garde. We study the memes of the Alt-right because they are the most significant tool to its growth and public presence. As Phillips notes, "mainstream pop culture…is overrun with the brainchildren of subcultural trolls."[98] If we seek to understand the ways the Alt-right has gained a public platform and considerable presence, we cannot treat it as a small group that is only talking to a small number of Americans. Rather, we must understand how Alt-right messages reflect and impact broader patterns of public discourse.

Alt-right memes are central rhetorical artifacts in the battle for social and political change. These images can encapsulate and repeat the patterns of the status quo. These images can also subvert those patterns by twisting and turning their logics. Yet, at root, the persuasive principles of Alt-right memes work by attracting viewers to the possibility of radical change, an undoing of the status quo. 4chan and reddit users describe being red pilled by memes as a specific process. Audiences begin with a sort of humorous or ironic orientation to these images and over time come to learn some "truth" espoused on the boards. Memes, then, are positioned as a way to normalize the radical ideal. What was once humorous or ridiculous can be deemed commonplace. Indeed, users often post queries on these boards and forums asking to be "red pilled," to be shown memes that upturn their assumptions on particular topics. In these instances, memes are pursued as forms of knowledge in and of themselves. They are seen as powerful images, capable of radicalizing those who are smart enough to grasp the truth they portend. The pursuit of lulz, then, supplies the gateway to the radicalization of meme enthusiasts on /pol/ and r/the_donald/. These discursive actions hold severe impacts for external audiences.

Lulz in Public Culture: Ironic Hatred Is Still Hatred

Whether or not the ideological affinity is genuine, the creation of Alt-right memes in /pol/ and r/the_donald/ is often predicated on a drive for lulz. The goal is not focused on direct engagement but rather users often interact with one another obliquely, with trolling or other forms of lulz. Memes developed on /pol/ and r/the_donald/ may enact such lulzy patterns but deploy these images with a particularly insidious force. That is, memes that spread white nationalism, promote the agenda of Donald Trump, or encourage misogyny effectuate a large shift in public culture regardless of their felicitous intent.

Public discourse is first changed via the deployment of and engagement with white nationalist or other extremist memes within these boards. Users create outlandish memes under the guise of lulz. These memes do not necessarily indicate personal beliefs but rather enable users to espouse the idea that they are not "really" white nationalists while nevertheless contributing to the preponderance of messages within a certain board. In these instances, radical memes are instances of memetic *détournement* that supply cover for radical imagery and messages. In effect, the standards of the board uphold white nationalism, misogyny, and the like even if users proclaim they operate differently in their everyday lives. One user on 4chan posted a comment that encapsulates this ironic distance well. This user wrote, "My best post in this place 'what do you pretend to be on /pol/ and what are you in real life?' and the start [*sic*] majority of people said 'I'm pretending to be a national socialist, but really I'm more of a centrist.' We're all pretending here. Don't forget who you are, and the infinite love and compassion you are capable of as a human being."[99] As in this example, users thus differentiate between their "real" selves and the persona they embody on these sites. Their /pol/ persona is a national socialist while their real self is a centrist that can embrace the love and compassion essential to the human experience. This separation of selves can enable /pol/ users, at least, to spread repugnant messages in one location while they hold onto some sacred offline "self" that is not tainted by such hatred. Yet, the distinction—if it actually exists—may be erased as they spend more time on these sites. More importantly, from a rhetorical perspective, that distinction bears little significance if the culture of the board encourages the continuation of vile advocacies and organizes ongoing actions to spread white nationalism.

One cannot forget that /pol/ and r/the_donald/ are sites that organize and propagate messages about white nationalism and other forms of hate. Even if users insist that their actions are for the lulz, these sites are nevertheless used to create better memes for the proliferation of toxicity. Users vociferously debate how to best use memes, how to best present white nationalism to the public, and how to troll the mainstream public into retreat. That such debate may be engaged by users who don't *actually* aim to embolden white nationalism is beside the point. As B.L. Ware and Wil A. Linkugel pointed out, audiences are sometimes unable to distinguish between the persona and the person when the individual so closely embodies the mask they wear.[100] In these sites, it is often the anonymity or pseudonymity of digital users that withers the distinction.[101] Users in online forums as well as outside audiences cannot always grasp the difference between the mask espousing white nationalism and the self-identified centrist posing as such. As marked by the previous post, that difference can erode even for individual users themselves. Moreover, the work of publicly proclaiming white nationalism in both enclaved digital spaces and beyond still creates the conditions through which users devise stronger public relations efforts, on the ground actions, and most commonly, better memes. Thus, memetic *détournement* becomes the rhetorical framework that allows users to proliferate extreme forms of discourse as just for the lulz. Yet, these memes and actions do not spread half-hearted white nationalism or misogyny. Instead, the circulation of such memes becomes a rhetorically functional, and palpable, white nationalism.

The gap between the inventional purpose and the image's circulation widens as memes move across the social. Pointedly, white nationalist and other extremist messages do not so easily travel with ironic playfulness. Instead, these vicious messages and images can never truly be ironic. White nationalist, misogynist, and other hateful memes circulate these ideas and certainly attract an audience who finds affinity with these claims, even in jest. In this way, despite the pretentions of the original user claiming ironic distanciation, that irony is itself a form of racism given that the user seems to presume that they can singularly determine the meaning of memes regardless of context. Yet, as memes spread, contexts shift. Once such memes circulate across other digital outlets, that image nevertheless promotes white nationalism.

The increased visibility and proliferation of these messages on a host of platforms widens the boundaries of acceptability. Users on Facebook, Twitter, and comments sections on mainstream media sites become accustomed to seeing memes of this nature. Memes from /pol/ and r/the_donald/ certainly migrated from these digital enclaves to both Twitter and Facebook. Moreover, dozens of accounts on both of these sites created memes akin to those found on 4chan and reddit. As we detail in the next chapter, these memes were often Russian purchased ads that mirrored political discourse already popular on social media. In this sense, users were quite accustomed to seeing political memes, and more pointedly, were often exposed to more extremist memes that promoted white nationalism, misogynist, and other messages of hate. These kinds of memes become normal to a certain extent and suggest that white nationalism is a common set of claims that social media users experience. While these images may not recruit users in direct ways, they become a way to render banal the violent and dehumanizing messages that ultimately undergird white nationalism proper.

Extreme messages are often normalized through repeated exposure and it is through frequency that outsiders can potentially be radicalized by memes. That is, even though we cannot know how many individuals may have been persuaded or influenced by virtue of memes, we do know that the nature of public discourse was radically changed via the proliferation of Alt-right memes. The nature of public discussion shifted such that white nationalist and similar claims became more common. Indeed, shocking imagery facilitated this change by bolstering journalistic coverage and public attention. The circulation of those messages heightened that impact. Therefore, to grasp how these memes widened the resonance of Alt-right claims, the work of circulation must be explored.

Notes

1. Ashitha Nagesh, "Secret Nazi Code Kept Hidden by 'milk' and 'Vegan Agenda,'" *Metro*, February 21, 2017, http://metro.co.uk/2017/02/21/secret-nazi-code-kept-hidden-by-milk-and-vegan-agenda-6463079/.
2. Nagesh, "Secret Nazi Code Kept Hidden by 'milk' and 'Vegan Agenda.'"
3. Nagesh, "Secret Nazi Code Kept Hidden by 'milk' and 'Vegan Agenda.'"
4. Alex Swerdloff, "Got Milk? Neo-Nazi Trolls Sure as Hell Do," *Munchies*, February 21, 2017, https://munchies.vice.com/en_us/article/kbka39/got-milk-neo-nazi-trolls-sure-as-hell-do.
5. Swerdloff, "Got Milk? Neo-Nazi Trolls Sure as Hell Do."
6. Swerdloff, "Got Milk? Neo-Nazi Trolls Sure as Hell Do."
7. Wyatt Pahr, *He Will Not Divide Us ("Nazi" Party FRIDAY NIGHT) Hwndu Hewillnotdivideus Racist Milk*, *YouTube*, February 5, 2017, https://www.youtube.com/watch?v=dTy6f_HyuQU.
8. Jack Smith IV, "Milk Is the New, Creamy Symbol of White Racial Purity in Donald Trump's America," *Mic*, February 10, 2017, https://mic.com/articles/168188/milk-nazis-white-supremacists-creamy-pseudo-science-trump-shia-labeouf; Swerdloff, "Got Milk? Neo-Nazi Trolls Sure as Hell Do"; Kelly Riddell, "Milk: The New Symbol of Racism in Donald Trump's America," *Washington Times*, March 17, 2017, https://www.washingtontimes.

com/news/2017/mar/17/milk-new-symbol-racism-donald-trumps-america/; Nagesh, "Secret Nazi Code Kept Hidden by 'milk' and 'Vegan Agenda.'"

9. Sam Kestenbaum, "Got Nazis? Milk Is New Symbol of Racial Purity for White Nationalist," *Forward*, February 13, 2017, https://forward.com/fast-forward/362986/got-nazis-milk-is-new-symbol-of-racial-purity-for-white-nationalists/.
10. Ryan M. Milner, "FCJ-156 Hacking the Social: Internet Memes, Identity Antagonism, and the Logic of Lulz," *The Fibreculture Journal* 22 (2013).
11. Milner, "FCJ-156 Hacking the Social."
12. Whitney Phillips, *This Is Why We Can't Have Nice Things: Mapping the Relationship Between Online Trolling and Mainstream Culture* (Cambridge, MA: MIT Press, 2015), 27–28.
13. Gabriella Coleman, *Hacker, Hoaxer, Whistleblower, Spy: The Many Faces of Anonymous* (Brooklyn, NY: Verso Books, 2014), 31.
14. Coleman, *Hacker, Hoaxer, Whistleblower, Spy*, 33.
15. "Shitposting," *Know Your Meme*, n.d., accessed April 9, 2018, http://knowyourmeme.com/memes/shitposting; Andrew Griffin, "Shitposting: What is the Bizarre Online Behaviour That Could Win Donald Trump the Election," *Independent*, September 23, 2016, http://www.independent.co.uk/life-style/gadgets-and-tech/news/what-is-shitposting-donald-trump-us-election-2016-palmer-luckey-a7326111.html.
16. Wayne C. Booth, *A Rhetoric of Irony* (Chicago, IL: University of Chicago Press, 1974), ix.
17. Kenneth Burke, *A Grammar of Motives* (Berkeley: University of California Press, 1969), 503.
18. Certainly, disavowal is a term of art for psychoanalytic scholars. Our use of disavowal here most closely aligns with Freud who defined the term as "the attitude which fitted in with the wish and the attitude that fitted in with reality exist side by side." On our view disavowal is to recognize and then look away—wherein the wish to be seen as not racist nevertheless feeds the wish to participate in racist discourse without consequence. Given the numerous theoretical angles needed to analyze the work of lulz, we are simplifying our discussion of disavowal to this footnote so as to not unduly burden the prose with the addition of Freud. See Sigmund Freud, "Fetishism," in *Contemporary Film Theory*, ed. Antony Easthope (New York: Routledge, 2013), 27.
19. Phillips, *This Is Why We Can't Have Nice Things*, 97.
20. George Lipsitz, *Possessive Investment in Whiteness* (Philadelphia, PA: Temple University Press, 1998).
21. On ironic racism, see Dustin Bradley Goltz, *Comic Performativities: Identity, Internet Outrage, and the Aesthetics of Communication* (New York: Routledge, 2017); Hélène Frohard-Dourlent, "Someone's Asian in *Dr. Horrible*: Humor, Reflexivity, and the Absolution of Whiteness," in *Joss Whedon and Race: Critical Essays*, ed. Mary Ellen Iatropoulos and Lowery Woodall III (Jefferson, NC: McFarland & Company, 2017), 283–297; Leslie A. Hahner and Scott J. Varda, "Yarn Bombing and the Aesthetics of Exceptionalism," *Communication and Critical/Cultural Studies* 11, no. 4 (2014): 301–321.
22. Guy Debord, *Society of the Spectacle* (Detroit, MI: Black & Red, 1967).
23. Phillips, *This Is Why We Can't Have Nice Things*, 68.
24. "Meme Magic," *Know Your Meme*, n.d., accessed August 29, 2017, http://knowyourmeme.com/memes/meme-magic.

25. Abby Ohlheiser, "'We Actually Elected a Meme as President': How 4chan Celebrated Trump's Victory," *Washington Post*, November 9, 2016, https://www.washingtonpost.com/news/the-intersect/wp/2016/11/09/we-actually-elected-a-meme-as-president-how-4chan-celebrated-trumps-victory/.
26. Paul Spencer, "Trump's Occult Online Supporters Believe 'Meme Magic' Got Him Elected," *Motherboard*, November 18, 2016, https://motherboard.vice.com/en_us/article/pgkx7g/trumps-occult-online-supporters-believe-pepe-meme-magic-got-him-elected.
27. Spencer, "Trump's Occult Online Supporters Believe 'Meme Magic' Got Him Elected."
28. Morgan Quaintance, "Cultic Cultures," *Art Monthly*, March 7, 2017.
29. Quaintance, "Cultic Cultures," 7.
30. Ryan M. Milner and Whitney Phillips, "Dark Magic: The Memes That Made Donald Trump's Victory," *US Election Analysis 2016*, http://www.electionanalysis2016.us/us-election-analysis-2016/section-6-internet/dark-magic-the-memes-that-made-donald-trumps-victory/.
31. Andrew Marantz, "Trolls for Trump," *New Yorker*, October 31, 2016, http://www.newyorker.com/magazine/2016/10/31/trolls-for-trump; Cooper Fleishman, "Inside the White Supremacist Alt-Right's Terrifying Election Celebration," *Mic*, November 9, 2016, https://mic.com/articles/159070/alt-right-donald-trump-victory-celebration-racist-pepe-memes-anti-semitism-white-surpremacy-4chan-8chan-reddit.
32. Phillips, *This Is Why We Can't Have Nice Things*, 10.
33. Olivia Nuzzi, "How Pepe the Frog Became a Nazi Trump Supporter and Alt-Right Symbol," *The Daily Beast*, May 26, 2016, http://www.thedailybeast.com/articles/2016/05/26/how-pepe-the-frog-became-a-nazi-trump-supporter-and-alt-right-symbol; "Here's How Two Twitter Pranksters Convinced the World That Pepe the Frog Meme Is Just a Front for White Nationalism," *Daily Caller*, September 14, 2016, http://dailycaller.com/2016/09/14/heres-how-two-twitter-pranksters-convinced-the-world-that-pepe-the-frog-meme-is-just-a-front-for-white-nationalism/.
34. Nuzzi, "How Pepe the Frog Became a Nazi Trump Supporter and Alt-Right Symbol."
35. Nicole Hemmer, "Tweedy Racists and 'Ironic' Anti-Semites: The Alt-Right Fits a Historical Pattern," *Vox*, December 2, 2016, https://www.vox.com/the-big-idea/2016/12/2/13814728/alt-right-spencer-irony-racism-punks-skinheads.
36. John Lechte, "Julia Kristeva and the Trajectory of the Image," in *Psychoanalysis, Aesthetics, and Politics in the Work of Julia Kristeva*, ed. Kelly Oliver and S.K. Keltner (Albany: SUNY Press, 2009), 84. Contemporary uses of this tactic include culture jamming—the events and images of ad busters, ®™ark, and more.
37. Simon Sadler, *The Situationist City* (Cambridge, MA: MIT Press, 1999).
38. Cole Stryker, *Epic Win for Anonymous: How 4chan's Army Conquered the Web* (New York: The Overlook Press, 2011); Heather Suzanne Woods, "The Rhetorical Construction of Hacktivism: Analyzing the Anonymous Care Package" (master's thesis, Baylor University, 2013).
39. Aja Romano, "How the Alt-Right Uses Internet Trolling to Confuse You into Dismissing Its Ideology," *Vox*, November 23, 2016, https://www.vox.com/2016/11/23/13659634/alt-right-trolling.
40. Vincent Kaufmann, "Angels of Purity," in *Guy Debord and the Situationist International: Texts and Documents*, ed. Tom McDonough (Cambridge, MA: MIT Press, 2004), 292.

41. Kauffman, "Angels of Purity," 292.
42. Kauffman, "Angels of Purity," 292.
43. Jack Bratich, "Memes, Movements, and Meteorology: Occupy Wall Street and New Mutations in Culture Jamming," in *Culture Jamming: Activism and the Art of Cultural Resistance*, ed. Marilyn DeLaure and Moritz Fink (New York: NYU Press, 2017), 322–47; Toby Heys and Andrew Hennlich, "The Art of Conservative *Détournement*," *Érudit*, no. 88 (2009/2010): 61–64.
44. George Michael, "The Rise of the Alt-Right and the Politics of Polarization in America," *Skeptic* 22, no. 2 (2017): 9–18.
45. Tom McDonough, "Introduction: Ideology and the Situationist Utopia," in *Guy Debord and the Situationist International: Texts and Documents*, ed. Tom McDonough (Cambridge, MA: MIT Press, 2004), ix.
46. Heys and Hennlich, "The Art of Conservative *Détournement*," 61.
47. Douglas Haddow, "Meme Warfare: How the Power of Mass Replication Has Poisoned the US Election," *The Guardian*, November 4, 2016, https://www.theguardian.com/us-news/2016/nov/04/political-memes-2016-election-hillary-clinton-donald-trump.
48. Heys and Hennlich, "The Art of Conservative *Détournement*," 61.
49. Romano, "How the Alt-Right Uses Internet Trolling."
50. Romano, "How the Alt-Right Uses Internet Trolling."
51. Milner, "FCJ-156 Hacking the Social."
52. Ryan M. Milner, *The World Made Meme: Public Conversations and Participatory Media* (Cambridge, MA: MIT Press, 2016), 218.
53. Milner, *World Made Meme*, 219.
54. Milner, *World Made Meme*, 219.
55. Anonymous, "Get Your Shit Together," Comment, *Politically Incorrect*, February 2, 2017, 4chan.org/pol/.
56. Phillips, *This Is Why We Can't Have Nice Things*, 31.
57. Leslie A. Hahner, "The Riot Kiss: Framing Memes as Visual Argument," *Argumentation and Advocacy* 49, no. 3 (2013): 151–66.
58. Anonymous, "Alt-Right General," Comment, *Politically Incorrect*, August 15, 2017, 4chan.org/pol/.
59. "Richard Bertrand Spencer," *Southern Poverty Law Center*, n.d., https://www.splcenter.org/fighting-hate/extremist-files/individual/richard-bertrand-spencer-0.
60. Anonymous, "Get Your Shit Together."
61. Anonymous, "Get Your Shit Together."
62. Conslurvative, "I Just Want to Point out How Impressive This Sub Is," Comment, *The Donald*, October 2017, reddit.com/r/The_Donald/comments/72ouvb/i_just_want_to_point_out_how_impressive_this_sub/.
63. Phillips, *This Is Why We Can't Have Nice Things*, 146.
64. Adrienne Massanari, "#Gamergate and The Fappening: How Reddit's Algorithm, Governance, and Culture Support Toxic Technocultures," *New Media & Society* 19, no. 3 (2017): 333.
65. Massanari, "#Gamergate and The Fappening," 333.

66. Justa_buncha_letters, "The Great Meme War, 2017," Comment, *The Donald*, August 15, 2017, reddit.com/r/the_donald.
67. Kalle Lasn, *Culture Jam: The Uncooling of America* (New York: William Morrow & Company, 1999), 123.
68. Whitney Phillips, Jessica Beyer, and Gabriella Coleman, "Trolling Scholars Debunk the Idea That the Alt-Right's Shitposters Have Magic Powers," *Motherboard*, March 22, 2017, https://motherboard.vice.com/en_us/article/z4k549/trolling-scholars-debunk-the-idea-that-the-alt-rights-trolls-have-magic-powers.
69. Phillips, Beyer, and Coleman, "Trolling Scholars Debunk."
70. Phillips, Beyer, and Coleman, "Trolling Scholars Debunk."
71. SPOAD, "This Is Not Right. Meme the Truth Out," Comment, *The Donald*, August 13, 2017, reddit.com/r/the_donald.
72. SPOAD, "This Is Not Right." This moment also speaks to how earlier instances of *détournement* unfolded given that artists and their novel viewpoints were integral to creating imagery that might interrupt the spectacle.
73. SPOAD, "This Is Not Right."
74. Anonymous, "Alt-Right General."
75. Anonymous, "Alt-Right General."
76. Kerry Walters and Robin Jarrell, *Blessed Peacemakers* (Eugene, OR: Cascade Books, 2013), 83.
77. Kalle Lasn, "Culture Jamming," in *The Consumer Society Reader*, ed. Juliet Schor and Douglas Holt (New York: New Press, 2011), 421.
78. Lasn, "Culture Jamming," 421.
79. Anonymous, "MEME WAR – Operation Pearl Harbor," Comment, *Politically Incorrect*, August 15, 2017, 4chan.org/pol/.
80. Mark Simone, Twitter Post, January 4, 2018, 8:06 AM. https://twitter.com/MarkSimoneNY/status/948948730362941440.
81. Avery Thompson, "Why the Eastern U.S. Is So Cold Right Now," *Popular Mechanics*, December 29, 2017, https://www.popularmechanics.com/science/environment/a14517105/why-the-eastern-us-is-so-cold-right-now/.
82. Scott Martelle, "It's Winter. It's Cold. For Trump, That's Evidence Against Global Warming," *Los Angeles Times*, December 29, 2017, http://www.latimes.com/opinion/opinion-la/la-ol-trump-twitter-global-warming-20171229-story.html.
83. Scott J. Varda, "Drew Ali and the Moorish Science Temple of America: A Minor Rhetoric of Black Nationalism," *Rhetoric & Public Affairs* 16, no. 4 (2013): 685–717.
84. Phillips, *This Is Why We Can't Have Nice Things*, 121–22.
85. Anonymous, "How Come Right Wingers Are so Good at Memeing?," Comment, *Politically Incorrect*, February 2, 2017, 4chan.org/pol/.
86. Anonymous, "Memetic Missiles General—Katniss Edition /MMG/," Comment, *Politically Incorrect*, February 1, 2017, 4chan.org/pol/.
87. Jeremy Engels, *Enemyship* (East Lansing: Michigan State University Press, 2010), 5.
88. Anonymous, "MEMETIC MISSILES GENERAL: Pt 23 //MMG Temp OP," Comment, *Politically Incorrect*, February 2, 2017, 4chan.org/pol/.
89. Anonymous, "MEMETIC MISSILES GENERAL: Pt 23 //MMG Temp OP."

90. Anonymous, "DMG CONTROL Alt Right," Comment, *Politically Incorrect*, August 13, 2017, 4chan.org/pol/.
91. Phillips, *This Is Why We Can't Have Nice Things*, 68.
92. Milner, *The World Made Meme*, 219.
93. Anonymous, "Memetic Missiles General," Comment, *Politically Incorrect*, November 12, 2017, 4chan.org/pol/.
94. Anonymous, "Its All Fun and Memes until You Tweet This," Comment, *Politically Incorrect*, January 5, 2018, 4chan.org/pol/.
95. ZionHalcyon, "It Is Time for a MAGAEVOLUTION!," Comment, *The Donald*, September 14, 2017, reddit.com/r/the_donald.
96. Anonymous, "ALRIGHT BRO RED PILL THE FUCK OUT OF ME. I'M READY," Comment, *Politically Incorrect*, January 5, 2018, 4chan.org/pol/.
97. Anonymous, "How Do I Unswallow the Red Pill," Comment, *Politically Incorrect*, January 5, 2018, 4chan.org/pol/.
98. Phillips, *This Is Why We Can't Have Nice Things*, 22.
99. Anonymous, "How Do I Unswallow."
100. B. L. Ware and Will A. Linkugel, "The Rhetorical Persona: Marcus Garvey as Black Moses," *Communication Monographs* 49, no. 1 (1982): 50–62.
101. Emily van der Nagel and Jordan Frith, "Anonymity, Pseudonymity, and the Agency of Online Identity: Examining the Social Practices of r/Gonewild," *First Monday* 20, no. 3 (2015).

· 4 ·

HOW THE ALT-RIGHT MOVES

Memes as Tactical Circulation

Memes are potent persuasive mechanisms for users on 4chan and reddit, who deploy these images as forms of tactical engagement. Yet, memes gain additional rhetorical traction as they move to sites outside their typical birthplaces. Indeed, memes are powerful persuasive mechanisms predominantly because of their circulation. Memes are designed to move and attract greater audiences. Some memes are more effective than others in this regard. Leading into the 2016 election and continuing into the present day, meme enthusiasts on 4chan and reddit have capitalized on the network culture that helps memes find—and create—new audiences. The networked nature of media platforms fashioned an ideal rhetorical situation for Trump to compose rhetorical messages that could gain traction with the nationalistic, nihilistic, and often xenophobic moods of supporters. Memes helped disseminate, distribute, and amplify these dispatches to ever widening publics. In this way, Alt-right memes impacted both the content and norms of public discourse by acting as key media nodal points in the Alt-right ecosystem. Most importantly, memes carried Alt-right messages—or else disrupted alternate, competing discourses—to diffuse audiences and conjoined those peoples who would otherwise remain unaffected.

This chapter explores how some memes circulated with diverse audiences and marshaled those addressed by such images into sympathetic relation with the Alt-right. We elucidate how Alt-right memes moved across traditional media; enclaved and social media such as 4chan, reddit, and Facebook; and a newly developed media infrastructure tailor-made for disseminating the messages of the Alt-right—which we call the Alt-right ecosystem. Although seemingly innocuous or mundane, memes were often the connective tissue between all three of these media channels. Moving expeditiously between each arena, memes facilitated the broader travels of Alt-right content. Memes translated covert political expressions to the mainstream and then back again. There were several important effects of this memetic circulation. Perhaps most obviously, memes became a central communicative component of the 2016 election of Donald J. Trump. Trump—who favored Twitter and other direct modes of communication during his candidacy—used Alt-right memes to address would-be voters and to turn meme lovers into political agents in the digital sphere and elsewhere. Moreover, the weaponization of memes in the present tense has pernicious impacts that will influence democratic politics for years to come. To wit, we argue that the popularization of Alt-right memes created the conditions of possibility for Russian interference in the 2016 US presidential election. Circulated through Alt-right ecosystems, memes became the medium through which disinformation campaigns thrived and discursive chaos reigned. The Internet Research Agency took up that model of political action as a template, manufacturing related memes that may have significantly influenced not only the US election, but other events, including Brexit.

To engage this argument, we first detail theories that reconcile traditional models of content dissemination with the affordances of new media, drawing especially on the insights of Tiziana Terranova on network culture.[1] Second, we describe the impact of networked processes on the circulation of Alt-right memes, focusing on algorithms as rhetorical agents of influence. In the case of the 2016 election, algorithmic logics not only facilitated the travels of messages and memes across media channels, but served an epistemological and persuasive function. Third, we analyze the networked media ecosystems exploited by the Alt-right in the 2016 campaign, at the moment of Trump's victory, and thereafter. Finally, we illustrate how the weaponization of memes by the Alt-right cleared a pathway for the Russia-linked Internet Research Agency to spread discord through memes.

Circulation in Network Culture

Like other memes, Alt-right memes rely on circulation to reach and engage their audiences. Circulation, as a concept and as a modality for disseminating content, has become increasingly important for communication and media theorists to interrogate, given the rise of networked technologies that challenge traditional models of content distribution predicated on hierarchy or resource density. Circulation describes how information flows in the present moment. Rather than moving from a singular, concentrated point to another, content moves in a non-linear fashion across and sometimes against apparent distributive schemas. In so doing, circulation names how the connected components of a network move content forward and back across nodes of connectivity expeditiously and with seemingly little physical infrastructure or resources required.

Scholars of media and communication have documented a transformation in the way content is distributed. New media technologies, global expansion, and the apparent rapidity of present-day symbolic exchange contributes to this shift. One significant characteristic of this change is a wider net of content creation and dissemination. For some, network connectivity has enabled egalitarian modes of technical infrastructure, benefitting those without previous access to traditional media processes and infrastructures.[2] For instance, in their 2005 analysis of Occupy Wall Street, Joel Penney and Caroline Dadas note that networked technologies allow activists to create "a geographically dispersed, networked counter public that can articulate a critique of power outside of the parameters of mainstream media," partially as the result of the "digital circulation of texts," broadly conceived.[3] Now, those with access to basic tools and an internet connection can become agents of media production and circulation. And although networked technology's influence on access to media creation and dissemination is often overstated (as in the riot of essays and thinkpieces that indicate that the internet or social media "caused" the uprisings of the Arab Spring), it is hard to deny that influence outright.

Given network culture, the key watchword for media and communication theorists may no longer simply be dissemination or distribution, but rather circulation. For rhetorical scholars, circulation of content challenges several foundational components of the rhetorical situation and posits new questions for rhetorical criticism itself. Eric S. Jenkins argues that communication scholars ought to prioritize "modes" as "manners of engagement or interfacing that structure the specific actualizations" of "particular texts in specific contexts."[4]

Rather than focusing on the dualism of either text or an audience prepared to receive it, Jenkins' model foregrounds "the interfacing between text and audiences."[5] Modes are theoretically akin to affect, which suggests that they are "pre-subjective and pre-objective" in that they "express the circulating energies of contemporary existence rather than re-presenting the interests of particular rhetors."[6] Jenkins' model shares some affinity with the "rhetorical circulation" model proposed by Catherine Chaput. "Understand[ing] rhetoric as circulating rather than situated," Chaput maintains, means shifting critical perceptions to the dynamic, constant exchange of rhetoric through "an evolving ecological space of signifying and becoming."[7] Chaput contends that,

> This ontological shift takes us from the rhetorical situation as a temporarily and spatially fixed site of exigency, constraints, and discourse to rhetorical circulation as a fluidity of everyday practices, affects, and uncertainties. Unhinged from its role in negotiating political agency, rhetoric bursts through its site-specific bounds, circulates, and gives value to everyday practices, just as the constant circulation of production and consumption generates political economic values.[8]

From this perspective, the rhetorical situation foregrounds the way networked processes alter the dynamics of communication.

Network culture upsets scholarly traditions regarding the fixity of both transmission and meaning. For Terranova, "network culture" is a way to describe the shiftiness, liminality, and inherent contradictions characteristic to a period of "information overload."[9] For our purposes, these features outline a new terrain for collective action unbound by traditional components of persuasion or communication. Those wishing to foment collective action in network culture must take into account what Terranova calls the "centripetal" and "centrifugal" forces endemic to the network.[10] These bi-valent forces operate simultaneously, creating a discursive and material "topology" that at once coheres and dissolves.[11] Such processes approximate the movement of memetic content as produced, disseminated, and (re)produced by leaning into chaos as a mode of rhetorical invention and distribution. As a heuristic, network culture names how human and nonhuman agents generate memetic content. This theoretical framework assumes in advance the polysemy and antagonism of memetic content as productive of cultural change.[12] In network culture, modes of rhetoric are unfixed, constantly negotiated, and fluid. In particular, memes are articulated through dynamic information flows that disrupt traditional communication models. As Terranova maintains, in contemporary network culture, "[w]e are no longer mostly dealing with information that is transmitted from a source to a receiver, but also increasingly with informational dynamics—that is, with the relation between noise and signal, including microvariations, entropic emergencies and negentropic emergencies, positive feedback and chaotic processes."[13] As such, analysis of memetic content must be attentive to the dynamism of informational flows.[14] In this chapter, we analyze informational processes that produce the conditions of possibility for that change, pointing out where these processes facilitate the actions of the Alt-right.

Studying memes as mobile modes of address troubles the idea that rhetoric operates in a structurally predetermined way, in a specific place, with an intended audience determined in advance. Memes are rhetorically powerful via affective flows and circuitous movement, with audiences that only ever briefly exist in their own right before dissolving back into a larger collectivity. As Jenkins puts it: "[c]irculation continually alters situations and contexts by varying the rhetors, audiences, exigencies, and constraints."[15] Understanding symbolic exchange as autopoetic demonstrates the generative components of circulation. Namely, circulation invites the articulation of new avenues of persuasion and meaning-making. The continual movement of the rhetorical situation gives life to memes as a modality of rhetoric. That is, although circulation of a text may introduce uncertainty, memes may leverage "the uncertainty generated by the circulation and intermingling of frameworks for inventional purposes."[16] Because the task of the critic is to trace how "circulation can serve as an organizing principle for rhetorical theory and criticism,"[17] following the travels of memes is key to analyzing how memes rhetorically address audiences, often as sites of continual and rapid invention. Our perspective on memes suggests that memetic content is not bound by a particular fixed meaning determined in advance or accurately decoded by all receivers. Rather, we see memes as a mode of address that "supports and encloses the production of meaning."[18] Memes become an important mechanism for human and nonhuman agents to negotiate meaning through networked relationality.

Centralizing the network in the study of memes suggests that the form and function of the rhetorical audience shifts. Whereas past audiences might be constituted (or otherwise conjured) through a locality relative to a rhetor and/or a rhetorical act, network culture commonly engenders a dislocation between rhetor, rhetoric, and audience wherein these roles continually shift. James Alexander McVey and Heather Suzanne Woods argue that the "organized yet open-ended circulation of texts" produces a "consortium of individuals, each of whom is hailed and brought into a collectivity as a possible public....Because of a public's contingent and timely nature, the hailing of strangers and their constitution into a public is liminal, transitional, and transformational."[19] These publics and counterpublics need not be organized in relation to a shared ideology. Rather, network culture prompts the development of diffuse publics according to shared interest or affinity across discursive milieus. As a rhetorical text, memes may provide an audience momentary coherence despite diffusion and dislocation. The travels of memes demonstrate that networked audiences are transformational exactly because they are liminal, or, perhaps because their configuration is always becoming and partial. This rearticulation of the audience is an inherently rhetorical issue, as memes speak along and across multiple discursive fields: to those who witness or watch, to those who create anonymously and share, and to those who retweet or repost. The multiplication of rhetors, the interactivity thereof, and the blurring of rhetorical intention adequately depicts the modality of memes as circulated, which almost always requires audience uptake and recreation.

Memes also challenge how scholars imagine context and temporality. In circulation, memes seem to slip from one situation to the next, dragging both content and context along with them. Memes also defy the supposed temporal configuration of a rhetorical situation; the demand for a rhetorical response moves as do the constraints given memetic flow. In network culture, fixity is both fleeting and ultimately impossible. Information flows endemic to the network encourage the diffusion of a text. As Terranova indicates, "one of the major points of departure that distinguishes the Internet from other modern decentralized media...is that messages are not beamed or transmitted through a channel, but broken down and let loose in the network to find their destination."[20] Network culture's communicative flow is "diffuse and chaotic" and characterized by "gradients of openness and closure." A such, the temporal configurations of memetic flow are altered by the structures of the network.[21] Memes oscillate velocities up and down; they disseminate rapidly at some points in some contexts, and they die away in others. Memes, then, travel through the rhythms of sharing, the movement between and amongst nodal points, the shared relationally amongst friends and strangers who become co-conspirators in the creation of memetic content that flows beyond any one persons' fingertips or line of sight. Memes have a tempo that is rhythmic, intoxicating, overdetermined, yet agential. They invite the masses to dance or—more precisely—to orchestrate the melody.

The Hybrid Circulation of Alt-right Memes in Network Culture

Models of circulation are shaped by a new era characterized by increased participation, rapidity, and algorithmic amplification. Older models of distribution have not disappeared. Rather, they have been augmented by distributed media. As Henry Jenkins, Sam Ford, and Joshua Green suggest, the present moment involves "an emerging hybrid model of circulation, where a mix of top-down and bottom-up forces determine how material is shared across and among cultures in far more participatory (and messier) ways."[22] There is a complex relationship between traditional media producers and those who take up that content, not only by sharing it, but by "remixing" or "recreating" it. What's new, according to this updated model, is the ability for increased user engagement with a text.

Alt-right memes are an exemplar of this updated, hybrid model. As new and traditional modes of media production and circulation cohere, those who make, share, or view memes may rearticulate their relationship to the text, moving from consumer of information to a more participatory role. Insofar as memes invite engagement, memes ask users to become producers or at least re-creators of content. Alt-right memes are built from this participatory model. They are fashioned in digital communities but also invite others to use the inventional possibilities of these memes—either through the easy reworking of the digital macro (through a number of meme-making sites) or by sharing these memes on social media sites. Alt-right memetic texts, then, become less fixed and more fluid, more memetic in modality if not in content proper. Participatory cultures are key to this change in media flow. Members of the public are not simply "consumers," Jenkins et. al. write, but "people who are shaping, sharing, reframing, and remixing media content in ways which might not have been previously imagined. And they are doing so not as isolated individuals but within larger communities and networks, which allow them to spread content well beyond their immediate geographic proximity."[23] The shift from distribution to circulation leverages the affordances of the community over the individual; the shifting network over a pointed geographic crystallization; and engagement and creation over passive reception.

Another important aspect of internet culture is the ability for people to reach likeminded individuals unbeknownst to them, hybridizing the local and global through circulation. As Terranova argues, the "particularly dynamic" nature of the internet sets it apart from other network models. Because it is a "form linking the bounded with the unbounded, the local with the global," the internet reworks conceptions of spatiality but also of social and political relation.[24] Social media is one milieu in which this plasticity between local and global is revealed. While social media is oftentimes used to connect with friends, another important use is to communicate with strangers.[25] Memes, which can be personal enough to travel locally among friends but general enough to attract the shared interest of global strangers, may form a public among known and unknown parties that increases the probability of sharing. For the Alt-right, this stranger relationality offers possibilities for attention as well as recruitment and activation. Moreover, Alt-right memes close the gap between enclave and public, by stitching the two together through shared attention to memetic texts.

Alt-right collectivities rely on networked platforms where content is produced and then amplified outward. That some texts—including memes—circulate more easily or widely than others is supported by media theories about networked connectivity. Forums such as reddit and 4chan encourage the rapid creation of new content (sometimes known as OC), which may then be shared, taken up, or remixed. Rhetors on these platforms often reflexively shape messages according to the structure in which they hope messages will disseminate.[26] For example, different social media privilege selected modalities of communication and suggest various forms of addressivity. Twitter, with its character limit, lack of edit function, and rapid "in real time" updates, serves texts that are brief, impactful, and searchable.[27] Moreover, Twitter's sorting processes deliver amplified communicative media to selected subjects. The intent of these algorithmic logics is to curate *relevance* for users, sorting what—and who—is valuable.

In effect, Alt-right rhetors assess networked infrastructures and processes before designing moments of address. By virtue of their addressivity and flexibility, memes are a useful discursive tool for circulating content in networked publics. Alt-right memes evoke both the global and the local, leaning on the affordances of nodal points in the network to produce rhetorical effects in sections of the network. For instance, crafting memes in friendly digital sites can then support memetic transfer in places where distribution is organized through relevance algorithms. Forms of address differ in these spaces, but memes can morph and flex to meet the needs of different platforms. In this way, the creation and movement of memes affirms Robert Hariman and John Louis Lucaites' argument that "media and messages of the public sphere cohere not by virtue of their content alone, which is always shifting, but because of shared properties of design, addressivity, and circulation."[28] Memes' varying influence and uptake are impacted by their circulation in some sites over others. Because the infrastructure of a platform or mediated sphere influences both addressivity and how texts circulate, it is worthwhile to attend to the rhetoricity of non-human agents and logics that contribute to the circulation and uptake of some memes over others.

Platforms and Algorithms: Knowing What to Know

Like most digital messaging on platforms, Alt-right memes circulate in part due to algorithmic logics that amplify some content over others. Although they may appear neutral or without intent, algorithms are profoundly political agents because they sort and select amongst a variety of data in a way that is necessarily partial and partisan. Investigating the technical elements of some platforms (including the algorithms that make them function, the design protocols that shape user interaction, and so on) from a critical communication perspective reveals the traces of agents who designed and coded them. As such, a rhetorical analysis of platforms renders apparent the human processes of technological abstraction that might otherwise seem banal or even objective. Ken Hillis, Kylie Petit, and Michael Jarrett contend that "[t]echnologies are ideas in built form and they contain within them the archeology of their history, including not only traces of their utilitarian purposes, but also of the philosophical ideas and cultural desires that propel their invention, manufacture, and social and geographic diffusion."[29] Importantly, algorithmic logics are often black-boxed, that is, obfuscated or made less visible to the outside. As Fenwick McKelvey notes, "[a]s it stands now, algorithms leave little room for debate about the forms of cultural, economic, and social control they exert."[30] This black-boxing, too, prevents people from recognizing the human elements embedded and encoded into technology because the features of technologies are made to seem innate, objective, and neutral in their capacities. Algorithmic logics are not only instrumental, but curate the circulation of digital messages, including memes.[31]

Algorithms enable the amplification of memes and indicate the political stakes involved in managing flows of information. Hillis, Petit, and Jarrett argue that Google has become "consecrated" as an epistemological agent—one that has shaped the nature of both knowing and finding. The authors trace the ways "Google has become so naturalized it no longer seems to have an origin."[32] Google functions as an agential actor, one that cannot be seen as neutral. Google rhetorically acts through an assemblage of modes, including programmers, mathematicians, everyday searchers, corporate elements, branding agents, and so on. Algorithms are, in part, rhetorical by selecting and privileging some content over others. As these authors argue, Google's PageRank function promotes itself as objective ("you can't buy our rankings") and virtuous ("do no evil" as company policy), yet PageRank and Google have shaped digital actors' ways of knowing and seeing in profound ways. Google is a political agent in part because it helps us determine what is worth knowing. In relationship to search queries, Paul Baker and Amanda Potts maintain that algorithms may "inadvertently reproduc[e] stereotypes" by creating a feedback loop between what others have searched and what users find when they use Google's auto-completion software.[33] In other words, algorithms both amplify and tacitly endorse privileged patterns as they aid and abet message circulation.

As rhetorical processes central to network culture, algorithmic choice and circulation directly impacts the constitutive nature of Alt-right memes. Because "data is persistently messy,"[34] it must be encoded into a language that is receivable by the machine that processes it. Algorithms are productive because they help users decide what is most relevant when presented with infoglut. Tarleton Gillespie argues that "we need not resort to such muscular theories of ideological domination to suggest that algorithms designed to offer relevant knowledge also offer ways of knowing—and that as they become more pervasive and trusted, their logics are self-affirming."[35] As Gillespie suggests, rather than focusing on discovering algorithms' "'effect' on people," scholars ought to instead investigate the "multidimensional 'entanglement' between algorithms put into practice and the social tactics of users who take them up."[36]

The Alt-right—comprised of, at the very least, a few savvy and well connected users—appears particularly aware of the power of algorithmic amplification for expanding audience reach. In chapter one, for instance, we mentioned how pro-Trump internet denizens, some of whom identified with the Alt-right, effectively gamed reddit's algorithm through technically verboten but still in practice concentrated upvoting/downvoting of key content. In response, reddit changed the algorithm responsible for determining top content. We suggested that reddit's alteration of the algorithm indicates leadership's significant concern about Trump supporters and Alt-right activists' ability to influence culture on the site. But beyond any intentionality, the Alt-right's messages—and therefore the configurations of politics in digital public spaces—have been influenced by platforms that rely on choosey algorithms to decide what content is relevant to produce newsfeeds, front pages, comment sections, and more.

The Alt-right has mobilized a variety of new media platforms to organize, carry out, and communicate its varied goals. In particular, the Alt-right has used the affordances of new media platforms to make significant gains in achieving its desired outcomes, many of which contest PC culture, counter the apparent liberalization of mainstream media, and rearticulate an insular, xenophobic politics against expansive globalization. Drawing on the structural capacities of new media to (1) bring together individuals in distant locales,[37] (2) rapidly circulate information with little start-up capital required on the part of interested participants,[38] and (3) organize people based on shared interest or affinity,[39] the Alt-right has used a variety of new media platforms to effectively augment its ability to intervene into the realm of the political. Because the Alt-right works both "online and offline," Nathan Jurgenson might call these types of movements "augmented revolutions" that are characterized by the "implosion of atoms and bits" such that "the advantages of digitality—information spreads faster, more voices become empowered, enhanced organization and consensus capabilities—intersect with the importance of occupying physical space with flesh-and-blood bodies."[40] In other words, the virtual capacities of the digital (made available by commonly-accessible platforms) have profoundly boosted the Alt-rights' capacities for organizing and agitating both in and beyond the digital sphere.

In many ways, the Alt-right has organized by capitalizing on the logic of complaint that fuels much platform discourse. In part because of their positive understanding as spaces for organizing change or political action, platforms appear to signify an egalitarian ethos, a dangerous connotation given the capitalist logics from which platforms emerge and are at play. Jodi Dean has postulated that increased, networked circulation of apparently political commentary has failed to reach those with their hands on the levers of power. For her, democratizing media offered little in the way of actually building a progressive and durable democracy. Dean suggests that the circulation of complaint has functioned as a release valve, off-putting some of the populace's anxieties with and against politics proper in a pseudo-political milieu: constantly circulating, networked texts. She notes that "we might express this disconnect between engaged criticism and national strategy in terms of a distinction between politics as the circulation of content and politics as official policy."[41] Unfortunately, these two modalities of politics operate parallel to one another, never the two to meet: "these components of a political system seem to run independently of the politics that circulates as content."[42] The ultimate impact of this airing of grievances is grim: despite increased circulation of petitions (content), politics as official policy needs only to recognize their apparent right to circulation, not take them seriously (or into account when developing policy). For Dean, then, "the message was not received. It circulated, reduced to the medium."[43]

On our view, Dean's characterization of endless, unanswered circulation of political complaint is profoundly accurate. The stunning success of the Alt-right in the 2016 election and beyond is at least in part reliant upon harnessing the capacities of endless circulation, which, paired with platform logics and algorithmic amplification, led the Alt-right to deftly construct a dangerously effective version of what Terranova might call "a topological formation."[44] In other words, the Alt-right rhetorically engineered a durable yet flexible configuration of discourses, infrastructures, and processes that offered coherence despite dissonance. As Terranova argues, "[t]he politics of network culture are…not only about competing viewpoints…but also about the pragmatic production of viable topological formations able to persist within an open and fluid milieu."[45] Memes were—and are—a central part of that rhetorical strategy. Attempts at political coherence or activation must reconcile with the chaotic flows of information central to network culture. Memes—as conduits of content but also as sites for negotiating meaning—are a pragmatic response to the "potential indeterminacy of information flows" endemic to the network.[46]

Over and against "mainstream" conservatives who have not yet cracked the code of internet culture, the Alt-right has leveraged the affordances of digital media for a fascist, white nationalist articulation of politics. Importantly, memes are nodal points where the various, constitutive components of networked platforms merge together. In the next section, we analyze the modes of memetic circulation enjoyed by the Alt-right. We describe how the Alt-right's use of memetic media in constructed ecosystems amplified the Alt-right's messages and altered the formation of the public both on and offline. We focus on the affordances of digital media for (1) finding like-minded individuals, (2) turning strangers into affiliates or co-conspirators, and (3) evading detection when critiquing reality structures.

The Weaponization of Memes in Alt-right Ecosystems

Retrofitting Already Extant Platforms

The Alt-right is depicted (relatively accurately) as an internet-savvy consortium of individuals who use the digital sphere to connect with one another and to organize politically. The "internet-savvy" part of this description is not inconsequential. Rather, the Alt-right has formed and developed alongside—and with the aid of—technological mediation. Perhaps most generally, the Alt-right's rise was parallel to and sometimes amplified by the growth of internet culture. Moreover, the Alt-right as a burgeoning movement benefitted from the memetic affordances of the internet, in which hate speech can move rapidly and often without retribution. According to Matthew N. Lyons, "The Alt-right's rapid growth partly reflected trends in internet culture, where anonymity and the lack of face-to-face contact have fostered widespread use of insults, bullying and supremacist speech."[47] More specifically, individuals associated with the Alt-right have connected their persuasive strategies to those that are especially successful in the digital sphere. Sometimes, the Alt-right has taken rhetorical techniques or discursive styles from internet culture and adapted them.[48] Memes are the penultimate example. With memes in circulation, discursive fields or platforms need not be ideologically-affiliated with the Alt-right to be useful. Many of the platforms used by the Alt-right before, during, and after the 2016 election did not have an explicit politics in favor of the Alt-right. Rather, memetic discourse from the Alt-right circulated on social media mainstays and even via mainstream media. These apparently politically-neutral structures (such as Facebook, Twitter, YouTube, even established parts of reddit and 4chan) served as an ideal canvas for the Alt-right to acquire persuasive techniques and test them in the environment of their origins.

One of the ways that the Alt-right influenced public discourse is by linking Alt-right or far right websites and platforms with those that appear politically neutral or even left-leaning. Sometimes these websites, platforms, and networks are ideologically agnostic—at least in conceptualization or perception. Yet that appearance is carefully constructed and discursively negotiated. The rhetoric of neutrality (or more acutely: information freedom) gestures towards Alt-right claims for liberty against regulation. In an essay on free and open source software (FOSS), Gabriella Coleman offers a related claim about the apparently non-political nature of "hacker aesthetics," evidenced by discourses surrounding FOSS. For her, although "[p]olitical intent and subjectivity are indeed noticeably absent in the constitution of the free software and open source movement," the attempt to enact political agnosticism evidences a clear valence.[49] In network culture, many platforms operate similarly; demands for free speech against censorship acquiesce to a libertarian ethos of "freedom"—of speech, of content, of circulation. For our purposes, apparently agnostic websites are indispensable to the Alt-right cause even if they don't explicitly boast Alt-right (or far right) monikers. Rather, what makes them attractive for Alt-right memetic dissemination is their apparent political ambivalence and the related tendency toward "freedom"—or, in the case of platforms in general, the unstated premise that platforms are egalitarian and central to the democratic process (and that regulation would disintegrate that democratic ethos). As the chapter on Pepe indicates, audiences can be activated by politicized content that doesn't appear political. Memes are especially subject to seeming politically neutral because they read as humorous. In this regard, memes may be especially influential on platforms that espouse neutrality.

Moreover, rapid transmission of far right memes has become increasingly difficult to discern as the Alt-right rearticulates neutral symbols for political purposes. As *Wired* reports, "[e]ven as [the Alt-right's] memes morph into militaristic propaganda, this loosely organized troll army inhabiting extremist corners of social media, 4chan, and Reddit has adopted a new tactic: claiming mundane objects like milk, the peace symbol, and the LGBTQ flag as symbols of white supremacy."[50] In network culture, the proliferation of polysemous texts that circulate rapidly causes a crisis of meaning that visibly delinks signifier from signified. As a result, "images are not representations, but types of bioweapons that must be developed and deployed on the basis of a knowledge of the overall informational ecology."[51] Alt-right memes that play with the non-fixity of the sign are a pragmatic example of this weaponization. Recoding the signification of common symbols with novel meaning is a profoundly rhetorical action, and on its own, is not necessarily worthy of alarm. However, the choice of symbols—Pepe, echo parentheses—is profound insofar as it indicates that the Alt-right is attempting to take non-political symbols and associate them with far right ideologies.

Such a move has at least two possible, pernicious effects: first, coding neutral and frequently-used symbols like milk (even for trolling purposes) into a symbol for the Alt-right has a naturalizing effect. Or, as *Wired* puts it, "If anybody who drinks milk might be a Nazi, the idea of someone being a Nazi starts looking more pedestrian."[52] Second, and more importantly, the Alt-right can use these strategies to induce chaos. The type of humor associated with trolling is predicated on pranks, trickery, and "baiting." The Alt-right knows that it can introduce false flags in memetic format, inviting journalists who are still trying to figure out what the Alt-right even is to report on the false flag as if it were true. Not all shadowy memes or rearticulated symbols represent white supremacy, but some of them *do*.[53] Again: this is a rhetorical problem. If no one knows what symbols mean, how does communication about them occur? Sense making becomes a nearly insurmountable task. Memes that don't make sense (and therefore appear foolish or pedantic) can actually be effective tools of sense making, including harbingers for Alt-right messages. Memes, then, are a significant part of a disinformation campaign that causes confusion at one turn while advancing white supremacist logics at another. Their slipperiness, their rapid circulation, their inherent invitation for uptake, make them crucial for transferring white supremacist ideologies from far right sites like Breitbart to apparently non-political sites in the Alt-right ecosystem.

Audiences seeking refuge from politics may find themselves engaging with content that is explicitly political but otherwise obscured by the seemingly non-political nature of the site or message. These locations are often focused on content creation and dissemination. Platforms such as Imgur, Know Your Meme, and other meme generators are potent spaces for Alt-right interpellation precisely because they appear to be politically neutral. There are several in-roads to activation, operating subtly at multiple levels. Each website offers opportunities to learn about memetic content and to participate in the invention of memes. The memes made through these seemingly innocuous generators ultimately become fodder for weaponized messages by the Alt-right. Moreover, because memes require both innovation and iteration—knowing how to create appropriate content—networked websites become fabricators of both epistemological and rhetorical innovation. Given that memes require users to both *know* and then *create* a given generic image, these websites direct users to the lineage of the referent, empowering them to successfully deviate from it to fashion something new. Engaging in meme creation is an exercise in meaning-making, but also in learning the bounds of a playing with the sign. From this perspective, sites such as Know Your Meme perform an important political function for the Alt-right. Insofar as they encourage rhetorical invention and invite users to play with meaning, they prime participants to engage with the Alt-right as a collectivity. Moreover, they may offer, even inadvertently, ways to use "images as *bioweapons*, let loose into the informational ecology with a mission to infect."[54]

In network culture, political activation is a tenuous task. Those looking to engage in politics (or any collective enterprise) must strike a delicate balancing act, paying close attention to informational flows and processes that make such collectivity possible. As Terranova notes, "[t]he production of collective modes of organization…requires not only a knowledge of social and psychological dynamics of informing a collective mode of production, but also an active engagement with the larger ecology of the Internet—screening out the junk, balancing the passive energy of the lurkers with the hyperactivism of the regular posters and keeping the vandals out."[55] In network culture, balancing the "centripetal" and "centrifugal" lends durability to processes of collectivity.[56] Or, more precisely, finding equilibrium—however temporary—staves off the "centripetal dissolution" of projects that operate within the bounds of "entropic dynamics of the network milieu."[57] From our perspective, meme generating and disseminating sites such Know Your Meme and Imgur are exemplars of projects that productively lean into the chaotic, entropic characteristics of the internet, encouraging the creative proliferation of meaning in accordance with the memetic genre.

The Alt-right has associated itself with adjacent parts of this creative digital culture. For example, Steve Bannon, once a campaign strategist for Trump and executive chairman of Breitbart, learned how to organize "kids" playing World of Warcraft.[58] According to Joshua Green, who interviewed Bannon extensively, World of Warcraft was not only a business opportunity for Bannon, but a way to tap into a virulent (and sometimes explicitly violent) masculinity largely unimpeded by regulation or cultural response and amplified through algorithms. "Bannon was captivated by what he had discovered while trying to build the business," Green argues, "…an underworld he hadn't known existed that was populated by millions of intense young men (most gamers were men) who disappeared for days or even weeks at a time in alternate realities."[59] Bannon's interest in these gamers extended beyond their affinity for games to their ability to collectively organize and use their mass and might to influence major institutions. Green notes that Bannon "later confirm[ed]…[that] this luciferous insight gave him an early understanding of the size and strength of online communities, along with an appreciation for the powerful currents that run just below the surface of the Internet."[60] The goal was turning gamer affect into political affect. Bannon himself told Green that, "These guys, these rootless white males, had monster power…. It was the pre-reddit" but equally as powerful.[61] Knowing how important internet culture would be for the Alt-right, Bannon hired Milo Yiannopoulos, another major player in the Alt-right, to reach the youth.[62]

Gamers would prove to be a fertile population for recruitment to the Alt-right. The Alt-right reached out to gamers across myriad platforms. Although World of Warcraft was the catalyst for Bannon's persuasive campaign, it was certainly not the only place to find latent Alt-right activists. In his *Normie's Guide to the Alt-right*, Andrew Anglin notes that the Alt-right is a "new type of White nationalist movement began to form on the internet," constructed because of a "collision" of "different online subcultures" who "came together" because they arrived at "common conclusions."[63] Several of these communities either overlapped with or shared affinity with gaming culture (although certainly not all gamers agree with the Alt-right or were activated by it). Anglin himself argues that,

> Gamergate provided a direct entry-point to what is now called the Alt-right, as it was made-up of young White men who realized they were being disenfranchised by feminism and political correctness.... Gamergate is notable in that they had some pretty serious successes in fighting off attempts to maintain their hobby as a White male affair (though Daily Stormer is the only site which has actually gotten a feminist fired from a video game company).[64]

Here, Anglin notes at least three important connections between Gamer Gate participants and Alt-right activists. First, and foremost, he notes commonality in identity and affect, wherein Gamer Gate and the Alt-right supply a space of unification and solidarity for "disenfranchised" white males. Second, Anglin notes that both Gamer Gate and Alt-right activists share a conservative and inherently reactionary view to what may be called "PC" or "SJW" culture. From this account, gains on behalf of women and people of color are a direct attack upon both masculinity and whiteness as well as a signifier of PC culture. Third, Gamer Gate and the Alt-right share both strategies and tactics (e.g., one goal is to maintain white masculinity; a tactic is to get feminists fired, usually through online campaigns, sometimes threatening sexual violence to the object of the campaign). Importantly, memes were central to both projects.[65]

The latent public emblematized by gamer culture bespeaks the ways users understand the power of their communities. Both 4chan's and reddit's algorithmic front page construction paired with their status as supposed "deep dark corners of the internet" combine to turn some forums into echo chambers. Such echo chambers are extremely useful for conjuring support for hit campaigns. Ian Sherr and Erin Carson note that "[a]ttack groups are as old as civilization and they form for all sorts of reasons, from economic hardship to racial friction to political and religious differences. Groups like the Ku Klux Klan usually formed around people's homes among like-minded friends. In this connected age of ours, it happens inside the echo chambers of Twitter, Reddit and message boards like 4Chan."[66] Platform cultures influence how people who use those platforms see the world, and how they come together to create new worlds.

Developing a Dedicated Alt-right Ecosystem

While the Alt-right organized new messaging strategies in its enclaves, it also operationalized adjacent networks to 4chan and reddit. These sites include Alt-right-affiliated mainstays such as Breitbart, Fox News, The Blaze, InfoWars, *Washington Examiner*, as well as Alt-right branded websites including AltRight.com and the National Policy Institute (NPI), an Alt-right "think tank." These platforms shuttled information back and forth across the distributed network, or Alt-right ecosystem, such that information from far right websites spread throughout the digital sphere. Some of the content made its way to mainstream social media, including Facebook and Twitter, where it was taken up, retweeted, or referenced by traditional media outlets unaffiliated directly with the Alt-right. This web of content producers, disseminators, and remixers had a significant impact on public discourse before, during, and after the election. A March 2017 study indicated, for instance, that a "right-wing media network" not only dominated the production of outsider discourse, but significantly altered popular conceptions of politics during that time. The authors of the study argue that,

> The 2016 presidential election shook the foundations of American politics. Media reports immediately looked for external disruption to explain the unanticipated victory—with theories ranging from Russian hacking to "fake news." We have a less exotic, but perhaps more disconcerting explanation: Our own study of over 1.25 million stories published online between April 1, 2015 and Election Day shows that a right-wing media network anchored around Breitbart developed as a distinct and insulated media system, using social media as a backbone to transmit a hyper-partisan perspective to the world. This pro-Trump media sphere appears to have not only successfully set the agenda for the conservative media sphere, but also strongly influenced the broader media agenda, in particular coverage of Hillary Clinton. While concerns about political and media polarization online are longstanding, our study suggests that polarization was asymmetric.[67]

The polarization of content depicted in the study relies on the movement of content from Alt-right echo chambers into more public streams. As a topological formation, these partisan sites are concentrations of shared ideological views—or, at the very least, affinities according to common politics—which not only organize partisan discourse, but distribute it outward using algorithmically-amplified social media. This study, which "analyzed hyperlinking patterns, social media sharing patterns on Facebook and Twitter, and topic and language patterns in the content," concluded that Breitbart served as the "center of a distinct right-wing media ecosystem, surrounded by Fox News, the Daily Caller, The Gateway Pundit, the *Washington Examiner*, Infowars, Conservative Treehouse, and Truthfeed."[68] These partisan sites deftly orchestrated a media one-two punch; even as they claimed that more traditional media outlets such as the *New York Times* and *Washington Post* were liberal "fake-news" and thus not to be trusted, these networked sites produced disinformation campaigns that both muddied the water and constituted an "internally coherent, relatively insulated knowledge community, reinforcing the shared worldview of readers and shielding them from journalism that challenged it."[69] Importantly, many of these websites and platforms are less than twenty years old, signaling a shift in modern conservatism in terms of content, tone, and media strategy.[70] Unlike traditional news sources, nodes in this right-wing ecosystem are strategically equipped to take advantage of the network for disseminating content.

Although the rise of the echo chambers that immerse users have long been a concern, the rapid formation of an Alt-right ecosystem is a significant threat to democracy: the construction of a volatile and highly effective propaganda machine that renders other vantage points suspect. The Alt-right has been patently successful because it understands and exploits the post-"Truth" components of network culture where signifier and signified are subject to collective reimagining. Moreover, its' success has been augmented by knowledge of the way circulation functions both temporally and in terms of content. Taking advantage of algorithmic amplification, the rapidity of sharing on social media, and a distrust of traditional institutional structures,[71] the Alt-right has organized its discourse effectively around paranoia, with very little startup resources required. Breitbart, and websites like it, are central nodal points in building the requisite network for information warfare.

As a result of this stunning success, the Alt-right faces a seismic backlash. Visibility has been a double-edged sword for the Alt-right, offering the opportunity to gain followers and advance an agenda. At the same time, the Alt-right's public presence has drawn criticism. Under public pressure, members of the Alt-right responded to accusations that they were aiding and abetting a new form of white supremacy. Platforms, including Facebook, reddit, and Twitter, have all altered key processes, parts of their infrastructure, and/or their terms of service in response to criticism that they are harboring white supremacists. A "series of purges" has driven some Alt-righters away from mainstream platforms.[72] In late 2017, under pressure from critics, Twitter started removing some users' "verification" checkmarks—signs that typically demarcate the legitimacy of a profile or account. Among the first to lose their verification checkmarks were controversial Alt-right spokespersons Richard Spencer and Jason Kessler, organizers of the now infamous Alt-right rally in Charlottesville.[73] Around the same time, popular Alt-right troll Baked Alaska (Tim Gionet) was permanently banned for violating Twitter's rules.

Twitter's about-face on free speech for white supremacists was variously represented in the news: one reporter shared a text they received from a Twitter employee mandating that the company would support "No more Nazis."[74] A *Rolling Stone* reporter suggested that the policy changes were too limited, and may have given both Twitter and the Alt-right a publicity boost.[75] Breitbart noted that Twitter was acting unfairly, leaving "violent" far left accounts up. Others maintained that Twitter's so-called purge was misinformed censorship that would embolden the Alt-right. As journalist David Frum contends, "[i]t's precisely the perception of arbitrary and one-sided speech policing that drives so many young men toward radical, illiberal politics."[76] Facebook also acted to curb the Alt-right's reach in late 2017, though it did so under the banner of fake news or hate speech.[77]

In response to this backlash, the Alt-right has partially receded from public view. It has returned to alternate spaces to regroup and debate strategy. One such space, Gab, has offered harbor for the Alt-right under the banner of promoting free speech and fighting censorship. Content on Gab routinely references Alt-right memes such as "The Deplorables" and Pepe. It also shows significant overlap with reddit and 4chan in both style and content. As *Wired* journalist Emma Grey Ellis reports, even the logo for Gab is decidedly Pepe-esque. Ellis describes the relationship between the Alt-right and Gab thusly:

> To the group calling itself the Alt-Right, which is really another word for white supremacists, any moderation looks like censorship. Their anger at being supposedly sidelined and silenced has spawned hashtag campaigns, think pieces, and now, a brand-new social media platform, Gab. Its primary schtick is promising an end to

> censorship. But by sequestering itself, Gab has managed to sideline it [*sic*] members further into an echo chamber so far removed from the rest of the conversation that its message has no chance of reaching unfamiliar ears.[78]

The use of Gab alone is not a long-term strategy, as the Alt-right also strategizes recruitment outside the echo chamber of likeminded individuals. However, Gab may be an ideal space to plan the next intervention. Moreover, Gab may be the right place to radicalize individuals before unleashing them on the wider public.

The Alt-right takes advantage of the affordances and limitations of network culture. Memes are central to this strategy, for several reasons. Memes circulate quickly, linking disparate parts of internet culture together. Memes invite participation from strangers, incorporating more and different people into this amorphous, politicized mass that can then act in concert or independently. Moreover, because memes are both a vehicle for expression and negotiate expression, memes are a key locale for collective meaning-making, however partial and temporary. Because of their non-fixity and invitation to play with the sign, memes are also a useful tool for weaponizing overtly supremacist messages and renegotiating covert or neutral symbols to include white supremacist messages. Finally, memes serve as "connective tissue" between networked nodes, including Alt-right mainstays, antagonistic enclaves, and mainstream media. In particular, the Alt-right's use of memes unites mainstream and enclaved groups into a coherent social formation that is effective despite its internal inconsistencies. Given these qualities, the Alt-right's networked strategy laid the groundwork for Russian operatives to influence the 2016 presidential election.

Alt-right Meme Networks and Russian Imitation

Although popular culture often represents the Alt-right as a new configuration of older movements, the Alt-right is neither new nor a simple reorganization of older white supremacist, Nazi, or xenophobic collectives. Around the same time Trump "grab[bed] 'em by the pussy," an entire ecosystem of platforms, websites, think-tanks, networks, and social media were being formed with the Alt-right at the center. Thus, while Trump's campaign has offered a raised platform for the Alt-right, the Alt-right is not synonymous with Trump, nor did its media strategy begin when Trump announced his candidacy for the highest office in the land. Rather, in recent years, Trump and the Alt-right have enjoyed a co-productive, symbiotic relationship with one another.

The Alt-right's media configurations exceed Trump as candidate. Indeed, Harvard's Joan Shorenstein Fellow Zack Exley notes that "Donald Trump's presidential win has been variously attributed, with justification, to the Clinton campaign's flaws, FBI Director James Comey's last minute letter, Christian conservatives who were willing to overlook Trump's personal conduct, disillusioned working-class whites, and other factors. Largely overlooked has been the right's decades-long media effort, which now includes a more incendiary and radical component."[79] In an essay for *Wired*, Ellis describes the quiet but coordinated effort by far right contingencies to create a media empire. The concerted, well-thought out, and intellectual media strategy is complicated and nuanced. And while the networked affordances of the internet are a significant component of this strategy, the weaponization of media exists beyond the internet proper. As Ellis argues,

> The term "Alt-Right" probably makes you think of Twitter or a dark subreddit, or 4chan, or some social medium occupied by meme-slinging, Trump-supporting, unapologetically bigoted provocateurs. You probably don't think of a PO box in Whitefish, Montana. But that's the Alt-Right's street address. More precisely, it's where you send mail to the National Policy Institute, the think tank that built the movement.[80]

To be sure, parts of the Alt-right's media strategy include the incorporation of traditional media institutions (e.g., think tanks), which are then connected to a larger network, including digital platforms.

Several writers have suggested that the media campaign that helped Donald Trump win the 2016 election was organized through polarizing websites and platforms. At the very least, the audiences that received information about the candidates in the 2016 election did so through vastly different channels, relying more heavily on social media platforms than ever before. That users obtained news from vastly different sources, and with little regard to alternate points of view, is not new. In 2011, Eli Pariser published a book on the "Filter Bubble," so named for the bubble that users find themselves in when information is personalized to them. Even then, as Pariser notes, "to some extent we've always consumed media that appealed to our interests and avocations and ignored much of the rest."[81] However, the filter bubble is novel in three ways. First, the filter bubble affects the individual. In contradistinction to mediated messages that draw together based on interest or affinity, filter bubbles are profoundly lonesome spaces. As a "centrifugal force" filter bubbles are "pulling us apart."[82] Second, like many influential but hidden technological forces, "the filter bubble is invisible," even beyond the apparent division of partisan politics. The machinic logics that produce filter bubbles rely on data collected about individuals, with and without their consent, in such a way that users may not be able to access the data collected about them. Moreover, because they are invisible, and not openly partisan, they appear "unbiased, objective, true."[83] Pariser is clear that these logics are not any of these qualities, but are black-boxed (that is, hidden) enough that users may not know that they are biased. Third, and finally, filter bubbles are not willingly chosen by a particular user. Rather, personalized filters choose content to cater to one's interests. The troublesome part is that if users don't recognize a filter bubble, they are perhaps unable to grasp how their perception is altered by it. One of Pariser's overall claims is that filter bubbles are likely to proliferate, especially given their obfuscated nature, and the for-profit aims of the companies who use them.

A half decade later, Joshua Benton declared those filter bubbles weaponized. "I used to be something of a skeptic when it comes to claims of 'filter bubbles,'" Benton wrote, "[b]ut I've come to think that the rise of fake news—and of the cheap-to-run, ideologically driven aggregator sites that are only a few steps up from fake—has weaponized those filter bubbles. There were just too many people voting in this election because they were infuriated by made-up things they read online."[84] Benton acknowledges the significant effects weaponized filter bubbles have on the constitution of public discourse—and of the democracy that relies upon it. Both Benton and Pariser believe this to be a political but non-partisan issue. In other words, these authors assert that the issue of a weaponized filter bubble effects both people of the liberal and conservative persuasion. Benton, for instance, calls out those "ideologically driven aggregator sites" but does not explicitly name them. Similarly, he mentions that his post-election newsfeed has been dominated by "liberal friends from college or media" in part because "Facebook's algorithm isn't putting" his conservative friends on his feed. Importantly, both Pariser and Benton demonstrate that human agency is only one facet in the increasing polarization of media. Like algorithmic logics that lurk beneath the surface of mediated user interfaces, filter bubbles appear banal (if they are even perceived at all) and are assumed ideologically neutral. The filter bubble demonstrates that there is something new to the assumption of polarization; that it is not just individuals who exercise free will to bury themselves in news streams that support their interests. But, current scholarship fails to grasp the pernicious use of informational warfare according to a particular ideological valence. More pointedly, neither take into account the tactical weaponization of algorithmic logics to produce filter bubbles that then encapsulate digital citizens in a cocoon of increasingly valenced misinformation.

The 2016 election is an exemplar of this weaponization of digital media. Yochai Benkler and colleagues note, for instance, that "While concerns about political and media polarization online are longstanding, our study [about the 2016 election] suggests that polarization was asymmetric."[85] This study reveals that audiences supporting Clinton also favored traditional media outlets supplemented by "more left-oriented online sides."[86] On the other hand, "pro-Trump audiences paid the majority of their attention to polarized outlets that have developed recently, many of them only since the 2008 election season."[87] In other words, although the networks constituted through Alt-right memetic discourse are relatively new, they are effectively weaponized. The far right has been patently successful at directing users' attention toward misinformation, scandals, and half-truths, in effect undermining the claims of conventional media outlets and institutions. For this reason, traditional efforts at persuasion, including "fact-checking" endeavors, are hardly effective.[88] And while the mainstream media attempts to correct falsehoods, Alt-right echo chambers amplify them, circulating them wildly. Then, as mainstream media outlets report on the misinformation, the falsehoods gain a secondary boost. In the context of the 2016 election, the effects of this rhetorical strategy are asymmetrical. Although Clinton clearly attempted to engage the digital sphere, she was no match for a candidate whose appeal came not from experience or veracity, but from sensation and complaint. Trump's message simply worked better for his target audience within the digital sphere. His messages were dramatically magnified in the Alt-right ecosystem given the feedback loops operating.

The Alt-right relied upon networked processes and infrastructures to translate a relatively small, minoritarian worldview into a larger, powerful movement. Trump benefitted from and at times, capitalized on, this ecosystem and networked strategies. The tactics employed by key members of the Alt-right suggest that networked media were—and still are—central to the functioning of the Alt-right as a collective. Figures of the Alt-right are plentiful, including Steve Bannon and Milo Yiannopoulos. Yet, perhaps no one has been as deft with Alt-right strategy as Andrew Anglin. Anglin is characterized by *The Atlantic* reporter Luke O'Brien as a vegan hippie teen radicalized into an "American Nazi," and, eventually, "the Alt-Right's most vicious troll and propagandist."[89] The Southern Poverty Law Center suggests that Anglin's website, The Daily Stormer, is "aptly" named after Nazi propaganda with Anglin himself described as a sophisticated and "prolific Internet troll and serial harasser."[90] Anglin indeed seems talented at organizing the Alt-right using the affordances of digital media. In an article on The Daily Stormer, Anglin suggests the need to harness the capacities of the platform. He argues, "[w]e will need a platform which allows us to organize and collectively promote our agenda. This may be in the form of a political party, or it may be through an organization which acts to influence the existing Republican Party. We need real organization, and it needs to be based on a platform which is approved by the mob."[91] To be clear, Anglin is not talking about platform as in digital platform. But, Anglin is describing the affordances of digital media and the creation of alternative sites of organizing, especially via 4chan.org/b/ and /pol/.

The deployment of messages across platforms to leverage "the mob" fashions the boundaries of this extremist discourse and impacts public culture. Moving the Overton Window, then, requires a dramatic rethinking of reality, and, in some cases a radical dissociation from it. Memes are productive because they are antagonistic media that invite innovation even as they recognize the boundaries of previously established cultural dynamics. Memes exist in—and thrive upon—the liminal. And memes are inherently participatory, inviting users to engage productively within that contradiction. In this way, memes are an ideal medium for the Alt-right: open enough to invite user engagement with low barriers to entry and little risk, yet closed enough to direct the meaning of a text toward the goals of the Alt-right as a collectivity. Moreover, another contradiction of memes—that they are productive messages but also, as a result of the form's succinct and incited nature, unsettling in effects—can be useful for a movement looking to undermine conceptions of what is real and what is not. In this way, memes can foment conspiracy—with material effects.

For instance, in late October, only a few days before the 2016 election, a post appeared on Facebook accusing candidate Clinton of running an underground, underage sex ring.[92] The conspiracy caught fire quickly. As the *New York Times* reports,

> Within hours, menacing messages like "we're on to you" began appearing in his [the owner of Comet Ping Pong pizza place] Instagram feed. In the ensuing days, hundreds of death threats—one read "I will kill you personally"—started arriving via

> texts, Facebook and Twitter. All of them alleged something that made Mr. Alefantis's jaw drop: that Comet Ping Pong was the home base of a child abuse ring led by Hillary Clinton and her campaign chief, John D. Podesta.[93]

The scandal became known as #Pizzagate and the incident is an exemplar for how conspiracies spread in network culture. Wikileaks had posted John Podesta's emails, obtained under nefarious pretenses. Within a month of this release, anons on 4chan /pol/ and redditors on r/the_donald/ began piecing together a conspiracy about Podesta's connection to a Washington, D.C. pizza place. The New Nationalist, a far right website that routinely produces anti-Semitic reports on the "Zionist Scheme" and "corrupt…global media," was among the first to "uncover" the #Pizzagate scandal. The report itself reified the ecosystem, linking to posts on r/the_donald/, Imgur, and other sites. #Pizzagate moved expeditiously through Alt-right mainstays like InfoWars as well as mainstream social media such as Facebook and Twitter. The conspiracy was complicated. An investigation by *Rolling Stone* notes that "it took the better part of a year (and two teams of researchers) to sift through the digital trail. We found ordinary people, online activists, bots, foreign agents and domestic political operatives. Many of them were associates of the Trump campaign. Others had ties with Russia."[94] In addition to amplifying disturbing "fake news," #Pizzagate prompted a North Carolina man armed with several weapons to open fire in the Comet Ping Pong pizza restaurant where the supposed pedophilia ring occurred.

The timing of the conspiracy was kairotic, likely opportunistic: a day before the Pizzagate post set ablaze the internet conspiracy, the FBI announced that it would review new information pertaining to the case against Hillary Clinton, who had been investigated for using a private email server, despite then-FBI head James Comey saying that such use was not, in fact, criminal.[95] The choice to announce the renewed investigation was momentous, and not only because it appeared to be a partisan intervention into the 2016 election, with great consequences.[96] Even if the so-called "Comey Letter" was not the silver bullet that proved Clinton's proclaimed corruption—indeed, it did not even rise to the level of "reopening" the case[97]—just the announcement that there were "pertinent" emails related to the case ignited the controversy afresh. The media inaccurately deemed the case "reopened," with tweets sharing that headline retweeted thousands of times before several media outlets "walked" that language back.[98] The veracity of the claims did not matter much. Later that day, at a rally, Trump referred to the Comey letter to thunderous cheers from his supporters. He noted at the time, "I have great respect for the FBI for righting this wrong. The American people fully understand her corruption and we hope all—all—justice, will finally be served."[99] Later in the rally, he suggested that the Clinton email investigation would be "the biggest political scandal since Watergate. And I am sure it will be properly handled from this point forward."[100] To be clear, Trump's campaign had long been issuing messages with Clinton's alleged corruption as a central theme; that she was suspect (even criminal) fit neatly into the right's assertion that Clinton was a Washington insider abetted by cronyism.

The polarizing version of this narrative, one more specific to the Alt-right, but with some traction with rank and file Republicans, was that Clinton had made backdoor deals, participated in highly suspect activities in her various political roles, and that she was not to be trusted. #CrookedHillary would become a central organizing component, often described through memes. These themes would continue, but in a new, and more unsettling format. In particular, Russian operatives would mirror Alt-right conspiracy discourses, employing memes to shuttle divisive disinformation among network nodal points. Using the networked strategies of the Alt-right as a template, the Internet Research Agency (IRA) set in motion a meme-centric campaign to disrupt the 2016 US presidential election.

In 2012, then-FBI Director Robert Mueller claimed that "down the road, the cyberthreat…will be the number one threat to the country."[101] At the time, Mueller and other security leaders diagnosed the threat as one of quickly-developing technologies, cyber-hacks, and intellectual property rights. Russia and China were among the biggest concerns.[102] By 2017, the public became aware that Mueller's insights were prescient. In short order, the US would investigate Russia's purported meddling into the 2016 election. Mueller himself would lead the investigation, charged to determine whether or not Russia had interfered and whether or not US citizens—including members of the Trump campaign, were involved in any capacity.[103] That investigation continues at the writing of this book.

On the 16th of February, 2018, Mueller announced an indictment against the IRA, a Kremlin-linked media organization. The forty-page indictment listed not only the IRA in general but twelve individuals associated with the IRA. Most broadly, the indict included allegations that the IRA "knowingly and intentionally conspired with each other (and with persons known and unknown to the Grand Jury) to defraud the United States by impairing, obstructing, and defeating the lawful functions of the government through fraud and deceit for the purpose of interfering with the U.S. political and electoral processes, including the presidential election of 2016."[104] The IRA's methods were decidedly digital. The indictment indicates that IRA employees engaged in what we call memetic warfare, crafting social media accounts that seemed to belong to US citizens, creating "thematic group pages" on hot-button political issues such as race, religion, and immigration, and using Facebook advertising platforms to reach over a hundred million Americans.[105] Some ads "focused on divisive social issues such as race, gay rights, gun control and immigration," issues that Trump's campaign had highlighted as central to the 2016 election.[106] Examples include various iterations of "Down With Hillary!," "Lock Her Up!," and references to secure borders or #BLM (Black Lives Matter).[107] The ads appeared in the newsfeed of at least 10 million people.[108] The IRA's work was extensive and targeted swing states.[109]

Memes were central to this process as they served as an important method by which the IRA spread apocryphal information. That the IRA had used memetic content had been introduced several months earlier by news reports about "Russian Facebook ad[s]."[110] Leslie Shapiro of the *Washington Post* directly notes the linkage between the IRA-produced content and memes as traditionally conceived (e.g., text macros).[111] She writes that "[a]mong the ads released by lawmakers, there's a wide variety of content, tone, and visual style. While some mimic Internet memes intended for easy consumption and sharing, others take the form of more-traditional campaign-style ads or promoted events."[112] However, even those "more-traditional campaign-style ads or promoted events" that Shapiro codes as non-memetic share striking similarities with memes: they often include images that directly reference a basic meme template. Even those images that don't read as "meme" betray memetic influence, wherein images have been altered or provide a template for others to alter them. Yet the memetic components of the so-called Russian ads were not limited to images, proper. Sometimes, the Russian advertisements took advantage of the format by which memes are shared. The IRA, for instance, imitated Facebook events to sow discord. The *New York Times* describes the IRA as an institution "known for using 'troll' accounts to post on social media and comment on news websites."[113] Images and actions from the IRA mimicked trolling discourses such as an orchestrated event to "Steal Minnesota's lakes."[114] These fake users posed as Americans and purchased ad space that, according to Facebook's Joel Kaplan, "appeared to amplify political issues across the political spectrum."[115]

Russian-based accounts created and propagated memes related to—if not explicitly referencing—the election.[116] Using now familiar meme formats, including self-referential images and politically-charged, often humorous text-based messages, many of these memes disseminated conservative, often xenophobic, homophobic, and misogynistic messages far and wide.[117] The memes may have been more effective than the ads were at targeting users and spreading virally. Creating and participating in social media groups, meme-producers generated content that appeared home-grown to unsuspecting Facebook users, who may have shared the images such that they held more reach than reported ads. Whereas ads are somewhat regulated and therefore limited commercial endeavors organized by social media sites, memes are vociferously self-circulating persuasive artifacts. After all, memes moving through purchased ad space don't require citation, nor do they reference from whence they came

Emblematic of Russian memetic mimicry of the Alt-right is the Heart of Texas Facebook page, a propaganda site designed by the IRA to galvanize far right advocacy groups in Texas. Named in reference to a geographic region in Texas, the page had nearly a quarter of a million followers and "boasted more followers than the official Texas Democrat and Republican Facebook pages *combined*."[118] Content on the page organized real world protests in major cities and circulated petitions on far right political issues (See Fig. 4.1).[119] In a number of ways, the Heart of Texas page is similar to broader efforts from the IRA—posts and content mirrored already existent far right discourse to galvanize adherents. Yet, what proves significant about the Heart of Texas Facebook page is that the "advertising" images on this site were functionally memes that mimicked Alt-right content. The page predominantly posted images in keeping with those originally manufactured on 4chan: still images overlaid with impact font or similar styles.

Figure 4.1: Heart of Texas Flag.

The use of memes on this page is significant because it illustrates how Russian agents attempted to create animosity among strangers mobilizing a particular ecosystem of discourses. In other words, memes had been successful in influencing politics elsewhere, and could be put to use in this Facebook group. The Heart of Texas Facebook page motivated a considerable audience who took pleasure in the simplistic humor of memes. But, more importantly, this page demonstrates that Russian hacking efforts retooled memes in the same way that the Alt-right had—by weaponizing conservative ideas through the circuitous routes of networks. Without the ongoing work of the Alt-right and the power of memes generally, the IRA could not have been successful. Of course, it is difficult to say which came first given that Russian trolls had infiltrated at least reddit, if not other sites, for years.[120] On such sites, those trolls did not simply influence discourse. They also honed their meme-making skills. They then opportunistically unleashed those messages on the most powerful social media networks, Facebook foremost among them. In so doing, the IRA organized seemingly grassroots campaigns to breed chaos and malcontent, apparently using the Alt-right's memetic weaponization strategy as a template. As Samuel C. Wooley and Philip N. Howard wrote, in some places Facebook is a "monopoly platform for public life."[121] Unleashing the persuasive power of these meme-making abilities on *the* source for information proved incredibly compelling. Just as with the Heart of Texas page, this form of "Computational propaganda is one of the most powerful new tools against democracy."[122]

To be sure, Russian activities imitated Alt-right memes used to influence the 2016 election. While all candidates were targeted by the IRA, a large swath of these memes favored Donald Trump and a majority of the language used by the IRA directly refer to Alt-right talking points. The connection is clearest on the subject of Hillary Clinton's alleged criminal activity. The IRA indictment indicates, for instance, that "Certain ORGANIZATION-produced materials about the 2016 U.S. presidential election used election-related hashtags, including: '#Trump2016,' '#TrumpTrain,' '#MAGA,' '#IWontProtectHillary,' and '#Hillary4Prison.'"[123] Like other hashtags, these are organizing texts that align information and people, amplifying content using Twitter's hashtag-friendly algorithmic logics. Second, the Alt-right and the Russians share a central function: the production of disinformation campaigns to compel strangers into acting in concert. The Alt-right has been roundly criticized for spreading patently false narratives, often via memetic media. The IRA took up that mantle with great success.

Russian content extends and expands the Alt-right's rhetorical strategy. It is important to note that we are not arguing that the Alt-right and the IRA were in cahoots with one another, although there is some evidence that Russian operatives directly promoted Alt-right content, including amplifying Alt-right messages from Breitbart.[124] Nor are we convinced that Trump was directly involved with any Alt-right linkages to Russia, proper. However, Trump has certainly aggrandized the efforts of Russian troll accounts espousing an Alt-right agenda by retweeting and showing appreciation to "the largest fake Twitter account run out of Russia…"[125] Moreover, when confronted with Russian meddling allegations, Trump borrowed far right, Alt-right, and IRA strategies meant to spread disinformation and prompt citizens to question basic tenets of reality—including the veracity of news.[126] Trump has continued this strategy for well over a year with varying degrees of effectiveness. A March 2018 tweet by Trump shares syntactical and contextual affinity with discourse from the Alt-right on 4chan and Twitter as well as Russian operative discourse: "The Mueller probe should never have been started in that there was no collusion and there was no crime. It was based on fraudulent activities and a Fake Dossier paid for by Crooked Hillary and the DNC, and improperly used in FISA COURT for surveillance of my campaign. WITCH HUNT!"[127] Once more, the President's discourse relies on memes used by both the Alt-right and Russian trolls (#CrookedHillary) and invites users to disengage with media he disagrees with as "fake." It is not necessarily that the IRA and the Trump campaign or administration are working together. Rather, their discursive strategies are *compatible*. They are linked to one another. They mirror one another. And they continue to amplify one another in and through the algorithms of circulation, even if no intentional collusion is apparent.

If any one of the allegations against the Russia-linked IRA proves to be true, the United States will have to reckon with the fact that a foreign government has significant influence on its elections. The Mueller investigation is tasked, in part, with finding out whether or not the Trump administration colluded with Russia. Even in the present moment, and likely for months or years to come, internet experts, politicians, and average citizens are still assessing what memes were weaponized by Russians, and when. Kathleen Hall Jamieson has recently asserted that such disinformation campaigns were likely sufficient enough to shift the outcomes of the election.[128] Those messages we know are Kremlin-linked either tip their hand with slip-shod construction or are linked to social media accounts or groups traced back to the IRA.[129] Altogether, the alleged interference of the IRA in the 2016 election occurred by circulating shareable and remixable content via networked platforms, including Facebook, Twitter, and Instagram.[130] Regardless of whether or not Trump or his campaign staff abetted Russian interference, one thing seems clear: the Alt-right's use of memes have become so influential and ingrained in culture that they have changed the nature of political discourse, to the benefit of Donald Trump.

Memetic Media, Circulation, and Politics in Network Culture

In April 2018, Mark Zuckerberg, CEO of Facebook, voluntarily provided testimony to Congress on his service. Although the questions from lawmakers were mixed, Zuckerberg answered concerns about data security, privacy, and Facebook's role in the 2016 election. As the *New York Times* reports,

> There were glimmers of a partisan divide: Senator Ted Cruz, Republican of Texas, asked about Facebook's handling of conservative media, including content related to Glenn Beck and a Fox News personality; Democrats probed Mr. Zuckerberg on how quickly Facebook responded to Russian meddling.[131]

In his testimony, Zuckerberg confirmed that Russian operatives had infiltrated the platform. What's more, he noted, there was a possibility that Russian-produced content—including images and image-based ads—was still circulating on Facebook. Zuckerberg also indicated that Facebook was "working with" the Mueller investigation, though the extent of its cooperation was confidential and could not be shared during the open session.

Although Zuckerberg did not explicitly mention Alt-right or Russian memes, both he and lawmakers gestured toward the complex relationship among network culture, the memes used by the IRA on Facebook, and the 2016 election. For instance, in response to a question about possible Russian interference, Zuckerberg noted that, "there are people in Russia whose job it is…to try to exploit our systems and other Internet systems, and other systems, as well. So this is an arms race, right? I mean, they're going to keep on getting better at this…."[132] Zuckerberg's response is telling insofar as its organized around militarism and escalation in the digital public sphere. Here, Russian operatives have weaponized the affordances of network culture to the tune of nearly 500 fake accounts and pages on Facebook alone, many of which are organized through memetic content.[133] Unlike advertisements, whose reach can be tracked for monetization purposes, memetic content produced or shared by those accounts and pages may have captured the attention of over a hundred million Facebook users in the United States alone.[134] In this sense, Facebook advertisements are only the most visible representations of Russian memetic media.

While it is certainly disturbing, our concern is not only that Russian operatives potentially meddled in the 2016 US election (and other elections), although we are largely convinced of that. Most broadly, our concern is that an outside campaign mobilized the significant affordances of memetic content as part of a strategic disinformation campaign—to great effect. More pointedly, we contend that the Alt-right's weaponization of memetic content to spread disinformation and discord is a strategy that has been replicated, in part or in whole, by Russian operatives in the 2016 election. The theatre in which this memetic warfare occurs is not limited to a particular geopolitical entity or state. Rather, the stage for what Zuckerberg deems the arms race is decidedly more diffuse, temperamental, and rhetorically powerful; it is network culture itself.

Network culture is defined by shifting contexts, mobile audiences, and discursive connections that cannot be determined in advance. Network culture is characterized by the durable openness of the milieu itself. For this reason, those wishing to partake in collective action must take into account the inherent bounds of collectivity on the internet, balancing the centripetal and centrifugal forces that afford coherence and prompt its dissolution. Network culture reworks traditional modes of influence; persuasive endeavors cannot rely on the rhetorical situation to be dependable given increased circulation. The familiar constructs—exigence, audience, constraints, and even the rhetor—become unfixed in the network. As such, networked circulation prompts a rethinking of traditional persuasive mechanisms and outcomes.

In this chapter, we outlined the growth of a networked Alt-right collectivity, bolstered by linked platforms and memes that circulate between them. This ecosystem includes Alt-right mainstays but also more surprising suspects: apparently egalitarian platforms such as social media and even mainstream media sources. Enter Alt-right memes, born in digital communities, sometimes jokingly, sometimes in earnest. It's hard for an outsider to tell the difference between the two, and that's the exact point. These memes are perfunctory, imminently digestible, and persuasive without seeming so. Moving between enclaves and dominant publics, and occasionally picked up by the mainstream media, memes gain cultural salience as a form of persuasion that need not rely solely on formal mechanisms: reason, rationality, sound argumentation. Rather, these pithy agents reproduce best in spaces where citation is not needed or even expected. The banality of the meme is its greatest weapon. After all, they're *only* memes.

Alt-right memes disseminated during the 2016 election prompt us to reimagine politics given network culture, in which the veracity of claims may matter less than the circulation of complaint and irony. Memes—which travel expeditiously, propagate easily, and transmit constitutive content to collectives still in the making—are ideal rhetorical devices for networked cultural configurations. As a rhetorical form, they are inherently invitational, prompting the creation and dissolution of publics who engage with them. They are also effective at reimagining politics while appearing trivial. Memes connect public spaces and counterpublics, drawing covert content into the mainstream. Perhaps most importantly, memes can shape strangers into shared socio-political relation even absent ideological affinity. In sum, memes function politically even as they appear apolitical. When weaponized, they can influence structures that seem otherwise impenetrable.

Notes

1. Tiziana Terranova, *Network Culture: Politics for the Information Age* (Pluto Press, 2004).
2. Nathan Jurgenson, "When Atoms Meet Bits: Social Media, the Mobile Web and Augmented Revolution," *Future Internet* 4, no. 1 (2012): 86.
3. Joel Penney and Caroline Dadas, "(Re)Tweeting in the Service of Protest: Digital Composition and Circulation in the Occupy Wall Street Movement," *New Media & Society* 16, no. 1 (2014): 88.
4. Eric S. Jenkins, "The Modes of Visual Rhetoric: Circulating Memes as Expressions," *Quarterly Journal of Speech* 100, no. 4 (2014): 443.
5. Jenkins, "The Modes of Visual Rhetoric," 443.
6. Jenkins, "The Modes of Visual Rhetoric," 443.
7. Catherine Chaput, "Rhetorical Circulation in Late Capitalism: Neoliberalism and the Overdetermination of Affective Energy," *Philosophy & Rhetoric* 43, no. 1 (2010): 21.
8. Chaput, "Rhetorical Circulation in Late Capitalism," 6.
9. Terranova, *Network Culture*, 1.
10. Terranova, *Network Culture*, 69.
11. Terranova, *Network Culture*, 69.
12. Terranova, *Network Culture*, 3.
13. Terranova, *Network Culture*, 7.
14. Terranova, *Network Culture*, 8.
15. Jenkins, "The Modes of Visual Rhetoric," 445.
16. Leslie A. Hahner, "The Riot Kiss: Framing Memes as Visual Argument," *Argumentation & Advocacy* 49, no. 3 (2013): 162.
17. Mary E. Stuckey, "On Rhetorical Circulation," *Rhetoric & Public Affairs* 15, no. 4 (2012): 610.
18. Terranova, *Network Culture*, 9.
19. James Alexander McVey and Heather Suzanne Woods, "Anti-Racist Activism and the Transformational Principles of Hashtag Publics: From #HandsUpDontShoot to #PantsUpDontLoot," *Present Tense* 5, no. 3 (2016).
20. Terranova, *Network Culture*, 64.
21. Terranova, *Network Culture*, 64.
22. Henry Jenkins, Sam Ford, and Joshua Green, *Spreadable Media: Creating Value and Meaning in a Networked Culture* (New York: NYU Press, 2013), 1.

23. Jenkins, Ford, and Green, *Spreadable Media*, 2.
24. Terranova, *Network Culture*, 52, 34.
25. McVey and Woods, "Anti-Racist Activism and the Transformational Principles of Hashtag Publics."
26. Penney and Dadas, "(Re)Tweeting in the Service of Protest," 85.
27. Penney and Dadas, "(Re)Tweeting in the Service of Protest," 86.
28. Robert Hariman and John Louis Lucaites. *No Caption Needed: Iconic Photographs, Public Culture, and Liberal Democracy* (Chicago, IL: University of Chicago Press, 2007), 27.
29. Ken Hillis, Michael Petit, and Kylie Jarrett, *Google and the Culture of Search* (New York: Routledge, 2013), 9.
30. Fenwick McKelvey, "Algorithmic Media Need Democratic Methods: Why Publics Matter," *Canadian Journal of Communication* 39, no. 4 (2014): 599.
31. Algorithms, including those associated with Google, Facebook, and others, may also be productive of a particular subject, organized through logics that suggest the performance of self, online and off.
32. Hillis, Petit, and Jarrett, *Google and the Culture of Search*, 3.
33. Paul Baker and Amanda Potts, "'Why Do White People Have Thin Lips?' Google and the Perpetuation of Stereotypes via Auto-Complete Search Forms," *Critical Discourse Studies* 10, no. 2 (2013): 187–204.
34. Tarleton Gillespie, "The Relevance of Algorithms" in *Media Technologies: Essays on Communication, Materiality, and Society*, ed. Pablo J. Boczkowski and Kirsten A. Foot (Cambridge, MA: MIT Press, 2014), 170.
35. Gillespie, "The Relevance of Algorithms," 188.
36. Gillespie, "The Relevance of Algorithms," 184.
37. Lee Rainie and Barry Wellman, *Networked: The New Social Operating System* (Cambridge, MA: MIT Press, 2012), 11–12.
38. Jennifer Earl and Katrina Kimport, *Digitally Enabled Social Change: Activism in the Internet Age* (Cambridge, MA: MIT Press, 2011), 10.
39. McVey and Woods, "Anti-racist Activism and the Transformational Principles of Hashtag Publics"; Jeffrey S. Juris, "Reflections on #Occupy Everywhere: Social Media, Public Space, and Emerging Logics of Aggregation," *American Ethnologist* 39, no. 2 (2012): 266; Nathan Rambukkana, "#Introduction: Hashtags as Technosocial Events" in *#Hashtag Publics: The Power and Politics of Discursive Networks*, ed. Nathan Rambukkana (New York: Peter Lang, 2015), 15.
40. Jurgenson, "When Atoms Meet Bits," 86.
41. Jodi Dean, "Communicative Capitalism: Circulation and the Foreclosure of Politics," *Cultural Politics* 1, no. 1 (2005): 51–74.
42. Dean, "Communicative Capitalism," 52–53.
43. Dean, "Communicative Capitalism," 52.
44. Terranova, *Network Culture*, 100.
45. Terranova, *Network Culture*, 68.
46. Terranova, *Network Culture*, 68.

47. Matthew N. Lyons, "CTRL-ATL-DELETE: An Antifascist Report of the Alternative Right," in *CTRL-ALT-DELETE*, ed. K. Kersplebedeb (Montreal: Kersplebedeb Publishing and Distribution, 2017), 13.
48. Niko Heikkilä, "Online Antagonism of the Alt-Right in the 2016 Election," *European Journal of American Studies* 12, no. 2 (2017).
49. Gabriella Coleman, "The Political Agnosticism of Free and Open Source Software and the Inadvertent Politics of Contrast," *Anthropological Quarterly* 77, no. 3 (2004): 508.
50. Emma Grey Ellis, "The Alt-Right's Newest Ploy? Trolling with False Symbols," *Wired*, May 10, 2017, https://www.wired.com/2017/05/Alt-Rights-newest-ploy-trolling-false-symbols/.
51. Terranova, *Network Culture*, 141.
52. Ellis, "The Alt-Right's Newest Ploy?"
53. "Fact Check: Did a White House Intern Make the 'White Power Hand Gesture?," *Snopes*, January 4, 2018, https://www.snopes.com/fact-check/intern-white-power-hand-gesture/.
54. Terranova, *Network Culture*, 142.
55. Terranova, *Network Culture*, 69.
56. Terranova, *Network Culture*, 70.
57. Terranova, *Network Culture*, 70.
58. Mike Snider, "Steve Bannon Learned to Harness Troll Army from 'World of Warcraft,'" *USA Today*, July 18, 2017, https://www.usatoday.com/story/tech/talkingtech/2017/07/18/steve-bannon-learned-harness-troll-army-world-warcraft/489713001/.
59. Joshua Green, *Devil's Bargain: Steve Bannon, Donald Trump, and the Nationalist Uprising* (New York: Penguin, 2017), 83.
60. Green, *Devil's Bargain*, 83.
61. Green, *Devil's Bargain*, 145.
62. Snider, "Steve Bannon Learned to Harness."
63. Andrew Anglin, "A Normie's Guide to the Alt-Right: Version 3," *The Daily Stormer*, September 4, 2016, https://www.stormfront.org/forum/t1175673/.
64. Anglin, "A Normie's Guide."
65. Ian Sherr and Erin Carson, "GamerGate to Trump: How Video Game Culture Blew Everything Up," *CNET*, November 27, 2017, https://www.cnet.com/news/gamergate-donald-trump-american-nazis-how-video-game-culture-blew-everything-up/.
66. Sherr and Carson, "GamerGate to Trump."
67. Yochai Benkler *et al.*, "Study: Breitbart-Led Right-Wing Media Ecosystem Altered Broader Media Agenda" *Columbia Journalism Review*, March 3, 2017, https://www.cjr.org/analysis/breitbart-media-trump-harvard-study.php.
68. Benkler *et al.*, "Study: Breitbart-Led Right-Wing Media Ecosystem Altered Broader Media Agenda."
69. Benkler *et al.*, "Study: Breitbart-Led Right-Wing Media Ecosystem Altered Broader Media Agenda."
70. Benkler *et al.*, "Study: Breitbart-Led Right-Wing Media Ecosystem Altered Broader Media Agenda."
71. "Americans' Trust in Mass Media Sinks to New Low," *Gallup*, September 14, 2016 http://news.gallup.com/poll/195542/americans-trust-mass-media-sinks-new-low.aspx.

72. Katie Zavadski, "American Alt-Right Leaves Facebook for Russian Site VKontakte," *The Daily Beast*, November 3, 2017, https://www.thedailybeast.com/american-alt-right-leaves-facebook-for-russian-site-vkontakte.
73. Kerry Flynn, "The Reckoning of the Alt-Right on Twitter Has Begun," *Mashable*, November 16, 2017, https://mashable.com/2017/11/16/twitter-Alt-Right-ban-accounts-verification-policy/#x24KP_3pdgqF.
74. Flynn, "The Reckoning of the Alt-Right."
75. Bob Moser, "How Twitter's Alt-Right Purge Fell Short," *Rolling Stone*, December 19, 2017, https://www.rollingstone.com/politics/news/how-twitters-Alt-Right-purge-fell-short-w514444.
76. David Frum, "Suspending Alt-Right Twitter Accounts Doesn't Fix Anything," *The Atlantic*, November 16, 2016, https://www.theatlantic.com/politics/archive/2016/11/twitter-censorship-will-only-empower-the-Alt-Right/507929/.
77. "Facebook, Twitter Issue Policy Changes to Manage Fake News and Hate Speech," *NPR*, December 24, 2017, https://www.npr.org/2017/12/24/573333371/facebook-twitter-issue-policy-changes-to-manage-fake-news-and-hate-speech.
78. Emma Grey Ellis, "Gab, the Alt-Right's Very Own Twitter, Is the Ultimate Filter Bubble," *Wired*, September 14, 2016, https://www.wired.com/2016/09/gab-Alt-Rights-twitter-ultimate-filter-bubble/.
79. Zack Exley, "Black Pigeon Speaks: The Anatomy of the Worldview of an Alt-Right YouTuber," *Shorenstein Center on Media, Politics, and Public Policy*, June 28, 2017, https://shorensteincenter.org/anatomy-of-alt-right-youtuber/.
80. Emma Grey Ellis, "How the Alt-Right Grew an Obscure Racist Cabal," *Wired*, October 9, 2016, https://www.wired.com/2016/10/Alt-Right-grew-obscure-racist-cabal/.
81. Eli Pariser, *The Filter Bubble: How the New Personalized Web Is Changing What We Read and How We Think* (New York: Penguin, 2011).
82. Pariser, *The Filter Bubble*.
83. Pariser, *The Filter Bubble*.
84. Joshua Benton, "The Forces That Drove This Election's Media Failure Are Likely to Get Worse," *Nieman Lab*, November 9, 2016, http://www.niemanlab.org/2016/11/the-forces-that-drove-this-elections-media-failure-are-likely-to-get-worse/.
85. Benkler *et al.*, "Study: Breitbart-Led Right-Wing Media Ecosystem Altered Broader Media Agenda."
86. Benkler *et al.*, "Study: Breitbart-Led Right-Wing Media Ecosystem Altered Broader Media Agenda."
87. Benkler *et al.*, "Study: Breitbart-Led Right-Wing Media Ecosystem Altered Broader Media Agenda."
88. Chris Cillizza, "Why Fact-Checking Doesn't Change People's Minds," *Washington Post*, February 23, 2017, https://www.washingtonpost.com/news/the-fix/wp/2017/02/23/why-fact-checking-doesnt-change-peoples-minds/.
89. Luke O'Brien, "The Making of an American Nazi," *The Atlantic*, December 2017, https://www.theatlantic.com/magazine/archive/2017/12/the-making-of-an-american-nazi/544119/.
90. "Andrew Anglin," *Southern Poverty Law Center*, n.d., https://www.splcenter.org/fighting-hate/extremist-files/individual/andrew-anglin.

91. Anglin, "A Normie's Guide."
92. Amanda Robb, "Pizzagate: Anatomy of a Fake News Scandal," *Rolling Stone*, November 16, 2017, https://www.rollingstone.com/politics/news/pizzagate-anatomy-of-a-fake-news-scandal-w511904.
93. Cecilia Kang, "Fake News Onslaught Targets Pizzeria as Nest of Child-Trafficking," *New York Times*, November 21, 2016, https://www.nytimes.com/2016/11/21/technology/fact-check-this-pizzeria-is-not-a-child-trafficking-site.html.
94. Robb, "Pizzagate."
95. Anthony Zurcher, "What Was Clinton FBI Probe About?" *BBC News*, May 10, 2017, http://www.bbc.com/news/election-us-2016-37811529.
96. Nate Silver, "The Comey Letter Probably Cost Clinton the Election," *FiveThirtyEight*, May 3, 2017, https://fivethirtyeight.com/features/the-comey-letter-probably-cost-clinton-the-election/.
97. Silver, "The Comey Letter Probably Cost Clinton the Election."
98. Calderone, "News Outlets Dial Back Reports."
99. Donald J. Trump, "Campaign Rally in Lisbon, Maine," *C-Span*, October 28, 2016, https://www.c-span.org/video/?417634-1/donald-trump-campaigns-lisbon-maine.
100. Amy Chozick and Patrick Healy, "'This Changes Everything': Donald Trump Exults as Hillary Clinton's Team Scrambles," *New York Times*, October 28, 2016, https://www.nytimes.com/2016/10/29/us/politics/donald-trump-hillary-clinton.html.
101. Jason Ryan, "FBI Director Says Cyberthreat Will Surpass Threat from Terrorists," *ABC News*, January 31, 2012, http://abcnews.go.com/blogs/politics/2012/01/fbi-director-says-cyberthreat-will-surpass-threat-from-terrorists/.
102. Ryan, "FBI Director Says Cyberthreat Will Surpass."
103. Rebecca R. Ruiz and Mark Landler, "Robert Mueller, Former F.B.I. Director, Is Named Special Counsel for Russia Investigation," *New York Times*, May 17, 2017, https://www.nytimes.com/2017/05/17/us/politics/robert-mueller-special-counsel-russia-investigation.html.
104. *United States v. Internet Research Agency, LLC*, 1:18-cr-00032-DLF (D.D.C. Feb. 16, 2018), 2–3.
105. *United States v. Internet Research Agency, LLC*, 13; Alexis C. Madrigal, "Russia's Troll Operation Was Not That Sophisticated," *The Atlantic*, February 19, 2018, https://www.theatlantic.com/technology/archive/2018/02/the-russian-conspiracy-to-commit-audience-development/553685/.
106. Scott Shane and Vindu Goel, "Fake Russian Facebook Accounts Bought $100,000 in Political Ads," *New York Times*, September 6, 2017, https://www.nytimes.com/2017/09/06/technology/facebook-russian-political-ads.html.
107. Scott Shane, "These Are the Ads Russia Bought on Facebook in 2016," *New York Times*, November 1, 2017 https://www.nytimes.com/2017/11/01/us/politics/russia-2016-election-facebook.html; Leslie Shapiro, "Anatomy of a Russian Facebook Ad," *Washington Post*, November 1, 2017, https://www.washingtonpost.com/graphics/2017/business/russian-ads-facebook-anatomy/.
108. Elliot Schrage, "Hard Questions: Russian Ads Delivered to Congress," October 2, 2017, https://newsroom.fb.com/news/2017/10/hard-questions-russian-ads-delivered-to-congress/.

109. *United States v. Internet Research Agency, LLC*, 13.
110. Shapiro, "Anatomy of A Russian Facebook Ad."
111. Shapiro, "Anatomy of A Russian Facebook Ad."
112. Shapiro, "Anatomy of A Russian Facebook Ad."
113. Shane and Goel, "Fake Russian Facebook Bought $100,000 in Political Ads."
114. Adam Uren, "Minnesotans Respond to Wisconsin Plot to Steal Our Lakes," *Bring Me the News*, September 27, 2017, https://bringmethenews.com/life/minnesotans-respond-to-wisconsin-plot-to-steal-our-lakes.
115. Shane and Goel, "Fake Russian Facebook Bought $100,000 in Political Ads."
116. Ashley Hoffman, "Here Are the Memes That Russian Operatives Shared to Influence 2016," *Time*, November 1, 2017, http://time.com/5006056/russia-election-2016-memes/.
117. Scott Shane, "These Are the Ads Russia Bought on Facebook in 2016."
118. Casey Michel, "How the Russians Pretended to Be Texans—and Texans Believed Them," *Washington Post*, October 17, 2017, https://www.washingtonpost.com/news/democracy-post/wp/2017/10/17/how-the-russians-pretended-to-be-texans-and-texans-believed-them/.
119. Natasha Bertrand, "Shuttered Facebook Group Linked to Russia Organized Anti-Immigrant Rallies across Texas," *Business Insider*, September 13, 2017, http://www.businessinsider.com/facebook-group-russia-texas-anti-immigrant-rallies-2017-9.
120. Josh Horwitz, "Reddit's Most Popular Meme Forum Was a Hangout Spot for Russian Trolls," *Quartz*, April 11, 2018, https://qz.com/1249579/r-funny-reddits-most-popular-meme-forum-was-a-hangout-spot-for-russian-propaganda-trolls/.
121. Samuel C. Woolley and Philip N. Howard, "Computational Propaganda Worldwide: Executive Summary," *Computational Research Project*, November 2017, 3.
122. Woolley and Howard, "Computational Propaganda Worldwide," 7.
123. *United States of America v. Internet Research Agency, LLC*, 17.
124. Oren Dorell, "Breitbart, Other 'Alt-Right' Websites Are the Darlings of Russian Propaganda Effort," *USA Today*, August 24, 2017, https://www.usatoday.com/story/news/world/2017/08/24/breitbart-other-Alt-Right-websites-darlings-russian-propaganda-effort/598258001/.
125. Casey Michel, "Trump Personally Thanked Fake Twitter Account Linked to Russia," *Think Progress*, October 18, 2017, https://thinkprogress.org/trump-retweet-a-fake-twitter-account-149f3f9c1360/.
126. Donald J. Trump, Twitter Post, February 26, 2017, 12:16 PM, https://twitter.com/realdonaldtrump/status/835916511944523777.
127. Donald J. Trump, Twitter Post, March 17, 2018, 5:12 PM, https://twitter.com/realdonaldtrump/status/975163071361683456.
128. Kathleen Hall Jamieson, *Cyber-War: How Russian Hackers and Trolls Helped Elect a President* (New York: Oxford University Press, 2018).
129. Shapiro, "Anatomy of A Russian Facebook Ad."
130. *United States v. Internet Research Agency, LLC*, 7.
131. "Mark Zuckerberg Testimony: Senators Question Facebook's Commitment to Privacy," *New York Times*, April 10, 2018, https://www.nytimes.com/2018/04/10/us/politics/mark-zuckerberg-testimony.html.

132. Mark Zuckerberg, "Transcript of Mark Zuckerberg's Senate Hearing," *Washington Post*, April 10, 2017, https://www.washingtonpost.com/news/the-switch/wp/2018/04/10/transcript-of-mark-zuckerbergs-senate-hearing/?utm_term=.cb1c2dca4552.
133. Mike Isaac and Scott Shane, "Facebook's Russia-Linked Ads Came in Many Disguises," *New York Times*, October 2, 2017, https://www.nytimes.com/2017/10/02/technology/facebook-russia-ads-.html.
134. Tony Romm and Kurt Wagner, "Facebook Says 126 Million People in the U.S. May Have Seen Posts Produced by Russian-Government-Backed Agents," *Recode*, October 30, 2017, https://www.recode.net/2017/10/30/16571598/read-full-testimony-facebook-twitter-google-congress-russia-election-fake-news.

· 5 ·

SILENCING THE OPPOSITION

Memes as Warfare

On October 20, 2017, two signs were posted on the campus of Boston College. The signs featured a World War II-era image of Uncle Sam announcing the caption, "I want you to love who you are. Don't apologize for being white."[1] The small posters were placed by a known white supremacist organization and followed the vandalization of Black Lives Matter posters a few days prior.[2] By October 31, users on /pol/ proposed that members hang posters with the slogan "It's Okay to Be White" in various locales as a "'proof of concept' that a 'harmless message' would cause a 'massive media shitstorm (See Fig. 5.1).'"[3] Within days, in some cases hours, of this comment, posters proliferated. They were found on municipal telephone poles, within YouTube videos, and on stickers affixed in public places.[4] As anticipated, the images prompted immediate response. University administrators denounced the posters for their racist messages.[5] Op-eds sifted through the privilege and resentment displayed by such visuals.[6] Social media users railed against these dispatches and the individuals who supported this vitriol. While the posters, stickers, and YouTube videos were widespread, their circulation amplified uptake. Significantly, reactions to these images provided a greater media presence for such messages. In effect, public response had bolstered the signal of white supremacist propaganda.

Figure 5.1: It's Okay to Be White Poster.

By early November, Tucker Carlson, a conservative pundit, aired a segment on the posters, but his discussion did not focus on the racism of the images or the groups that placed the posters. Instead, Carlson accused the media reporting on the posters of an anti-white agenda. The *Washington Post* had covered one set of the images—ten identical posters found in Montgomery Blair High School in Maryland. Carlson suggested that coverage in the *Post* charged racism falsely. As he stated, "Being white by the way is not something you can control…Like any ethnicity, you're born with it. Which is why you shouldn't attack people for it, and yet the left does constantly—in case you haven't noticed."[7] As a conservative commentator, Carlson has long recited white supremacist fodder, at least since the removal of Bill O'Reilly in April 2017.[8]

Yet, this accusation was more pointed. As *Newsweek* argued, Carlson had used public reactions to underscore supposed threats faced by white people.[9] Claims that white people were under attack had already become an argument asserted by the far right, especially the Alt-right. In effect, Carlson became a *de facto* spokesperson for the Alt-right and warranted its "proof of concept" by claiming victimhood and exaggerating a "media shitstorm."

These posters were designed using the same principles as many of the memes created in /pol/ and r/the_donald/. As we have demonstrated throughout this volume, Alt-right memes are not simply messages espousing a direct line of advocacy. With these memetic posters and similar images, the message moves circuitously, bolstered by media flows and algorithmic amplification. In addition to disseminating Alt-right content, such modes of engagement labor to outrage others by anticipating frenzied counter-responses from political opponents. The ultimate goal is to create a reaction in liberals or the left that will further alienate mainstream and conservative audiences and thereby provide a larger media presence for the messages of the Alt-right. Just as with the "It's Okay to Be White" posters, the images did not simply communicate white pride to passersby. Instead, the posters were designed to provoke anger from university presidents, journalists, and others. That indignation justified, even weakly, the response of Tucker Carlson, who capitalized on their arguments to aggrandize the idea that whiteness was under attack. Carlson's response was part of a chain reaction formulated on 4chan: posters were manufactured in these sites, individuals placed posters publicly that invited backlash, which enabled Carlson to assert the need for white protectionism.

This chapter explains how some memes are crafted to alienate liberal and leftist audiences and incite overreaction, all for the benefit of the Alt-right. Using past outcry as a model for action, the goal is to predict how outside, and in particular, liberal audiences might react to a specific meme. While this chain reaction cannot necessarily be predicted or generated intentionally, there is nevertheless an anticipatory politics to memes of this ilk—a politics banking on alienation. Alt-right memes of this nature are designed to divide and conquer. Commonly, meme creators on 4chan's /pol/ and r/the_donald/ will craft memes to antagonize those who hold oppositional views. These audiences are often called "the left," compiling avowed democrats, socialists, and those pejoratively named "social justice warriors" (SJWs) into a set of outsiders who are goaded toward wrath via the messages of particular memes. Labeling of the left symbolically names a political opponent but also aims to antagonize those who materially enact some mode of leftist politics, principally: voting democrats, self-professed liberals, radical actors within social movements, or erstwhile campaigning progressives. In this endeavor, "the left" is a rhetorical term that compiles a group to both anger actors who often critique democrats (or the Democratic National Committee) and those establishment democrats who may not want to be associated with the far left (e.g., Antifa). The Alt-right gains tactical ground by labeling a diverse, and often oppositional, set of actors solely as "the left." As a case in point, members of r/the_donald/ deployed the term "Alt-left" to manufacture a violent, fascist understanding of left-wing activists.[10] In effect, labeling these heterogenous groups as "the left" constitutes an enemy both to antagonize those who have been deemed as such and to court mainstream actors to further demonize them. Our analysis thus highlights how Alt-right discourse rhetorically labels "the left" while simultaneously provoking outrage from a host of actors who respond to the Alt-right. Such machinations ultimately supply desired ammunition for its tactics of alienation.

A central component to this strategy is to characterize leftist outrage as institutional silencing, often through the lens of "political correctness." This scheme holds two key effects. First, the left becomes a reactionary, hysterical, and elitist formation that disallows the politics of the (white) everyman. Second, by highlighting how the left marginalizes far right advocacies, Alt-right enthusiasts become further attached to the privilege of whiteness and a sense of disenfranchisement. Such resonances broaden the divisions between the far right, mainstream conservatives and others. Ultimately, the rhetorical strategy at stake is one of alienation wherein division is leveraged for outside audiences. To understand the current work of Alt-right memes, scholars must grasp how its messages deploy alienation as provocation. Alienation has long been theorized as a rhetorical tactic that creates unity from the art of enemyship. The use of alienation by the Alt-right exacerbates a divide in the populace by redirecting the status of victimhood.[11] By digging deeper into these rhetorical efforts, scholars glean a stronger sense of how current responses to the Alt-right fail to mobilize effective resistance.

Alienation as a Wedge Issue

Alt-right memes operate through provocation and division. While we explored lulz as memetic motivation in chapter three, here, our interest focuses on the antagonism at stake in those memes designed to alienate the left. Specifically, we analyze how memes function as propagandistic messages that entrench political division—to the ultimate detriment of the *demos*. The necessary political conflict of the *agora*—wherein ideas are debated in the public theatre—is routed into a form of antagonism that breeds further contempt for the opposition. We take our cue from Chantel Mouffe who contends that agonism is essential to vigorous democracy—political differences ought not be erased but rather put into continual contestation. As she writes, "adversaries fight against each other because they want their interpretation of the principles to become hegemonic, but they do not put into question the legitimacy of their opponent's right to fight for the victory of their position."[12] She elaborates that agonism can often lead to antagonism. When democratic possibilities for identification with fellow citizens are not cultivated, citizens often turn against one another. In these instances, agonism gives way to antagonism—a zero-sum battle among citizens. Instead of engaging in democratic debate that sustains the necessary agonism of a vibrant democracy, citizens amplify divisions through antagonism. Set within a time and culture of extensive political enemyship, Alt-right memes intensify divisions among the populace. Often, these memes deploy shocking imagery to infuriate others. Those shock tactics aim to provoke outrage and thereby heighten political antagonism.

Shock tactics are a well-worn rhetorical strategy with an ignoble history. In response to the vicious propaganda of World War I, scholars began to take interest in how fear appeals, shocking imagery, and more influenced different populations.[13] Typically, propaganda scholars maintain that such messages manipulate information, emotions, and reasoning to goad the people into nationalistic, irrational, or ill-informed ways of thinking. In the field of rhetoric, for instance, J. Michael Sproule's research on war propaganda establishes how devious ploys inaugurated a public backlash against the use of such disinformation.[14] War-era tactics obfuscated the distinctions between emotion and reason to the detriment of deliberative politics. Propaganda's ability to manipulate the feelings of the populace was seen as an impediment to the possibilities of democratic action.

Shock tactics are part and parcel of the insidious nature of propaganda: these appeals often foster antagonism. Messages of this nature are problematic, especially during wartime, insofar as they stoke the public's fear and inflame division. Scholars of later periods of propaganda have denounced such outlandish stratagems. Cold War propaganda, for instance, preyed upon public distrust and used lies to fuel suspicion of the enemy.[15] Contemporary domestic propaganda often uses similar tactics to drive a wedge between the body politic, creating enemies out of an opposing political party, another socio-economic group, or others.[16] Overall, shocking images and messaging strategies are understood as a barrier to effective democratic processes. These images deter individuals from the highest ideals of the republic and expose the baser motivations that inhibit community building.

One of the reasons that shock tactics are dangerous is that they are often rhetorically effective where more ethical modes of argumentation fail. Recent studies of shock tactics, for instance, often praise these messages for cogently persuading audiences. In this research, shocking imagery or fear appeals command the attention of the audience and motivate behavioral modifications. Often, the goal is to induce cooperation or move attitudes to further extremes.[17] For instance, road safety persuasive messages regularly rely on shocking imagery and have been relatively successful in shifting perspectives on drunk driving or distracted driving.[18] A study on smoking cessation proved that shocking imagery diminishes the intention to smoke when individuals believe they have self-efficacy against the threat, or the ability to prevent smoking.[19] Some scholars even go so far as to suggest that shock tactics are necessary to change behavior given audience complacency.[20] One study from 2013 asserted that audiences had become "inherently more accepting of shock advertising than expected," especially when the cause was deemed worthwhile.[21] In this sense, shock tactics have become a significant persuasive strategy for provoking public conversations about social issues. As a result, shock tactics have re-emerged as a popular trend in marketing and elsewhere—downgraded from destructive propagandistic messages to a useful means of inciting cooperation.

Reactive outcomes are so common that these possibilities can be anticipated by persuaders. Studies of fear appeals often show that these messages can backfire—and do so with enough routine frequency that a particular type of response may be predicted. With most fear appeals, the aim is to target those individuals with limited knowledge of a given issue and install new attitudes based on their dramatic reaction to the appeal. Yet, fear appeals can induce the audience to recoil from the message and possibly engage in defiant behavior. For instance, Ioni M. Lewis and colleagues found that young males were less persuaded by physical threats (e.g., injury or physical impairment caused by drunk driving) as they may feel "less vulnerable" to such perils.[22] Other studies argue that audiences will reject shocking messages because they distrust the source, or employ counter-interpretations of the message.[23] Such a likelihood is echoed in earlier propaganda studies wherein disinformation strategies precipitated likely audience response.[24] This research evidences the anticipatory tactics at stake in shocking imagery. Some messages forecast the likely reactions of the audience to invite desired outcomes.

Recuperating the insidious aspect of fear-appeal propaganda, memes are often designed to create a backlash. As with our discussion of lulz, the goal is often to anger and offend outsiders. Yet, the anticipatory design of some memes is distinct from the lulz framework we described previously in that anticipatory messages aim to induce a specific response: leftist outrage. And it is this inducement to enmity that allows the Alt-right to further demonize the left to mainstream and conservative audiences. The memes analyzed in this chapter deploy shock and outrage for these purposes of alienation. Thus, while shock tactics and the like have long been used in propaganda, this chapter analyzes the specific rhetorical mechanisms at stake in Alt-right memes. Namely, these images turn agonism into antagonism through their astute understanding of predictable audience response.

The memes we study in this chapter are not crafted to merely attract those who hold similar beliefs but to anticipate and redirect outsider reactions. Memes are deft rhetorical artifacts precisely because they are polysemous and multifunctional. Yet, antagonistic memes often engage in trolling or other purposefully nefarious behavior by presenting shocking imagery. As memetic strategies from a given group endure, meme creators understand that their audiences are manifold. Within /pol/ and r/the_donald/, there are ample discussions of how to alienate outsiders with outrageous images. Many Alt-right memes seem to seek vitriolic responses. The messaging strategy of these memes cultivates discord or anger to drive a wedge between leftist and centrist audiences, at which point Alt-right memes may attract the interest and affiliation of these latent publics. Ultimately, Alt-right meme enthusiasts have operationalized the boomerang effect for the cause.

To grasp how this form of alienation works, it is important to explain the nuanced mechanisms of audience formation. If Mouffe and others are correct that alienation among peoples can produce toxic antagonisms, then the rhetorical invitations seeking such alienation must be studied. Rhetorical scholars have long analyzed how scare tactics foster alienation or identification among audiences. Kenneth Burke theorized that identification and alienation are joined in the same symbolic rhetorical tactic.[25] Burke argued that humans connect with one another to overcome their necessary separation. Symbolic identification expresses the drive to unite despite differences—alienation and identification are predicated on one another. Significantly, the alienation that drives a desire for identification is never subsumed; alienation urges audiences toward symbolic union. For Burke that alienation can be strategically used to separate and divide peoples. Scapegoating, for instance, is a way to bolster symbolic identification by exploiting the work of division.[26] Tyrants decry scapegoats as impediments to the success of the community. That rhetorical move jettisons a group from the community as it simultaneously congeals a new set of peoples as a collective. The Janus-coin to collective belonging, then, is division or alienation. Identification of a collective can rely on the violent exclusion of a set of others, often those others are already at risk given their marginal status. Rhetorical modes of address of this sort enable identification, yet that coming together may also dramatically alienate and imperil others.

The antagonism of politics is forged through such symbolic dialectics of identification and alienation. As Carl Schmitt famously argued, the political "can be understood only in the context of the ever-present possibility of the friend-and-enemy grouping."[27] The political is predicated on relations of similarity and difference. Conflict and contestation, or *agon*, is essential to the productive possibilities of democratic action. Democratic forms of governance rely on political differences to be agonistically debated. Yet, often agonism turns into antagonism and undermines foundational democratic praxis. Within such discursive machinations, groupings of friend and enemy are forged and re-forged. Agonism and antagonism are part and parcel of how citizens identify with one another and divide themselves from others. Political contestation, then, is situated within and against the ways peoples come together and separate themselves. On our view, those identifications and divisions are forged through rhetorical discourses and practices. Those operations include traditional actions such as voting, protesting, and lobbying but also extend to such practices as speeches, political advertisements, and even memes. Rhetoric—as material and symbolic action—is the key mechanism that enables and constrains identification and division among the populace.

The rhetorical work that generates friend-enemy distinctions impacts processes of democratic inclusion. Schmitt critiqued the foundations of liberal democracy to illuminate the paradox at the heart of liberal democracy: that enemyship both generated and undermined the people's democratic governance. Grand promises of inclusion are curtailed by the political implications of an "us" opposed to "them." Mouffe suggests that Schmitt stressed the argument "that the identity of a democratic political community hinges on the possibility of drawing a frontier between 'us' and 'them.'"[28] In this sense, "democracy always entails relations of inclusion-exclusion" and liberal theories of inclusion are unable to "tackle adequately" this boundary that "contradicts its universalistic rhetoric."[29] For Schmitt, this paradox undermines the foundations of liberalism and ensures its ultimate end. Inclusion cannot be offered when the political itself is premised on a symbolic jettison. For our purposes, the rhetorical articulation of the frontier—the friend and enemy—plays into the way the left is alienated and undercut by Alt-right discourse.

The rhetorical maneuvers of Alt-right memes both prey upon and redraw the lines between friend and enemy. This memetic process of identification is based on division—another audience is positioned as antithetical to the symbolic union of the Alt-right. Within this worldview, the left is the outside frontier that must be railed against. As we discussed in chapter two, such positioning enables the Alt-right to congeal as a collective and further shifts public discourse to the right. Yet, this positioning also alienates leftist perspectives from the mainstream. Alt-right memes inoculate viewers from such discourse and demonize the left to corral and curtail social advocacy. In this way, shocking memes invite left-wing actors to react in ways that reduce the efficacy of their influence with mainstream audiences. Rejoinders from the Alt-right or even the mainstream right further alienate and rework contemptuous responses. The left is caricatured as a monolith while particular reactions simultaneously reinforce such a stereotype. The Alt-right manages the nature of these interactions and thereby the terms through which effective response can occur.

Overall the effect is not simply to entertain members of the Alt-right—though such interactions do just that—but rather to lure mainstream or undecided audiences to denounce the left. Part of the allure of these memes, then, is to demonize the left in two ways. First, these memes caricature left-wing arguments and situate the left as ridiculous and bombastic. Second, these memes provoke reactions that—often regardless of their specific content—can be retooled for further mockery. In effect, these propaganda messages use alienation of the enemy to entrench cultural and social divisions. It is this divisive rhetorical enterprise that exacerbates the conditions preventing productive public discourse and fortifies political partisanship. Moreover, the Alt-right deploys these strategies of enemyship to attract those who may have no understanding of the origins or purpose of the message proper but are stirred by what may be seen as hyperbolic reactions. In this sense, the possibility of common ground is eroded and public discourse is remanded to that of ridicule. Indeed, the "triggering" of liberals is key to deploying identity-based claims that further the alienation of the left and widen the audience for Alt-right memes.

Liberals Are Easy to Trigger

Alt-right memes regularly paint the left as an enemy in broad strokes. The left is comprised of "snowflakes" who are too invested in their feelings and therefore easy to "trigger."[30] As a category of meaning, "snowflakes" references the idea that liberals see themselves as unique and special individuals. "Trigger" suggests that liberals can be aggravated or potentially traumatized by speech or actions that exclude them or fail to recognize their unique experiences. These terms draw upon a broader parody of the left as political correctness police: liberals are purportedly focused on correcting inappropriate language and offensiveness.[31] Moreover, triggered snowflakes are delicate, unable to get their hands dirty in the real politics of the day. In this depiction, the left is not pursuing arguments of inclusion or drawing attention to oppressive practices but exist instead as ill-informed, fascist thought police unable or unwilling to engage with politics as they operate for the (rhetorically constructed) majority. It matters not that there is an inherent tension in this characterization of the left—e.g., that leftists are somehow powerful enough to quash dissent but unable to engage in politics proper. What matters here is the rhetorical effects of this positioning: the location of the left as an elitist, out-of-touch group responsible for political division.

The overarching effect of this caricature is to create the grounds of opposition between the left and the Alt-right. If the left is demeaned as fascists that are inclusive of all ideas *but* those of the right, then they are hypocrites. Moreover, by demonizing the left, the Alt-right can proclaim moral ground: namely, that member's own identities (e.g., whiteness) or advocacies (e.g., traditionalism) are under attack. The so-called left's claims of oppression and exclusion are characterized as part and parcel of excluding others, especially the Alt-right. This discourse draws the lines of both engagement and enemyship. Meanwhile, larger issues of concern are superseded in the reclamation of identity claims by those who insist whiteness, maleness, and traditionalism are marginalized. Any response that denounces these advocacies is further proof of an ongoing war, with the left at fault.

Games of brinkmanship abound in political discourse, encouraging an embrace of a war within the nation. Mouffe describes how the fall of the enemy other—the Communist bloc—created the conditions in which liberal democracies would find an "enemy within."[32] She articulates how immigrants were disparaged as a threat to national identity by those claiming to be "pure" Europeans.[33] A number of factors motivated locating enemies within: from the rise of populist claims and a distrust of experts alongside the weakening of the press and the flailing actions of political parties.[34] Citizens began to not only distrust one another but to see oppositional political beliefs or certain identities as ultimate enemies. This internalized battle redirected nationalistic impulses toward incredible divisiveness. This same effect has occurred in the United States both historically and in the present moment. Current efforts to vilify an internal enemy (the left generally, and those for whom they advocate, in particular) proves evident in discourse both from internal groups and agents (e.g., the Tea Party) as well as from international parties (e.g., the Internet Research Agency). Longstanding political antagonism within the United States has generated a combative understanding wherein citizens of different political persuasions view one another as enemies. Taken together, this framework defined and has continued to define the relationships within American politics. There are two pernicious effects to such a framework of enemyship. First, such antagonism has heightened political division. Second, and relatedly, this framework of emnity exacerbates the conditions in which meme based propaganda could influence public discourse. Memetic propaganda strategies operationalize political divisions by aggrandizing the symbolism of enemyship. Meme warfare preys upon and entrenches a dogmatic divide between peoples to the detriment of the democratic experiment.

Memes have already been theorized as a key tool of enemyship, particularly as a form of psychological warfare. In Winter 2015, for instance, an entire issue of NATO's official *Defence Strategic Communications* journal attended to weaponizing the affordances of digital media. The journal contains a now well-circulated essay entitled "It's time to embrace memetic warfare." In it, Jeff Giesea notes the flexibility of the meme as a modality for transmitting information, whipping up emotion as propaganda, and even manipulating the psyche. For Giesea, memes are psychological warfare:

> Memetic warfare, as I define it, is competition over narrative, ideas, and social control in a social-media battlefield. One might think of it as a subset of 'information operations' tailored to social media. Information operations involve the collection and dissemination of information to establish a competitive advantage over an opponent. Memetic warfare could also be viewed as a 'digital native' version of psychological warfare, more commonly known as propaganda. If propaganda and public diplomacy are conventional forms of memetic warfare, then trolling and PSYOPs are guerrilla versions…The online battlefield of perception will only grow in importance in both warfare and diplomacy.[35]

Giesea suggests that memetic warfare is an incredibly useful supplement in the battle to reduce the influence of Daesh.[36] He understands memes as exemplary tools in the work of enemyship. As he wrote, "But for many of us in the social media world, it seems obvious that more aggressive communication tactics and broader warfare through trolling and memes is a necessary, inexpensive, and easy way to help destroy the appeal and morale of our common enemies."[37] Memes, then, define the enemy and set the stage for ongoing communicative battles.

Significantly, Giesea would later emerge as a spokesman for the Alt-right's public image strategy—one that depends heavily on exacerbating political divides. By 2016, Giesea would become well known as the "Man [Who] Helped Build The Trump Meme Army."[38] He is also one of the planners of the Deploraball and a co-founder, with conspiracy theorist and Alt-lite writer Mike Cernovich, of MAGA3X, a group dedicated to using social media amplification and memes to facilitate Trump's platform.[39] Giesea's efforts focused on memes that situated the left as those who censor and smear the Alt-right. In a radio interview for American University, Giesea described how the left marginalizes the Alt-right. As one commentator of the interview wrote, "In response to a question about why people may struggle when having conversations with white nationalists, he said, 'Even using the label white nationalist is a way to *otherize* someone, to *marginalize* them and to shut down any argument [emphasis added].'"[40] Giesea's positioning obviously claims victimhood for those who espouse white nationalism. Mirroring larger trends, these tactics appropriate the language and function of anti-discrimination. For instance, right leaning groups have filed cases demanding a right to discriminate, arguing that anti-discrimination laws impede their freedoms.[41] Legal and other advocacy strategies are reworked for regressive politics. But more importantly, the tactic establishes the lines of enemyship. Much as with Giesea's argument for foreign intervention, he distinguishes the left as an internal enemy—those who inhibit dialogue by labeling or otherizing. Giesea's memes often worked in similar ways. As such, Giesea's visual memes and discursive claims helped define the left as villains of the American *demos*, thereby shaping the ground of response.

For the Alt-right, memetic PSYOPS entrench disaffection and precipitate political alienation and isolation. The aim is to erode the so-called left's "safe spaces" such that individuals are goaded to respond publicly. This mode of engagement is central to the way /pol/ and r/the_donald/ users understand their work. As one /pol/ user posted,

> This is psychological warfare, to cause as much psychic damage as possible to them. Put another way, its removing the amount of ground they have to stand on, mentally speaking. It will elicit fear and paranoia in them; "even my bastions of liberal thought and ideas are turning against me!" This is fighting dirty, but it will definitely fuck with some people, further weakening the left. The left has been fighting dirty and have been corrupt for decades though, so its only fair IMO we act in self-defense for ourselves, our ideas, and our country. It is time we started using their psyop weapons against them.[42]

Giesea's discussion of PSYOPS bears strong affinities with this comment. The battle between the Alt-right and the left is positioned as a war reliant upon psychological weaponry. Here, memes are one way to fight dirty. These images are the weapon of choice in the battle for ideas. Carefully crafted memes enable the Alt-right to rework bastions of liberal thought into its own propaganda. In this comment, the left's tactics are lionized as effective counter intelligence while simultaneously appropriated for the work of the Alt-right. Memetic propaganda provokes liberals with their own tools and thereby gains "competitive advantage."[43] The left is remanded to a limited place of engagement—they are isolated tactically and psychologically.

If ostensible leftists or liberals react to this weaponry, their response becomes another form of psychological warfare. The Alt-right mocks counter actions to malign the left for moderate audiences, who are positioned to find such reactions abhorrent. One /pol/ member echoed the idea of psychic damage, writing, "Libs love seeing themselves as part of 'the Resistance,' witnessing a role reversal will at best fire up their neurons, at worst trigger them to no end."[44] The use of the word triggering indicates the second purpose of memetic enmity: to attract those who might be moved incrementally to the right and to repel those who are ostensibly disaffected by the meme. As encapsulated by one anonymous poster, "We're fine when it comes to pushing moderates to the right, the left is doing that for us with their riots. We need to get normies to share anti-left memes involving the things the left love to take away their escapism."[45] As made clear here, this propaganda often works by staying several steps ahead of the (leftist) target, by understanding how a certain group might respond and designing communiqués that capitalize on this thread of discourse. Prompting liberal reactions that might alienate moderates is, for the Alt-right, a successful PSYOPS intervention.

Provoking outrage has another important function. As we outlined at the start of this chapter, outside reactions amplify attention to Alt-right discourse. Anything that effectively compels an exaggerated reaction often broadens the scope of media coverage.[46] With the "It's Okay to be White" posters found across high school and college campuses (including at one of the authors' institutions), media attention proved of greater rhetorical consequence than the message itself. Once the media flagged arguments that could be construed by the Alt-right as anti-white, the terms of public deliberation shifted. Importantly, that shift was valanced against the left in favor of the Alt-right. Consider what happens to arguments about whiteness as Tucker Carlson is supplied opportunity to assess the main message of "It's Okay to Be White," while decrying censorship by school leaders. Carlson's coverage centers on the supposedly intractable nature of whiteness and obfuscates any other discussion on racism. Such reporting only further enables affective attachment to whiteness alongside the demonization of liberals. But more importantly, Carlson has bolstered a fallacious claim into one of national importance. The idea that liberals are shutting down free speech by policing particular identities and language has been popular in public discourse for quite some time.[47] With Alt-right memes, the left's exaggerated reaction is crucial to portraying the Alt-right as a movement with the power and agility to take down the fascism of the left. As Jared Holt, a research associate with People for the American Way told *Salon*, "Every time, someone on Twitter would take a picture of the sign and express that it was racist," those who put up or believed in the "alt-right posters," could "chalk that up as a win," because they want to convince people that "liberals are actively working against white people."[48] Trolling actions such as the posters cue the media to cover absurd proclamations of white supremacy on the terms demanded by white supremacists.

Repeatedly, memetic battles often demonstrate that the Alt-right has been relatively successful in determining the rules of engagement—even and especially when leftist memes are present. The lines of enemyship—the brandishing of claim and counterclaim—have been delimited by the use of memes to characterize the left in particular ways. Consider, for instance, a story from August 2017 entitled, "Trump Thanks Putin for Expelling U.S. Diplomats."[49] The story ran on all of *The Hill's* social media platforms. In the comments section of the article on Facebook, a meme battle erupted with apparently liberal memes winning the ground game. Comments often used memes as arguments against other commentators. One Trump supporter set the terms of engagement by writing, "Never mind me…I'm just here to watch the liberal tools meltdown! Thanks THE HILL! This is my daily comedy…you know many of them are having strokes and heart attacks over your constant posting of 'ShitToMakeLiberalsMeltdown right?'"[50] Responses to this user's repeated assertions of liberal intolerance and softness appropriated the language of "triggering" and brandished it against Trump supporters. Such engagement exemplified antagonism, not agonism, as none of the responses discussed the ideas of the article—consideration of the impact of the removal of diplomats or a robust interrogation of Trump's relationship with Putin. Instead, the memes themselves were a series of *ad hominem* attacks. These attacks accused liberals of being intolerant and easily triggered while Trump supporters were called ignorant. Given these responses, it seems that posters easily succumbed to simplistic patterns of enemyship. Ostensibly leftist responses did not undermine the snowflake caricature nor successfully reconfigure the nature of public discourse on the news. Of course, there is no way to know if those who effectively articulated the snowflake framework within this exchange are avowed white nationalists, members of the Alt-right, or Russian trolls. Yet, the memetic exchange indicates how oppositional actors have been pushed into defense with little effective offense.

Ultimately, stereotypes of the left and media savvy tactics create a groundswell of public attention that revels in the left's outrage. For instance, certain meme images appear regularly to strengthen the snowflake association. One snowflake meme is a still shot from *Willie Wonka and the Chocolate Factory*. The image voices Wonka (Gene Wilder) reading the caption "You're a special snowflake? Tell me about how unique that makes you" (See Fig. 5.2). Another includes an infant crying with the mouth contorted into a deep frown. That image is often coupled with phrases about "social justice warriors" and other insults that depict liberals, especially younger liberals, as unable to handle even the mildest of insults.[51] Captions read, "I'm so butthurt that trump won," and "I need a Safe Space. I need free tuition. I need people to value me just because I exist. I can't tolerate criticism. I require coddling."[52] The implication of these images suggests that liberals are not equipped to engage in acceptable political or public discourse without resorting to tears or outrage. In response to this cultural *mythos*, purposefully provoking the left has become a past-time for Alt-right social media users and others. With Alt-right memes, that provocation supplies a critical mass of public attention to revel in this caricature and entrench the battle lines. Indeed, *The Guardian* reported that the word "snowflake" had become the most popular insult of 2016.[53] As rebuke, the term leaves little room for deliberation insofar as "there's really no comeback to it."[54] If you say you are offended, you have proven that you are a snowflake. If you critique the term as a silencing mechanism, you have highlighted your aggrieved nature.

Given the popularity of the insult, it is not surprising that snowflake memes have proliferated. It seems that reveling in the mockery of purportedly entitled, young leftists has become exceedingly popular.

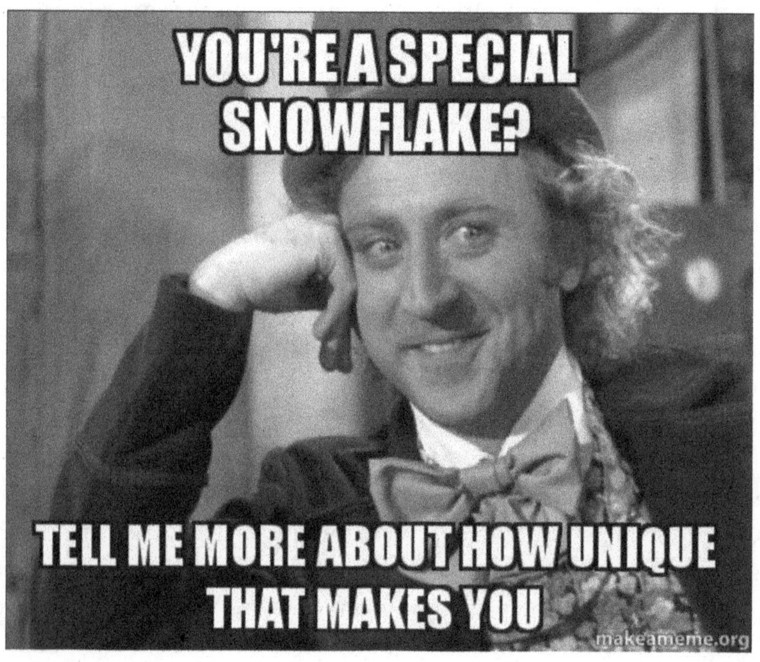

Figure 5.2: Snowflake Meme.

Triggering so-called liberals, then, has become part and parcel of the Alt-right memetic lobby. Alt-right memes often advertise the ways pro-Trump actions have triggered or melted snowflakes. One popular meme capitalizes on Trump's offensiveness to the left. A still shot of the film *It's a Wonderful Life* superimposes the caption, "Teacher says every time Trump tweets a snowflake melts."[55] Another meme contrasts a photo of James Van Der Beek crying with the phrase, "Stop making fun of me. I'm a delicate snowflake."[56] These memes are ubiquitous and located on nearly every social media platform and available for replication through a simple search. If these memes have successfully entrenched or amplified the claim of liberal sensitivity, nearly any critique against oppression is lodged as a mere complaint from a delicate snowflake unprepared for the "real world." Such framing has been so effective that others have used the metaphor to mark the supposed weaknesses of Trump supporters. After Mike Pence was booed at a *Hamilton* performance, a number of memes delighted in calling both Trump and Pence snowflakes.[57] The label has stuck to a multitude of public figures and political groups. In effect, the label of snowflake and the memes that embolden such name-calling have structured the way political discourse has proceeded. However, despite attempts to rework the snowflake meme, the Alt-right has been most successful at linking leftist politics to fragility and hysteria. At the same time that the left is critiqued for an affective attachment to politics, the Alt-right benefits from politics organized around sensational feeling.

Alt-right memes demonstrate that the antagonism of the political has been reworked to focus on resentment. Via memes, the right accuses the left of focusing on feelings to the detriment of rights. Others argue that the right is similarly melted by the injustice of asking them to value others. Altogether, the framework of the meme has set the tone of public discourse. Terms such as "triggered" and "snowflake" proclaim the political meaningless of public feelings while at the same time enshrining feelings as the very basis of social groupings. Each memetic volley revolves around the wounds of resentment. As Jeremy Engels writes,

> the politics of resentment is one of the most powerful forms of rhetoric ever developed for frustrating the aspirations of American citizens and perpetuating our feelings of victimhood. This rhetoric keeps citizens so weak that we find it difficult to do anything productive about our frustration. The result is a general acquiescence punctuated by explosions of hateful affect. The politics of resentment makes democracy less dangerous to elites, while creating the perfect context for citizens to turn violently on one another.[58]

With snowflake memes, citizens wield memetic content against one another circulating around feelings of resentment—highlighting their own wounds and ridiculing others. The Alt-right has been relatively successful at setting an agenda for public discourse, one that uses memes to flippantly refer to these virulent antagonisms, in effect carrying the wound of whiteness to great political lengths while dismissing the complaints of others.

Overall, the use of memes to trigger liberals directs the PSYOPS weapons significant to state security agencies against other citizens. Agonism is marshaled into antagonism via the circulation of targeted memes. These memes often mark the wounds of the Alt-right to justify its hatred of those individuals who ostensibly imperil the republic through their demands. From a rhetorical perspective, these memes code resentment into new visual forms. The wound of *feeling* marginalized, unappreciated, labeled, is carried by the frame of the meme and duplicates the logics of recognizability therein. Judith Butler refers to recognizability as the conditions in which subjects become recognized as such, when life is manifest to others.[59] For her, there are normative conditions of recognizability that are replicated in the circulation of frames of viewing. Audiences employ and develop ways of seeing or interpretations of images based on frames. Here, the palpable hatred that has erupted through the work of the Tea Party, Trump's "Deplorables," and others is deployed through memes. Whereas not all citizens will make their animus toward fellow Americans or others manifest through personal displays of public outrage, memes allow those resentments to travel in a rhetorical form that reworks anger into a humorous, ironic frame that invites broader resonance among some publics, and which sows division among others. But, of course, Alt-right memes display a particular brand of resentment, one fashioned on identification with whiteness and an insistence that white people have suffered such that their resentment is justified.

The Politics of White Resentment

Resentment has become an incredibly palpable political emotion—one that regularly generates the divisions of friend and enemy in the current climate. In 1998, J. M. Barbalet defined resentment as "an emotional apprehension of departure from acceptable, desirable, proper, and rightful outcomes and procedures."[60] As Barbalet wrote, resentment is not neutral but arises from a perceived threat to formal and legal rights. Significantly, whiteness is an ideological structure that often precludes the recognition of current systems as unequal. In effect, attempts to level the playing field for those without access often fashion an emotional, public response: that of resentment. In these instances, resentment "reveals an investment in the maintenance of privilege rather than to universal equality."[61] As Frantz Fanon presciently argued, "there is always resentment in reaction."[62] In his work on anti-blackness and colonialism, Fanon referenced those who endured subjugation. Yet, in the present tense, that reactionary resentment has been adopted by those who identify with whiteness—a dominant and privileged subject position—and who see themselves far afield from the privileges promised within late capitalism.[63] With the Alt-right, resentment becomes mobilized through memetic forms that *seem* to neutralize the emotional core of these political antagonisms. Yet, Alt-right memes circulate the sensation of resentment brought to bear by supposed subjugation, effectively inverting similar claims from marginalized peoples. Memes that demonize the left suggest that arguments against the right, or more pointedly, against the Alt-right, are entirely emotional. Yet, these same memes disavow the emotional resentment that motivates the work of white nationalism. As we mentioned previously, fidelity to a non-contradictory ideology is not required given rapid and circuitous flows of memetic media. Conflictual messages often propagate exceptionally well. By and large Alt-right memes are designed to move quickly—regardless of their allegiance to a particular worldview. The travels of some popular Alt-right memes generate a chain reaction predicated on an emotional investment. Such circulation evidences how rhetorical strategies of resentment effectively widen Alt-right claims for a general audience, one invested in the supremacy of whiteness.

It is seemingly undeniable that resentment has become the emotion at the core of US politics. Engels acknowledges that resentment has "long been recognized by philosophers, political theorists, and rhetorical scholars to be among the most potent of all political emotions associated with democracy."[64] Whereas at one point in history, resentment was a limited political emotion, now politicians embrace resentment to "turn citizens against one another."[65] In some sense, resentment is a justified political response to "injustice and broken promises."[66] Citizens express resentment toward one another or to political leaders given a structural blockade of their own ambitions. As it relates to the politics of white nationalism, resentment becomes a palpable form of political organizing, suturing individuals to a larger sense of disenfranchisement. Hua Hsu for the *New Yorker* writes,

> For poor and working-class whites, skin color no longer feels like an implicit guarantor of privilege. There is a sense that others, thanks to affirmative action or lax immigration policies, have nudged ahead of them on the ladder of social ascent. Their whiteness is, in fact, the very reason they suspect that they are under siege…they have begun to understand themselves in terms of identity politics. It almost doesn't matter whether their suspicions are true in a strictly material sense. The accident of white skin still brings with it economic and social advantages, but resentment is a powerful engine, particularly when the view from below feels unprecedented.[67]

Carol Anderson points out that, historically, any advancement for people of color has faced a tremendous backlash in the form of white rage.[68] White rage expresses resentment toward and uses violence against people of color to restore the purportedly lost place of whiteness. All the while, these forms of white supremacy, she argues, find ways to become more powerful, even if less overt.[69]

Memes have become the latest modality of white rage to mobilize resentment as a powerful political weapon. With Alt-right memes, resentment breeds antagonism among the *demos* such that opposition is ridiculed and minimized. In this latest tactic of enemyship, Alt-right modes of discourse constrain counter-attacks. As we demonstrated in chapter three, if outsiders participate in these same modes of response, their arguments are often unable to overcome the original terms of debate. Resentment in meme form, then, limits how actors typically counter white nationalists. From a rhetorical vantage point, the importance of the asserted divisions between the right and the left not only define friend from enemy but also illustrate the ways resentment hinders public discourse. As manifest in memes, resentment circles the victim status in such a way that political alliances are predicated on an attachment to woundedness.

Alt-right memes use several strategies to divide the *demos* and minimize rebuke. For instance, amplifying victimhood is a common meme strategy used to divide and conquer those who would censure the Alt-right. One meme in this vein uses the image of a disheveled history professor, who asks, "So you mean to tell me that if I say White Lives Matter I am racist?!?!?!"[70] In this image, a twisted logic proclaims name-calling as an act deserving of ridicule. The meme presumes that being called a racist is ludicrous if one is simply proclaiming that one's life matters. Despite only comprising thirteen percent of the population, black folks are thirty-one percent of those who are murdered at the hands of police, thirty-nine percent of that group have been killed but did not approach or attack a police officer or officers.[71] The White Lives Matter history professor meme sidesteps the motivation for the original rhetorical demand to value black lives.[72] The claim of racism is used to level the playing field such that violence against and the death of black citizens is rendered akin to being called a racist.[73] This image draws on the politics of victimhood as it simultaneously demeans those politics said to be predicated on victimhood. In effect, this meme marks lines of enemyship by amplifying the wound of ontological misrecognition.

The paradox of victimhood is often the mode of engagement central to these kinds of Alt-right memes. Such memes often lambast identity politics as claiming undeserved victimhood and yet that same victim status motivates these Alt-right memes and invites collective identification with the feeling of disenfranchisement. In rhetorical studies, Burke argues that rhetorical forms allow a community to demarcate itself through symbolic modes of identification and purification. One method is victimage where the impure element is jettisoned from the community; the other is to cleanse oneself of impurity through symbolic death.[74] There is a paradox at the heart of such purification rituals, such that absolution from the impurity is nearly impossible. In *A Grammar of Motives*, Burke writes about the nature of the *agon*, or dramatic conflict, wherein the protagonist is motivated by the nature of the antagonist.[75] Their motives pollute one another. Burke's analysis explains why pointed critique of violence and subjugation finds its mirror in the Alt-right. Moreover, with Alt-right memes, the status of victimhood pollutes the motives of the image itself. The victim is not the person who must demand recognition of their very life but the person who has been called a racist. Claiming marginalization by being called a racist is polluted by the original demand to recognize the evils of racism separating the community, commonly through violence and death. The politics of resentment come to the fore as the motive force for these imagaic attachments. Those who identify with the meme become attached to the demands entailed in recognizing one's life as valuable. That demand is based on resentment such that the same demand for others becomes illegitimate and situated as infringing on white lives. Ultimately, whiteness is sutured to the work of resentment via memetic address.

These reactionary memes circulate discourse undergirding white supremacy through a politics of resentment. Such frames of resentment travel to outside audiences, who then may use these frames to interpret social and cultural issues. For instance, the White Lives Matter meme forwards ways of understanding what counts as a legitimate claim of aggrievement—those proclaiming "black lives matter" or those called racist. Obviously, the stakes of these demands are dramatically uneven. Being called a racist does not imperil one's life whereas the structures of racism do extract life and liberties. The meme reroutes white privilege through the memetic structures of circulation we discussed in chapter four. As with historical enactments of white supremacy, these modes of rhetorical discourse have fashioned new ways to suppress progress and galvanize a collective will against such progress. With memes, mockery of the left or other modes of antagonism provide cover for novel white supremacist advocacies. Jason Wilson argues that members of the Alt-right don't just replicate white supremacy—they retool it. As he writes, "In other words, troll culture became a way for fascism to hide in plain sight."[76] Significant to this mode of white supremacy is the ability of the Alt-right to create normative ways of framing and justifying white supremacist advocacies. In this worldview, it is unjust to be called a racist simply because one values whiteness.[77] Similarly, claims made by those who fight systematic injustice are not salient means of making the nation great (again), but rather emblematic of those who choose victimhood. In effect, whiteness is to be preserved while so-called liberals and those who fight for "identity politics" are always already contrarian, even as both affirmative and negative understandings of this interplay are predicated on the dialectic of victimage.

Memes that outrage often do so by posturing the right as victims of the left. As Gillian Tett argues in the *Financial Times*, "The alt-right has swelled in power by presenting itself as a victim of elitist attacks, and the memes are so potent precisely because they are designed to be subversive and to bait their opponents into a reaction."[78] The strategy is a tautologically brilliant rhetorical construction that positions the beneficiaries of white supremacy as victims and simultaneously baits a response that entrenches the claim to victimhood. Virtually *any* response understood as a denouncement or ridicule warrants the original claim of marginality. In many ways, perceived ridicule fosters broader identification. These users often explicitly take a page from Saul Alinsky's playbook, *Rules for Radicals*: "The job of the organizer," Alinksy contends, "is to maneuver and bait the establishment so that it will publicly attack him as a 'dangerous enemy.'"[79] Alinksy himself has stated that "Today, my notoriety and the hysterical instant reaction of the establishment not only validate my credentials of competency but also ensure automatic popular invitation."[80] The rhetorical construction of the right as legitimate victims plays into a populist appeal for support. The claim suggests true radicals are the Alt-right, who are made victims by questioning progressive logics.

The proclamation of victimhood entrenches political polarization and pushes moderates further right. Matt Goerzen supplies a detailed explanation of the means through which this strategy works. He explains,

> To spread this conception to a wider audience, the Right hit on an effective strategy: they could exploit the liberal media's obsession with novelty and bleeding ledes to piggyback anti-liberal ideas into the mainstream on the back of "start-over monikers" like "alt-right" and transgressive memes like Pepe the Frog. And in so doing, they could mobilize existing antagonisms toward the political establishment, cultures of political correctness, and globalization, ultimately baiting the liberal media into revealing inconsistencies that could act as catalysts for their own, alternative platforms—or, as the Right might put it, effectively seizing the "memes of production."[81]

Indeed, by using shocking memes that position the collective as victim to a hysterical left, the Alt-right is able to both garner media attention and invite a predictable reaction. Simultaneously, these shocking messages bolster those antagonisms between political camps. By drawing on hatreds of political correctness and the establishment, those who would spread Alt-right memes create broader audience identification. Fledgling claims of distrust and marginality are aggrandized by inviting a whole host of audiences to identify with the tyranny of the left. In effect, those who associate with victimhood via white resentment amplify a sense of marginalization into one of utter disenfranchisement.

The success of this tactic is so well known that it was exploited by Russian operatives attempting to influence foreign democratic procedures. The Internet Research Agency placed a large number of advertisements on Facebook and Instagram that used identity politics in their appeals. The majority of ads placed in 2016 fanned division: bolstering nationalism in white, conservative voters through campaigns to make blue lives matter while simultaneously drawing attention to police brutality and invoking refrains of black lives matter.[82] Messages focused on a distrust of fellow citizens and the current injustices of the nation. For black voters, Russian strategies aimed to keep citizens away from the polls. For white voters, Russian messages stoked chauvinism and a fear of all immigrants and minorities.[83] Their ads "used vicious stereotypes and scare tactics: they mocked gays, smeared immigrants, invoked the devil, and portrayed Hillary Clinton as in league with Muslim terrorists."[84] These messages did not simply encourage citizens to vote for Trump—though they often did so—but rather sowed discord in favor of reactionary politics. As *Wired* reported of these advertisements and memes, "they tear at the parts of the American social fabric that are already worn thin, stoking outrage about police brutality or the removal of Confederate statues."[85] Russian propaganda drew on claims of victimhood and woundedness to bolster antagonisms and ultimately, push for the election of Donald Trump.

Given these specific tactical uses, memes can build on existing resentments through quotidian, often mundane modes of address. The memes that show up on one's Facebook, Twitter, or Instagram feed amplify existent modes of identification and cultivate distrust of one's fellow Americans. These images are not convincing audiences to radically change their worldviews overall. Instead, these images weaponize lines of alliances between friends and enemies. Alt-right memes specifically posit the left as jeopardizing the nation. Meanwhile, Russia augmented the right's hatred of the left while portraying the nation as one that, for democrats and other voters, was unworthy of saving. These images aggrandized and entrenched ongoing antagonisms. Memes of this sort anticipated angry reactions and used malevolent messages to upend the foundations for more inclusive deliberation. Often, these strategies revolved around the status of victimhood and claims of disenfranchisement. By positing the right or even conservative voters as victims and then provoking actions that proved that marginality, Alt-right memes effectively played out the politics of white resentment.

White Resentment Left Unchecked

Discussing the "Its Okay to be White" posters, journalist Amanda Marcotte suggested the overall strategy was to play up the status of victimhood. Whether disseminated via sticker, poster, tweet, or meme, Marcotte argued this message, "is part of a larger strategy aimed at garnering sympathy from mainstream conservatives, or 'normies': Rather than argue directly for racist or fascist beliefs, 'alt-righters' paint themselves as victims of 'political correctness,' playing directly to the conservative longing to believe that liberals are the intolerant bad guys in our national drama."[86] Political scientist Cas Mudde situates this phenomenon as having deep roots in the European far right. For decades, Mudde explains, this effort has redefined "who is the real victim" with "the argument…that political correctness has ruined everything, that minorities get everything and if white people speak out about it they're hit with political correctness."[87] These authors suggest, correctly, that the Alt-right reconfigures victimhood to attract a broader audience and entrench political division.

And yet a key part of this victimhood is the rhetorical hinge that enables this status to be claimed ostensibly legitimately: provocative techniques that alienate the so-called left. The status of victimhood is wrapped up in the antagonisms of political division and the work of white resentment. Mouffe claims that political antagonisms are predicated on sustaining the injuries of the party system and the treatment of compatriots as enemies, rather than people with whom one disagrees. For instance, the battle that rages in public discourse over terms such as "snowflake" or the idea that individuals can be "triggered" is a proxy war for the politics of resentment. The goal is to demean the other side such that the debate is one of pure enemyship. Agonism becomes antagonism and the battle lines remain entrenched with each new memetic PSYOPS weapon. Memes have become one way that the politics of white resentment circulates to broader audiences. These audiences are encouraged to take up normative frameworks that justify their own victimhood and strengthen partisanship and alienation of others. Memes help white resentment gain a stronger foothold in the public imagination, all while appearing glib and non-threatening.

Memetic weaponry entrenches the lines of attachment to white resentment. For instance, as we finished writing this chapter, one of us noticed that a conservative Facebook friend shared an image that was direct Russian propaganda—confirmed by the House in its investigation. When informed that this image was a Russian meme, this friend doubled down on the message of the meme, embracing its hatred of both Muslims and liberals while simultaneously proclaiming that "everything is Russia's fault these days," lamenting the removal of confederate monuments and prayer from public schools, and noting that "I just don't get it anymore."[88] This white, conservative citizen displayed all of the hallmarks of white resentment in one short post. He was attached to the feeling that he had lost something—he didn't "get it" anymore, his reality structure had been negatively impacted (if not totally upended), and he blamed these problems squarely on others, especially liberals and Muslims.[89] This, all the while eschewing the fact that he was amplifying Russian propaganda. Thus, even when memes are revealed to be false provocations, the resonance of white resentment they circulate proves intractable. The propagandistic meme was not removed, nor altered, but rather embraced for voicing white resentment—even if the former marine who posted it was a tool of the Russians.

Of course, this marine is not the only Facebook user who evidences the way memetic propaganda entrenches white resentment. In February 2018, CNN reporter Drew Griffin questioned a Trump supporter who had led a Facebook group entitled "Trump Team Broward County."[90] As a leader of this page, Florine Gruen Goldfarb had shared a number of Russian memes from the page "Being Patriotic."[91] When the reporter told Goldfarb that some of the images she had shared on Facebook were Russian propaganda, she said "I don't care if they were involved or not. That's, that to me that is the least important thing."[92] When pressed, she then refused to believe that she had shared Russian propaganda, claiming, "They were not Russians. I don't go with Russians."[93] She asserted repeatedly that all of her Facebook friends who participated were Trump supporters and not Russian trolls. Her insistence that everyone was a Trump supporter bespeaks the importance of the audience's attachment to their own authenticity, even when its (false) construction is laid bare. From this perspective, Goldfarb rejected the notion that such images were Russian given that Goldfarb could not understand herself as a pawn in the game of memes.

We must consider, then, that fact checking, the curtailing of Russian propaganda, or even the censorship of explicit white supremacist messages cannot undo the damage already done. Memes exacerbate existing antagonisms and attachments to the sense of marginalization expressed by the far right. Moreover, the popularity of Alt-right and adjacent memes hinder those modes of identification that foster robust democratic action. Indeed, as we will show in the conclusion, there is little broad understanding of the way memes play into antagonism or the available options for diminishing present divisions. As a result, we are left without the tools to change current crises or protect ourselves from outside actors. As scholars and as citizens, our goal in the final chapter, then, is to consider where we are and what we need to do to change today's dire circumstances.

Notes

1. Cassandra Arsenault and Keith Harrington, "White Supremacy Signs Appear on Boston College Campus Ahead of Protest," *NBC10 Boston*, October 20, 2017, http://www.nbcboston.com/news/local/White-Supremacy-Signs-On-Boston-College-Campus-451888233.html.
2. Madeleine D'Angelo and Alec Greaney, "Signs Supporting White Supremacy Appear at Starting Location of 'Silence Is Still Violence' March," *Heights*, October 20, 2017, http://bcheights.com/2017/10/20/signs-supporting-white-supremacy-appears-at-starting-location-of-silence-is-still-violence-march/.
3. "It's Okay to Be White," n.d., *Know Your Meme*, accessed January 26, 2018, http://knowyourmeme.com/memes/its-okay-to-be-white.
4. "It's Okay to Be White," *Know Your Meme*.
5. See, for example, "University of Regina is Removing 'It's Okay to Be White' Posters from Campus," *Regina Leader-Post*, November 23, 2017, http://leaderpost.com/business/university-of-regina-is-removing-its-okay-to-be-white-posters-from-campus; Abrielle Fulwider, "U Responds to 'It's Okay to Be White' Posters Found on Campus," *Daily Utah Chronicle*, November 10, 2017, http://dailyutahchronicle.com/2017/11/10/u-responds-to-its-okay-to-be-white-posters-found-on-campus/; Taylor Hartman, "Weber State Responds to 'It's Okay to Be White' Posters Found on Campus," *Fox13 Salt Lake City*, November 6, 2017, http://fox13now.com/2017/11/06/university-of-utah-responds-to-controversial-posters-found-on-campus/.
6. See, for example, Michael Harriot, "A Racist Flyer Might Cost Doug Jones the Election Because the Entire Democratic Party Is Trash," *The Root*, December 7, 2017, https://www.theroot.com/a-racist-flyer-might-cost-doug-jones-the-election-becau-1821065764; Nick Roll, "Campuses Plastered With 'OK to Be White' Signs," *Inside Higher Ed*, November 6, 2017, https://www.insidehighered.com/quicktakes/2017/11/06/campuses-plastered-%E2%80%98ok-be-white%E2%80%99-signs; Kianna Lanier, "Opinion: 'It's Okay to Be White' Posters Displayed throughout the Country," *The Cluster*, December 3, 2017, https://mercercluster.com/22952/opinions/opinion-its-okay-to-be-white-posters-displayed-throughout-the-country/.

7. Michael Edison Hayden, "'It's Okay to Be White': How Fox News Is Helping to Spread Neo-Nazi Propaganda," *Newsweek*, November 19, 2017, http://www.newsweek.com/neo-nazi-david-duke-backed-meme-was-reported-tucker-carlson-without-context-714655.
8. Carlos Maza, "Why White Supremacists Love Tucker Carlson," *Vox*, July 21, 2017, https://www.vox.com/videos/2017/7/21/16008190/strikethrough-white-supremacists-love-tucker-carlson.
9. Hayden, "'It's Okay to Be White': How Fox News Is Helping to Spread Neo-Nazi Propaganda."
10. Tim Squirrell, "Analysis of 500 Million Reddit Comments Shows How the Alt-Right Made the Alt-Left a Thing," *Quartz*, September 21, 2017, https://qz.com/1083444/analysis-of-500-million-reddit-comments-shows-how-the-alt-right-made-the-alt-left-a-thing/.
11. Wendy Brown, "Wounded Attachments," *Political Theory* 21, no. 3 (1993): 390–410.
12. Chantal Mouffe, *Agonistics: Thinking the World Politically* (Brooklyn, NY: Verso Books, 2013), 5.
13. J. Michael Sproule, *Propaganda and Democracy: The American Experience of Media and Mass Persuasion* (New York: Cambridge University Press, 1997); Thomas A. Hollihan, "Propagandizing in the Interest of the War: A Rhetorical Study of the Committee on Public Information," *Southern Speech Communication Journal* 49, no. 3 (1984): 241–57; Celia M. Kingsbury, *For Home and Country: World War I Propaganda on the Home Front* (Lincoln: University of Nebraska Press, 2010); Stuart Ewen, *Captains of Consciousness: Advertising and the Social Roots of the Consumer Culture* (New York: McGraw-Hill, 1976); Stewart Halsey Ross, *Propaganda for the Great War: How the United States Was Conditioned to Fight the Great War of 1914–1918* (Jefferson, NC: McFarland & Co, 1976); James J. Kimble, "Wither Propaganda? Agonism and 'The Engineering of Consent,'" *Quarterly Journal of Speech* 91, no. 2 (2005): 201–18; Harold D. Lasswell, *Propaganda Technique in the World War* (New York: Peter Smith, 1938); Arthur Ponsonby, *Falsehood in War-Time: Containing an Assortment of Lies Circulated throughout the Nations During the Great War* (New York: E.P. Dutton and Co., 1928); James Morgan Read, *Atrocity Propaganda, 1914–1919* (New Haven, CT: Yale University Press, 1941); Stephen Vaughn, *Holding Fast the Inner Lines: Democracy, Nationalism, and the Committee on Public Information* (Chapel Hill: University of North Carolina Press, 1980); Brett Gary, *The Nervous Liberals: Propaganda Anxieties from World War I to the Cold War* (New York: Columbia University Press, 1999).
14. Sproule, *Propaganda and Democracy*.
15. Ron Theodore Robin, *The Making of the Cold War Enemy* (Princeton, NJ.: Princeton University Press, 2001); Gary, *The Nervous Liberals*; Shawn J. Parry-Giles, *The Rhetorical Presidency, Propaganda, and the Cold War, 1945–1955* (Westport, CT: Greenwood Publishing Group, 2002); Nancy Bernhard, *U.S. Television News and Cold War Propaganda, 1947–1960* (New York: Cambridge University Press, 2003).
16. See, for example, Anthony DiMaggio, *The Rise of the Tea Party* (New York: Monthly Review Press, 2011); Geoffrey Kabaservice, *Rule and Ruin* (New York: Oxford University Press, 2012); Robert Faris *et al.*, "Partisanship, Propaganda, and Disinformation: Online Media and the 2016 U.S. Presidential Election," *SSRN Scholarly Paper* (Rochester, NY: Social Science Research Network, August 1, 2017), https://papers.ssrn.com/

abstract=3019414; Sheldon Rampton and John Clyde Stauber, *Weapons of Mass Deception* (New York: Penguin, 2003).

17. Sara Parry *et al.*, "'Shockvertising': An Exploratory Investigation into Attitudinal Variations and Emotional Reactions to Shock Advertising," *Journal of Consumer Behaviour* 12, no. 2 (2013): 112–21.
18. Ioni M. Lewis *et al.*, "Promoting Public Health Messages: Should We Move beyond Fear-Evoking Appeals in Road Safety?," *Qualitative Health Research* 17, no. 1 (2007): 61–74; Ioni Lewis *et al.*, "The Role of Fear Appeals in Improving Driver Safety: A Review of the Effectiveness of Fear-Arousing (Threat) Appeals in Road Safety Advertising," *The International Journal of Behavioral Consultation and Therapy* 3, no. 2 (2007): 203–222.
19. Simon Manyiwa and Ross Brennan, "Fear Appeals in Anti-Smoking Advertising: How Important Is Self-Efficacy?" *Journal of Marketing Management* 28, no. 11–12 (2012): 1419–37.
20. Özlem Sandıkcı, "Shock Tactics in Advertising and Implications for Citizen-Consumer," *International Journal of Humanities and Social Science* 1, no. 18 (2011): 42–50.
21. Parry *et al.*, "'Shockvertising.'"
22. Lewis *et al.*, "The Role of Fear Appeals in Improving Driver Safety."
23. Joseph Grandpre *et al.*, "Adolescent Reactance and Anti-Smoking Campaigns: A Theoretical Approach," *Health Communication* 15, no. 3 (2003): 349–466; James Price Dillard and Lijiang Shen, "On the Nature of Reactance and Its Role in Persuasive Health Communication," *Communication Monographs* 72, no. 2 (2005): 144–168; Stephen Bell, Andrew Hindmoor, and Frank Mols, "Persuasion as Governance: A State-Centric Relational Perspective," *Public Administration* 88, no. 3 (2010): 851–70; Stephen A. Rains and Monique Mitchell Turner, "Psychological Reactance and Persuasive Health Communication: A Test and Extension of the Intertwined Model," *Human Communication Research* 33, no. 2 (2007): 241–69; Sahara Byrne and Philip Solomon Hart, "The Boomerang Effect A Synthesis of Findings and a Preliminary Theoretical Framework," *Annals of the International Communication Association* 33, no. 1 (2009): 3–37.
24. See, for example, L. John Martin, "Disinformation: An Instrumentality in the Propaganda Arsenal," *Political Communication* 2, no. 1 (1982): 47–64; Faris *et al.*, "Partisanship, Propaganda, and Disinformation;" Alvin A. Snyder, *Warriors of Disinformation* (New York: Arcade Publishing, 1997).
25. Kenneth Burke, *A Rhetoric of Motives* (Berkeley: University of California Press, 1969), 22.
26. Kenneth Burke, *Permanence and Change* (Berkeley: University of California Press, 1984), 16.
27. Carl Schmitt, *The Concept of the Political* (Chicago, IL: University of Chicago Press, 2008), 35.
28. Chantal Mouffe, *The Return of the Political* (New York: Verso Books, 2005), 43.
29. Mouffe, *Return of the Political*, 43.
30. Rebecca Nicholson, "'Poor Little Snowflake'—The Defining Insult of 2016," *The Guardian*, November 28, 2016, http://www.theguardian.com/science/2016/nov/28/snowflake-insult-disdain-young-people; Julie Sprankles, "How To Respond When Someone Calls You A 'Snowflake,'" *Bustle*, April 28, 2017, https://www.bustle.com/p/how-to-respond-when-someone-calls-you-a-snowflake-51617; Faith Salie, "Who's the Snowflake? A Chilly Riposte to Political Insults," *CBS News*, July 9, 2017, https://www.cbsnews.com/news/whos-the-snowflake-faith-salie-a-chilly-riposte-to-political-insults/; Dana Schwartz,

"Why Trump Supporters Love Calling People 'Snowflakes,'" GQ, February 1, 2017, https://www.gq.com/story/why-trump-supporters-love-calling-people-snowflakes.

31. Geoffery Hughes, *Political Correctness: A History of Semantics and Culture* (Hoboken, NJ: John Wiley & Sons, 2011); Martin E. Spencer, "Multiculturalism, 'Political Correctness,' and the Politics of Identity," *Sociological Forum* 9, no. 4 (1994): 547–67; Norman Fairclough, "'Political Correctness': The Politics of Culture and Language," *Discourse & Society* 14, no. 1 (2003): 17–28; John K. Wilson, *The Myth of Political Correctness* (Durham, NC: Duke University Press, 1995).
32. Mouffe, *Return of the Political.*
33. Mouffe, *Return of the Political*, 4.
34. Mouffe, *Return of the Political.*
35. Jeff Giesea, "It's Time to Embrace Memetic Warfare," *Defence Strategic Communications* 1, no. 1 (2015): 68–76.
36. Giesea, "It's Time to Embrace Memetic Warfare," 68.
37. Giesea, "It's Time to Embrace Memetic Warfare," 69.
38. Joseph Bernstein, "This Man Helped Build the Trump Meme Army—Now He Wants to Reform It," *BuzzFeed*, December 30, 2016, https://www.buzzfeed.com/josephbernstein/this-man-helped-build-the-trump-meme-army-and-now-he-wants-t.
39. Josh Harkinson, "Meet Silicon Valley's Secretive Alt-Right Followers," *Mother Jones*, March 10, 2017, https://www.motherjones.com/politics/2017/03/silicon-valley-tech-alt-right-racism-misogyny/; Tyler Pager, "'DeploraBall' Highlights Worries over 'Alt-Right' Participation in Trump Presidency," *Boston Globe*, January 18, 2017, https://www.bostonglobe.com/news/politics/2017/01/18/deploraball-triggers-debate-over-alt-right-participation-inaugural-festivities/cvYYaUbw6PfPYJfRYzW3CN/story.html. The Anti-Defamation League deems Cernovich Alt-light, adjacent to the advocacies of the Alt-right. See "From Alt-right to Alt-lite: Naming the Hate," *Anti-Defamation League*, n.d., https://www.adl.org/resources/backgrounders/from-alt-right-to-alt-lite-naming-the-hate.
40. "Jeff Giesea, Master of the Meme," *Vanderbilt Political Review*, March 21, 2017, http://www.vanderbiltpoliticalreview.com/jeff-giesea-master-of-the-meme/.
41. Henry Gass, "Religious Liberty or Right to Discriminate? High Court to Hear Arguments in Wedding Cake Case," *Christian Science Monitor*, December 4, 2017, https://www.csmonitor.com/USA/Justice/2017/1204/Religious-liberty-or-right-to-discriminate-High-court-to-hear-arguments-in-wedding-cake-case.
42. Anonymous, "MEMETIC MISSILES GENERAL—Pt15," Comment, *Politically Incorrect*, February 3, 2017, www.4chan.org/pol/.
43. Giesea, "It's Time to Embrace Memetic Warfare," 69.
44. Anonymous, "MEMETIC MISSILES GENERAL—KATNISS EDITION _MMG," Comment, *Politically Incorrect*, February 1, 2017, www.4chan.org/pol/.
45. Anonymous, "MEMETIC MISSILES GENERAL—Pt15."
46. Mathew Ingram, "How Can Journalists Stop Providing Oxygen to Trolls and Extremists?," *Columbia Journalism Review*, May 24, 2018, https://www.cjr.org/the_new_gatekeepers/journalists-trolls-amplification.php.
47. See Wilson, *The Myth of Political Correctness*; Fairclaugh, "Political Correctness"; Spencer, "Multiculturalism, 'Political Correctness,' and the Politics of Identity."

48. Amanda Marcotte, "Alt-Right Snowflakes Play Victim, in Hopes of Mainstream Sympathy," *Salon*, November 9, 2017, https://www.salon.com/2017/11/09/alt-right-snowflakes-play-victim-in-hopes-of-mainstream-sympathy/.
49. Max Greenwood, "Trump Thanks Putin for Cutting US Diplomats: 'We Want to Reduce Our Payroll,'" *The Hill*, August 10, 2017, http://thehill.com/homenews/administration/346108-trump-thanks-putin-for-expelling-us-diplomats-we-want-to-reduce-our.
50. Greenwood, "Trump Thanks Putin for Cutting US Diplomats."
51. Greenwood, "Trump Thanks Putin for Cutting US Diplomats," Comment.
52. Greenwood, "Trump Thanks Putin for Cutting US Diplomats," Comment.
53. Nicholson, "'Poor Little Snowflake.'"
54. Nicholson, "'Poor Little Snowflake.'"
55. Mike Miles, "90 Miles From Tyranny: Every Time Trump Tweets, A Snowflake Melts…," *Blogspot*, December 2017, http://ninetymilesfromtyranny.blogspot.com/2017/12/every-time-trump-tweets-snowflake-melts.html.
56. Bearbear613, "The Best Snowflake Meme's and Responses:—Steemit," *Steemit*, December 2017, https://steemit.com/meme/@bearbear613/the-best-snowflake-meme-s-and-responses.
57. Nicholson, "'Poor Little Snowflake.'"
58. Jeremy Engels, *The Politics of Resentment: A Genealogy* (University Park: University of Pennsylvania Press, 2015), 13.
59. Judith Butler, *Frames of War: When Is Life Grievable?* (New York: Verso Books, 2009), 7.
60. J.M. Barbalet, *Emotion, Social Theory, and Social Structure* (New York: Cambridge University Press, 1998), 137.
61. Cynthia Levine-Rasky, *Whiteness Fractured* (Surrey, UK: Ashgate, 2013), 149.
62. Frantz Fanon, *Black Skin, White Masks* (New York: Grove, 2008), 222.
63. Barbalet, *Emotion, Social Theory, and Social Structure*.
64. Engels, *The Politics of Resentment*, 5.
65. Engels, *The Politics of Resentment*, 6.
66. Engels, *The Politics of Resentment*, 13.
67. Hua Hsu, "White Plight?," *New Yorker*, July 25, 2016, https://www.newyorker.com/magazine/2016/07/25/the-new-meaning-of-whiteness.
68. Anderson, *White Rage*.
69. Anderson, *White Rage*.
70. "White Lives Don't Matter," *Funnyjunk*, July 19, 2015, https://funnyjunk.com/White+lives+dont+matter/funny-pictures/5619969/.
71. German Lopez, "There Are Huge Racial Disparities in How US Police Use Force," *Vox*, December 17, 2015, https://www.vox.com/cards/police-brutality-shootings-us/us-police-racism.
72. Barbara A. Biesecker, "From General History to Philosophy: Black Lives Matter, Late Neoliberal Molecular Biopolitics, and Rhetoric," *Philosophy & Rhetoric* 50, no. 4 (2017): 409–30.
73. Stacey Patton, "Sorry, 'Deplorables': Being Called Racist Doesn't Mean You're Being Oppressed," *Washington Post*, September 15, 2016, https://www.washingtonpost.com/amphtml/posteverything/wp/2016/09/15/sorry-deplorables-being-called-racist-doesnt-mean-youre-being-oppressed/.

74. Kenneth Burke, "Dramatism," in *International Encyclopedia of the Social Sciences*, ed. David L. Sills (New York: Macmillan, 1968), 7: 445–52.
75. Kenneth Burke, A *Grammar of Motives* (Berkeley: University of California Press, 1969), 33.
76. Jason Wilson, "Hiding in Plain Sight: How the 'Alt-Right' Is Weaponizing Irony to Spread Fascism," *The Guardian*, May 23, 2017, http://www.theguardian.com/technology/2017/may/23/alt-right-online-humor-as-a-weapon-facism.
77. Biesecker, "From General History to Philosophy."
78. Gillian Tett, "Why the Alt-Right Is Winning America's Meme War," *Financial Times*, January 19, 2018, https://www.ft.com/content/be8ca142-fb0f-11e7-a492-2c9be7f3120a.
79. Saul Alinsky, *Rules for Radicals: A Practical Primer for Realistic Radicals* (New York: Vintage Books, 1971), 100.
80. David Weigel, "The Alinsky Model," *Slate*, January 26, 2012, http://www.slate.com/blogs/weigel/2012/01/26/the_alinsky_model.html.
81. Matt Goerzen, "Notes Toward the Memes of Production," *archive.is*, June 8, 2017, http://archive.is/VqFco.
82. Dylan Byers, "Exclusive: Russian-Bought Black Lives Matter Ad on Facebook Targeted Baltimore and Ferguson," *CNN Money*, September 27, 2017, http://money.cnn.com/2017/09/27/media/facebook-black-lives-matter-targeting/index.html; Nitasha Tiku, "How Russia 'Pushed Our Buttons' with Fake Online Ads," *Wired*, November 3, 2017, https://www.wired.com/story/how-russia-pushed-our-buttons-with-fake-online-ads/.
83. Tiku, "How Russia 'Pushed Our Buttons' with Fake Online Ads"; Byers, "Exclusive"; Casey Michel, "How the Russians Pretended to Be Texans—and Texans Believed Them," *Washington Post*, October 17, 2017, https://www.washingtonpost.com/news/democracy-post/wp/2017/10/17/how-the-russians-pretended-to-be-texans-and-texans-believed-them/.
84. Clay Farris Naff, "Call in the Robocops," *The Humanist* 78 (2018): 18–21.
85. "House Democrats Release 3,500 Russia-Linked Facebook Ads," *Wired*, May 10, 2018, https://www.wired.com/story/house-democrats-release-3500-russia-linked-facebook-ads/.
86. Marcotte, "Alt-Right Snowflakes Play Victim."
87. Maria Murriel, "The Alt-Right and White Outrage Around the World: An Explainer," *PRI's The World*, November 25, 2016, https://www.pri.org/stories/2016-11-25/alt-right-and-white-outrage-around-world-explainer.
88. Anonymous, "Cold Dead Hands (Photo)," Comment, *Facebook*, May 18, 2018.
89. Anonymous, "Cold Dead Hands (Photo)."
90. Ian Schwartz, "CNN Reporter Confronts Trump Supporter: Your Pro-Trump Group Was Infiltrated by Russians," *Real Clear Politics*, February 21, 2018, https://www.realclearpolitics.com/video/2018/02/21/cnn_reporter_confronts_trump_supporter_your_pro-trump_group_was_infiltrated_by_russians.html.
91. Schwartz, "CNN Reporter Confronts."
92. Schwartz, "CNN Reporter Confronts."
93. Schwartz, "CNN Reporter Confronts."

CONCLUSION

THE COMING MEME BATTLES

The 2016 election proved to be the first meme election—the contest announced the presence and power of memes as persuasive mechanisms for a host of audiences. The significance of memes has not abated since that fateful night in November. As the nation presses forward to future elections, memes have been mined as a resource for a host of advocacies, especially those courting young voters. By now, the ubiquity of memes makes them a near standard mode of address for a whole host of right leaning organizations and personalities. Conservatives—from top rated Fox News hosts and contributors, to free market promoting right-wing nonprofits, to sitting US Senators—have all appropriated the Alt-right's preferred mode of persuasion.[1] While memes are comparatively deployed less by the institutional left, firms like NextGen, a liberal data management and social media firm, and far left advocacy groups have increased meme deployments to sway voters and influence cultural thought.[2] As these brief memetic campaigns indicate, memes have become a crucial form of address in political advocacy. To that end, political and social campaigns must use memes effectively and broadly as part of an overarching strategy. Memes will continue to be a persuasive tool shifting politics and public culture in monumental ways. Given this, deployments of memes must be examined in their specificity and uniqueness. Using our skills as rhetorical critics, in this text, we have analyzed Alt-right memes to show how these images stultified public discourse and shaped national conversations.

We argued that memes function as a key form of political communication, that they are rhetorically effective, and that they challenge foundational deliberative norms. In particular, we suggested that memes serve an important persuasive purpose for the Alt-right, a loose collection of individuals on the far end of the conservative spectrum. This collective used memes to amplify its work, influence public culture, and abet Donald Trump's ascension to the presidency. In the case of the 2016 election, the Alt-right deftly orchestrated a form of informational warfare by harnessing the affordances of memes, the modes and processes by which they are created, and the infrastructures and platforms that support memetic circulation and dissemination. The memes crafted by the Alt-right evidence the rhetorical significance of iteration and resonance as they moved from enclaves such as 4chan and reddit to mainstream media—even the president's Twitter account. Memes addressed discrete audiences in divergent ways and allowed the Alt-right considerable dexterity and sophistication in its messaging. Memes are thus useful in effecting change in two powerful ways: by drawing people together into collectivities and by dividing them through chaos, confusion, and antagonism. Ultimately, this volume has demonstrated how memes are an agile, deft, and perhaps even dangerous form of communication—a fact that some politicians and their media managers seem to harness. So effective are memes for uniting and dividing people politically that they have become a key propaganda mechanism for Russian operatives attempting to influence US presidential (and other) elections.

Rhetorical criticism is essential to understanding memes of the Alt-right. The rhetorical functions of memes are plentiful: these images congeal the Alt-right as a collective, amplify its messages, proselytize to potential adherents, and alienate outsiders. Rhetorical criticism focuses on the work of particular persuasive tactics and our analysis here underscores how memes enable the Alt-right to respond to ongoing exigencies. Our use of rhetoric, then, does not seek to demystify the Alt-right and its *beliefs*—as the actions and agenda of the group cannot be assessed so simply. Instead, our goal has been to define and interrogate the *tactics* by which the Alt-right impacts public discourse. Given that the Alt-right has been remarkably successful in using memes to garner attention and influence public discourse, it is imperative for scholars to grasp how exactly the Alt-right has effectively deployed memetic rhetorical discourse. Examination of particular tactics offers a broader sense of how digital modes of propaganda and memetic discourse can move audiences. Indeed, studying the Alt-right's use of memes lends insight into how the political landscape has changed dramatically from its rhetorical efforts.

The Alt-right developed its memetic strategies in internet communities known for their status as meme manufacturers. Memes as we know them today were born in counterpublic enclaves such as reddit and 4chan, sites significant to the development of internet (counter-) culture. Although certainly not all (or even a majority of) users of 4chan and reddit espouse Alt-right perspectives, these sanctuaries of sarcasm helped incubate communicative practices that are now mainstays for extremist movements, aided by cultures that value free speech, anonymity/pseudonymity, and trolling. The functions of these spaces have filtered out to internet culture writ large. As we mentioned in chapter one, 4chan's work as an enclaved meme factory in tandem with reddit's sorting algorithms has been (and continues to be) effectively gamed by collectivities of people who work together politically—for lulz or otherwise.[3] Both reddit and 4chan function as producers, hosts, and disseminators of memetic content that may then be transported through algorithmically amplified circulation to the "outside world." The Alt-right has unleashed these affordances in powerful ways.

Memes are essential to the work of the Alt-right given that the collective is not necessarily drawn together through ideological affinity but rather congeals around a loosely shared politics and the circulation of particular memes. For the Alt-right, memes structure conversations on imageboards, generate publicity for the assemblage, and provide outreach for possible recruits. On our view, memes are the cardinal component of the Alt-right's internal communication and recruitment strategy. Memes are especially effective at gaining social traction in sites across the Alt-right's network, including 4chan and reddit, where memes already function as a basic communicative medium. Yet, the capacity of memes to influence public culture lies in their ability to circulate broadly. Memes slingshot throughout the digital ecosphere, slipping from more private sites to mainstream platforms. In so doing, memes hail new individuals' attention as they gain momentum on apparently agnostic platforms such as Facebook, Twitter, and Know Your Meme. These memes carry Alt-right messages to the mainstream through broad circulation. When journalists report on these phenomena, and cite exemplars of this communicative form, Alt-right memes get a third boost. In this way, the Alt-right harnesses one of the most important function of memes—their fungibility. Through their movement, Alt-right memes proliferate white nationalist and exclusionary politics in seemingly banal spaces, sites that may obfuscate their overtly political origins and trajectories. At the same time, by virtue of their invitational nature, Alt-right memes activate latent publics to participate in nationalist, xenophobic, and even fascist political acts. The results can be catastrophic. Although there is not a simple, linear causal relationship between Alt-right memes and the outcomes of the 2016 election, our analysis has shown that memes galvanized the Alt-right, stultifying political discourse even as they helped extremist counterpublics congeal.

Memes are effective in part because they superficially appear to be pithy, image-based jokes, rather than meaningful engagements with the world. However, from a critical perspective, memes are profoundly effective in that they rhetorically negotiate ambivalent meaning. Pepe—a cartoon frog brought to life by artist Matt Furie—has become one of the most important symbols for the Alt-right. Pepe is an ideal signifier for a loosely-conglomerated Alt-right. Like most memes, Pepe speaks to multiple publics. For Alt-right users on 4chan and reddit, Pepe signifies a relatively blank memetic canvas for Alt-right messaging: Pepe is a rallying point and a place to cohere despite significant differences. For larger, more mainstream publics, Pepe serves a metonymic purpose, standing in for the Alt-right writ large and offering some syntactical coherence. Although Furie has frequently, loudly, and even litigiously denounced white supremacist, Nazi, and Alt-right uptake of Pepe, Pepe's nefarious reach remains wide. So singular is the presumed relationship between Pepe and hateful messages from the Alt-right that Facebook enacted a special exception to its content reviewer instructions applying only to posts containing the famous frog.[4] Pepe both directs public attention to Alt-right advocacies and enables the Alt-right to appear as a singular force.

The white nationalist politics of the Alt-right are similarly obfuscated through ironic distanciation, or, what has sometimes been called "lulz." Pepe's traction has much to do with the work of ironic distanciation—a way for meme makers and replicators to separate themselves from backlash and vitriol by claiming ironic distance from it. Pepe, in particular, is so saturated in the ironic frame that deployment of a Pepe meme functions partially by befuddling layers upon layers of meaning. More generally, memes pursuing Alt-right lulz often work through memetic *détournement*, which names how memes come to serve as trollish resistance to status quo politics. While several scholars have analyzed "lulz," even concluding, as Whitney Phillips does, that the "lulz are dead,"[5] memetic *détournement* demonstrates its next iteration: flexibility to couple both spectacle for trolls and inclusion of "normies." This bivalent function of lulz is of great importance to the Alt-right, because it conjures new publics while remaining conversant with already extant ones. Simultaneously, trollish humor at the expense of others provides cover for circulating hateful content online. Today's memes are outfitted with layers of intertextual irony. Not all layers are visible to all people all the time and that's precisely the point. Speaking through multiple frames of reference and addressing different audiences via such modalities enables them rhetorical flexibility.

Alt-right methods and goals are often opaque for outsiders in that they regularly seek chaos or lulz rather than a specific goal. In this sense, chaos becomes a mode of rhetorical invention in confrontation with traditional, reason-based persuasive approaches. Shitposting as an evolution of lulz, for instance, has wielded significant impacts on public discourse, though it would be inaccurate to describe this tactic as inherently supporting a specific *telos*. Shitposting is used to disrupt digital conversations by dispersing focus through repeated memetic responses. This tactic, characterized by either sensationalistic or extremely banal content, can impact public discourse by diverting attention. Unlike more traditional deliberative schema, however, the tactic is predicated on chaos as the methodological optic. Studying Alt-right tactics in their specificity reveals how these advocates reach broader audiences with images that, at first blush, may seem nonsensical or even insignificant. A predominant aspect of the Alt-right's success has been to amplify its work via strategies that camouflage easily recognizable motives.

The Alt-right benefits from the network as an organizing material and symbolic configuration for the flow of information. Alt-right memes circulate well in the apparently politically neutral digital sphere. Recent rhetorical scholarship has taken on the concept of circulation as a way to challenge traditional conceptions of the rhetorical situation.[6] The circulation of messages via digital networks, in particular, has recreated the rhetorical situation, such that audiences, exigencies, and constraints are unfixed and unbounded. Memes—which are polysemous, overdetermined, and inherently invitational—thrive in such an environment. Memes productively lean into what Terranova deems the "centripetal" and "centrifugal" nature of the network because they simultaneously draw people, ideologies, and discourses together and offer opportunities to distinguish among them.[7] Memes are also tailor-made to travel rapidly across the myriad platforms the Alt-right uses. Memes shift quickly from enclaved sections of reddit and 4chan to Alt-right sites such as Breitbart and InfoWars as well as to mainstream social media sites. These varied components of the Alt-right ecosphere become an interconnected web for disseminating content, activating would-be Alt-right members, often evading detection as Alt-right discourses. Although Trump does not belong entirely to the Alt-right (and vice versa), the Alt-right deployed memes through this network of platforms to influence discourse regarding the 2016 election. Using this ecosystem, the Alt-right capitalized on polarization and circulated memes that further entrenched division. As evidenced by the mobilization of individuals for Alt-right causes, these memes resonated loudly and widely. Moreover, because they appear to be merely internet jokes, these memes evaded detection even as they sowed discontent.

The Alt-right crafted memes to exploit alienation and bolster political antagonisms. Alt-right users sought to foment "media shitstorms" that would both amplify their claims and position liberals in the least favorable light. These memes regularly provoked liberals and the left so that their public outrage inflamed existing divisions and further marginalized leftist advocacies. Often, these moments of provocation enabled Alt-right proponents to position themselves as attacked by the left—marginalized by those who usually seek inclusion. These claims simultaneously rely on and foster white resentment in audiences by stealing argumentative ground from those possessing rightful claims to oppression. Importantly, these tactics work within existing political antagonisms but also further entrench enmity. Democratic possibilities for change are obstructed as political opportunists fight for white supremacy, even white nationalism. As these opportunists succeed, democratic agonism is rendered nearly impossible.

The Alt-right's work was crucial in the maintenance of a network ripe for further toxic messaging. As evidence from Robert Mueller's investigation is released, it is increasingly clear that foreign agents took advantage of the political maelstrom present in the United States. In early 2018, Mueller named more than a dozen alleged conspirators working for three agencies with ties to the Kremlin. Using divisive rhetoric that appeared to mirror the Alt-right, the Internet Research Agency devised, funded, and carried out a coordinated media warfare campaign to the ultimate benefit of Donald J. Trump. While most media coverage of the Mueller investigation focused on the fact that Russian operatives advertised on Facebook, for us, the real story was the apparent success of information PSYOPS given the affordances of network culture. In particular, Russian agents seemingly capitalized on the polarization of digital media audiences and then weaponized it. Most importantly for our purposes, this discourse was often configured in an unlikely format: memes. Russian agents had already infiltrated 4chan and reddit. These agents learned how to meme in these spaces while simultaneously engaging in divisive psychological warfare.[8] The success of Russian propaganda was predicated on a toxic culture exploited and strengthened by the Alt-right.

Ultimately, this book supplies a roadmap to the rhetorical strategies of the Alt-right. Throughout this volume, we have suggested that rhetorical criticism is central to understanding how the Alt-right has stultified and shaped public discourse. The Alt-right is an assemblage that comes together and creates a stronger public presence through the work of memes. Its methods are diverse, using ironic distanciation, memetic *détournement*, provocation of outsiders, lulz, shitposting, and more to move audiences. These myriad tactics are amplified by the nature of networked circulation—a tool that the Alt-right has capitalized on dramatically. A wide set of social media users have been able to find affinity with Alt-right memes as these images flowed across their feeds. Moreover, even repulsion to such messages provided a signal boost to the Alt-right that aided the spread of such messages. Put simply, the Alt-right is playing a different game than "normies." They are winning the meme war, bigly. Scholarship that analyzes the specific ways the Alt-right uses memes must come to grips with these present circumstances to enable productive solutions.

Alt-Right Memes as Rhetorical Innovation

In outlining this roadmap to the rhetorical strategies of the Alt-right, we have contributed to the rhetorical study of public culture. Using memes as our textual focus of analysis suggests that these images cannot be treated merely as symptomatic signs that help scholars diagnose the cultic behaviors and principles of the Alt-right. Instead, using memes to analyze the Alt-right has allowed us to center on the ways the Alt-right persuasively addresses audiences and the means through which it has aggrandized a public presence. Memes are a key tool of the Alt-right in our current digital ecosphere and it is paramount to take these images seriously as modern forms of public address. Analyzing memes as textual artifacts enables scholars to follow the flow and circulation of discourse in ways that underscore the power and significance inherent to algorithmically-amplified networks of public discourse.

Memes are persuasive political devices that have significant effects on the way both publics and individuals understand and address pressing political topics. As we mentioned in the introduction to this volume, memes are oftentimes understood as distractions from political processes rather than rhetorical innovations productive of public deliberation and politics. When memes are taken seriously, they are often assumed to function through an irrational "meme magic." By analyzing their iconicity, rhetorical function, circulation, and uptake, we have shown that memes are an increasingly important mode of digital communication. Memes can have powerful political effects. Perhaps most obviously, memes that communicate about overtly political issues or specific candidates may influence not only political discourse but also voting habits. But, more insidiously, the ambiguous nature of memes suggests that even covertly political memes may be grounds for forming publics and influencing political culture more broadly. Thus, by studying memes in their concrete deployments, we have demonstrated how specific memes must be analyzed by scholars who understand their uses and impacts. To dismiss memes is to thoroughly misapprehend the nature of political communication in the present.

Pointedly, Alt-right memes shifted the nature and focus of public discourse regarding the election and entrenched a certain mode of white supremacist politics within mainstream discourses. Alt-right memes thus used memetic image politics to stultify public discourse. That is, the rhetorical uses of memes as invocations of lulz, deployments of *détournement*, provocations to outsiders, and more have shaped the way public conversations proceed. As political images, memes garner attention through their repetitive and frequent iterations across social media. The relatively short attention span of audiences is punctuated by these memetic, imagaic eruptions. It is not surprising that many mainstream media channels have now started covering popular memes, given that they, too, are attempting to capture a cultural *zeitgeist* (and thereby the public's attention) before that moment has elapsed. It helps that memes function well on almost any sized screen.

For the Alt-right, the way memes garner attention has enabled this collective to control the focus and flow of public discourse. In these deployments, Alt-right memes are designed to alienate and shake up the status quo. As such, provocative memes can be effective images even if they only create chaos rather than a specific political outcome. Given their Alt-right uses, memes are the pinnacle of image politics in the present cultural conjuncture. They are seemingly innocuous, often humorous images that captivate the public for a brief period. Though these images fly under the radar of those who might detect them as information warfare, they are nevertheless key forms of modern propaganda: they direct attention, influence audiences, and do so while seemingly offering only entertainment.

Because of the Alt-right's continuing successes, failure to robustly engage how Alt-right (or other) memes impact public discourse imperils democratic practice. The meme election of 2016 was certainly not the first event to mark the significance of memes in shaping public culture. In the spring of 2015, Russian propaganda and Alt-right imagery warned US citizens that a military exercise in Texas was planned to round up those who acted against the government.[9] As with more recent forms of Russian PSYOPS, much of this propaganda relied on memes to address audiences. Michael Hayden, former director of the National Security Agency and Central Intelligence Agency, reported to MSNBC's *Morning Joe* podcast that the Russians were testing the possibilities of interference.[10] The Russians were abetted by Alt-right discourses including Alex Jones's InfoWars and World Net Daily—sites whose ridiculous assertions were amplified via a series of social media memes.[11] The Jade Helm conspiracy's plot thickened when Governor Greg Abbott sanctioned the rumors and called in the National Guard to protect citizens. As Hayden observed, "At that point I'm figuring the Russians are saying, 'We can go big time.' And at that point I think they made the decision to play in the electoral process."[12] As we now know, Russia has been relatively effective in gaming political processes in the United States and elsewhere.[13] For instance, the Brexit referendum in the UK was bolstered by jingoistic, divisive tweets and other disinformation campaigns from the Russians.[14] Despite significant campaigning, including digital and print media campaigns, pro-Brexit messages prevailed, aided by a consortium of agents using propaganda to agitate towards chaos—or worse: outright xenophobic politics. These propaganda mechanisms are reliant on digital media aggregation, hashtag formations, and quite often, on memes. Most social media discourse is amplified if images accompany the text or are supplied on their own. Studying the advertisements released by Russia into the US evidences their reliance on images that look like memes to social media users.[15] Notice that the Alt-right helped the Russians generate outrage about Jade Helm. While these groups were likely not working together, their goals momentarily aligned: both sought to shift seats of power for their own agenda. Memes and other memetic social propaganda have played a significant role in undermining globally-recognized democracies, most famously in the UK and the US, but also across Europe.[16] This book has described and interrogated how those modes of memetic propaganda functioned.

Alt-right memetic propaganda often endeavored toward stronger forms of white nationalism, misogyny, and an injunction against any moves toward egalitarianism. That is not to suggest that the Alt-right specifically aims to create these ends. While some users may seek these goals, the Alt-right cannot be described as a singularity with one *telos*. Yet, considered as a non-cohesive whole, its discourse is often focused on the preservation of white privilege, the elimination of nearly all immigration, the ridicule of feminism, and more. The centrality of these discourses defines the work of the group—even if such definitions are delimited via outside observation. Moreover, Alt-right messages of resentment have achieved incredibly broad circulation. For its part, the Alt-right understands that bombastic, jingoistic, and hate-filled thematics enhances the circulation of messages and provokes outrage from outsiders. Outrage is functional: the Alt-right's modes of discourse are aggrandized via the circulatory rhythms of social media and traditional media networks. From this perspective, it is not surprising that political newsfeeds jump from one outrageous, clickable (and profitable) story to the next. It is also not surprising that enterprising politicians leverage this system through absurd messages that divert the public's attention. The absurdity of memetic discourse is not an error of these networks, it is a design principle. Networks amplify bombastic or otherwise extremist discourse to help facilitate engagement. Within a democratic context, that circulation also shapes how citizens communicate with one another.

Alt-right memes in particular travel across social media networks not only because of their offensive or radical content but also because of their affective resonances. Claims of white oppression and white resentment generally are not based in reality or facts. Nearly every study of the US continues to find massive advantage to whiteness and continued structural oppression for those excluded from its perceived contours.[17] Instead, white resentment is manufactured through affective resonances. If viewers can feel a *sense* of disenfranchisement or marginalization, that sensibility affords the meme stronger persuasive potential and greater circulation. Once again, this affective resonance will continually be used to enable the travels of memetic propaganda. This is true both because of algorithmic amplification—both users and machines bolster the signal of certain messages—but also because meme makers draw upon this affective resonance in their design principles. For instance, at a 2018 conference on social media use for police departments, the focus of discussion was on how to shape stronger public perceptions.[18] Yet, conference goers did not engage social media relations with the goal of bolstering public protections or communicating how departments were responsive to broader cultural changes, but instead emphasized viral content such as #hotcops memes.[19] These tactics speak to the affective sensibilities of police officers, with over seventy percent of white officers and over forty percent of black officers resentful of current media coverage of police brutality and corruption.[20] These officers are less likely to see high profile deaths of citizens as part of a pervasive issue and instead view them as "isolated incidents."[21] As a result, much of the social media tactics discussed at the conference did not deploy social media as a tool to communicate largescale changes but rather as a site to communicate those affective rhythms that distract the public from present antagonisms. As with the Alt-right, memes and other social media content once again punctuate and corral the flow of public discourse for police departments. More generally, memes travel broadly and impact public discourse often through those affective routes that shore up radical potentiality in favor of managing the manipulable public.

In terms of memes themselves, our findings cut against research that suggests memes unfurl original potential in each replication. Numerous scholars claim that memes are radical texts—images that can be moved to new locales and changed via their continual remaking and iterative qualities.[22] The open-access nature of memes, typically supported by sites that allow memes to be reconfigured in various forms, speaks to this potential. Yet, the Alt-right defies the radical potential of memes. Users have become adept at responding to moments of potential memetic resignification by shitposting and repeatedly deploying memes that shore up imagery and arguments the Alt-right has pilfered from others. For instance, efforts to reclaim Pepe have been ill-fated, not for lack of effort but rather from Alt-right backlash. In this way, Alt-right memes as rhetorical devices have resisted polysemous imagery given their repeated deployments. In the same way that Judith Butler argues gender is seen as essential given reification through a "set of repeated acts," memes become "regulated" via processes "of repetition" given the way this collective punctuates public discourse writ large.[23] In other words, memes are not politically neutral. Rather, they are constituted by and through the encultured media ecologies from which they are born and are circulated. In the present tense, those media ecologies routinely skew conservative. That is not to suggest that memes cannot be radical—they most certainly are in their denotative form—but the present conjuncture of discourse across networks and the rhetorical potency of Alt-right tactics belies the radicality of the form.

In this way, it is necessary for rhetorical scholars to add their perspective and unique methodologies in the study of networked publics. Rhetorical scholars are skilled in attending to larger generic forms as well as specific persuasive deployments that respond to on-the-ground conditions. As in this volume, our training as rhetorical critics has allowed us to illuminate moments when Alt-right memes adhere to memetic principles as well as the ways the Alt-right has innovated the memescape with its own strategy. Without attending to the persuasive functions of Alt-right memes, the current meme war will continue to be resoundingly won by the far right. Memetic discourse has enabled the Alt-right a considerable degree of control over the nature and focus of public conversations. Without robust consideration of the rhetorical, persuasive mechanisms fueling its success, other political parties and agents will be left in the present circumstances: unlikely or unable to fight back effectively.

Everyone's Got Dank Memes but the Institutional Left

We hope to have convinced the reader that the Alt-right weaponized memes as an effective rhetorical strategy for influencing public discourse, particularly in relationship to the 2016 election. Throughout our analysis, we have suggested that the Alt-right (and to some extent, more traditional conservative parties) have outmaneuvered the institutional left with memes. In this assertion, we have necessarily argued that memes are significant images to contemporary politics and public discourse. In this sense, 4chan and reddit are not simply sites where trolls speak to one another, but sites of strategic development where internet denizens develop novel ways to assert influence and shape public culture. Those who oppose the specific politics that have emerged from these sites must remember that tactical sophistication is essential to memetic operations. Indeed, if the left or moderates are to combat the Alt-right as it has been constituted through discourses on /pol/ and r/the_donald/, they must reconfigure their tactics.

While a number of political candidates have attempted to use memes or other social media for their gain, none have yet won the meme war (or even many battles) against the Alt-right. In the 2016 election, for instance, Donald Trump was not the only one who used memes. Jeb Bush, Ted Cruz, Hillary Clinton, and more all attempted to use memes to bolster the signal of their social media feeds.[24] Since then, candidates of both political parties have taken up the tactic, using memes with varying levels of effectiveness. For instance, the democratic nominee for Texas House District 63, Richard Wolf, created his own memes to support his candidacy. Brian Feldman lavished praise on the candidate's Facebook feed, calling him one of the "dirtbag left," with images that show a "combination of staunchly leftist politics and a refusal to adhere to the rules of respectful decorum and debate that traditional political operatives hold dear."[25] While there was some enthusiasm for the candidate on the page for the reddit podcast Chapo Trap House—a similar "dirtbag left" humor podcast—Wolf was unsuccessful in his run and lost the primary.[26] The moment, and the institutional left's use of memes writ large, demonstrates the ways meme battles have largely been lost to the right. As with Wolf, most candidates have not yet created memes that resonate with broad sets of users. When the institutional left deploys memes, they are often seen as inauthentic. As a result, institutional democratic candidates have not yet used memes in convincing ways.

As a case in point, Hillary Clinton showed a strong digital presence leading up to the 2016 election. Several times during the election cycle, she dominated news feeds with digital content. Dawn Chmielewski, writing for *Recode*, asserts that the now infamous "delete your account" tweet was effective in "throwing shade, social media style."[27] The "delete your account" quip was a response to then-candidate Trump calling her "crooked Hillary" after an Obama endorsement. With some 707,000 likes, it was perhaps one of Hillary's most successful memetic moments. Chmielewski characterizes the meme as an effective response to Trump, the troll. Yet, as any savvy social media user will tell you, it's generally best not to feed the trolls. Indeed, despite the success of "delete your account," more often Clinton's social media forays failed utterly, likely through the campaign's inability to anticipate counter response.

When Clinton attacked opponents, especially Trump, it often backfired. Clinton's characterization of Trump supporters as a "basket of deplorables," which she clarified as "racist, sexist, homophobic, xenophobic, Islamophobic," was a gaffe.[28] The backlash was swift and cutting. Clinton apologized for the comment, but tempered her speech of apologia with a fierce condemnation of the Alt-right ecosystem. "But lets be clear," she noted,

> what's really 'deplorable' is that Donald Trump hired a major advocate for the so-called 'alt-right' movement to run his campaign....It's deplorable that Trump has built his campaign largely on prejudice and paranoia and given a national platform to hateful views and voices, including by retweeting fringe bigots with a few dozen followers and spreading their message to 11 million people.[29]

On our view, Clinton's analysis of Trump's engagement with the Alt-right is largely accurate. The veracity of her claims is unquestionable. Yet, for the same reason that "fact-checking" Trump may not be convincing to his base, Hillary appeared unlikely to win over any new voters with her deplorables comment. Coupled with a slew of internet denizens who bolstered online support for Bernie Sanders, Clinton's message—although important—was drowned out by dank memes from the right.

Clinton failed to respond to far right deplorables memes in ways that aided her candidacy and this mistake emblematizes her problematic memetic strategy writ large. To be sure, many factors contributed to the downfall of Hillary Clinton as a presidential candidate. Her gender was a highly salient characteristic that influenced public perception, journalistic coverage, and more.[30] The country, still recovering from the Great Recession, was dealing with major growing pains in which the industries that had made the country wealthy—manufacturing, for instance—gave way to the knowledge economy (or even still: the "gig economy").[31] Racial tensions, stitched into the very fabric of the republic, were laid bare and exacerbated by economic inequality.[32] From our vantage point, however, it is clear that memetic discourse struck a central nerve in political systems. Those who had "dank memes"—and those who could deploy them effectively—had the ability to reach and activate latent audiences toward political participation. Clinton's campaign was strong in many communicative capacities. However, it did not enjoy the same memetic uptake as other candidates, to the ultimate detriment of her campaign. As Jennifer Grygiel wrote in a *New York Times* op-ed,

> Mrs. Clinton made a few attempts at using memes but struggled with the execution. In one notable attempt, she used a "Texts from Hillary" meme for her Twitter profile photo starting in 2013, perhaps hoping it would make her appear hip and internet-savvy. But the meme met with some ridicule and probably did not reach the swing voters she badly needed. Mrs. Clinton also attempted to use a meme on Election Day, generating a video that showed her participating in the "mannequin challenge," a meme that had recently gone viral. But she did this after that meme had already started to fade.[33]

Grygiel's analysis is adroit insofar as she outlines several problems with Hillary's memetic attempts. First, Clinton's use of memes seemed to dull their shine, rather than amplify them as Trump's did. Second, Clinton's use of memes was insular to the left and was unlikely to cross the digital aisle to latent or undecided voters. Third, her choice of memes was reactionary to the point of being antithetical to their aims. Memes have a short shelf life. Deliberating whether or not one should jump aboard a particular meme may mean that the meme decays in popularity. Given that deft use of memes signifies in-group status, deploying a meme too late is often worse than not participating at all. In Clinton's case, poor use of memes further positioned her as mainstream, institutional, and reactionary—not dank.

This lack of memetic dexterity from Clinton and others was noted by the Alt-right, who deployed memes to mock unsuccessful or uncool memes from the left.[34] This memeplex, called "The Left Can't Meme" served as a new vehicle to criticize the establishment left for being politically correct, and therefore, patently unfunny.[35] In a thread on r/the_donald/, user ZhonPepe used the site to crowdsource an answer about why the left fails at memeing. As summarized by ZhonPepe, "because the left is default politically correct and thus must often hide the truth, they have close to zero ability to use memes as impactful (spicy) propaganda to sway public opinion/perception," which "weakens their memes," and "allows for a situation where the right is able to trigger/traumatize people into swaying their opinion by revealing forbidden but often instinct-or nature-based truths."[36] On the other hand, the right is successful because they are not held to the same "PC" standards. For ZhonPepe,

> The spicy, radioactive, sharp venomous memes of the right penetrate deep because the ideas themselves are not allowed in PC mainstream culture, add on top of that an offensive/arousing picture worth a thousand words, and that is a one way communication device with effectiveness. Over time we got a recipe for a red congress, court, and president for several years.[37]

In other words, the right is effective in constructing dank, "spicy" memes that "penetrate" in a way institutional, deliberative discourse cannot. Here, ZhonPepe outlines several characteristics of memetic warfare we have described in this text. First, the author describes how Alt-right memes are by nature discursively counter-cultural, and therefore released from "PC" or traditional, deliberative rhetorical standards. Second, and relatedly, Alt-right memes often traffic in offensive images that function as an effective "one way communication device" given how they garner publicity across algorithmic networks. In this way, memes can be a dog whistle for white supremacist and xenophobic communities while also inviting normie/mainstream political affinity. Finally, Alt-right memes serve a variety of seemingly conflictual ends. Although memes are critiques of institutional "PC" culture, they can be productive of institutional ends, including the capture of high political offices in the US. In this comment by ZhonPepe, there is a clear sophistication to how Alt-right memes are deployed, a nuanced level of knowledge that informs this user's critique of the left. Democratic candidates have yet to consistently demonstrate a similar level of nuance.

So salient is the "left can't meme" meme that a fictitious, parody book emerged on Amazon entitled *Yes, We Can Meme: A Progressive-Left Playbook for Winning the Internet Meme Culture War*, "published" in July 2017 by "Dr. Stan Kerifeke," a "lecturer in popular culture at the Shadilay Institute."[38] On first blush, this text appears quite legitimate. It follows convention both in terms of format and political ideology. The front cover references leftist symbolism: the red, black, and white color scheme evokes communist or socialist thematics; the closed, raised fist gestures toward activist symbols; the title suggests affinity with Obama's iconic "Yes, We Can" campaign slogan. The book boasts dozens of customer reviews, apparently from those in opposition to the left. The first few sentences in the description outline that this book will "show you how to fight fire with fire and defeat 'Kekistan' once and for all."[39] Yet, this book is decidedly parodic. The "Shadilay Institute" is memetically linked to Pepe. Clicking on the "read more" portion of the description demonstrates that the "book is satirical…intended as a gift for humourless, regressive leftists from sensible people who understand internet culture on even the most basic level."[40] Here's the joke: that the "humourless, regressive leftist" might actually pay for this guidebook, realize that its contents are "kek" and sit fuming, thus cementing their own fate as a "normie."

Outside of this obvious Alt-right volume, there is popular support for the idea that the left is humorless—not just from the Alt-right or rank-and-file conservatives. Rather, a (if not *the*) dominant perception from non-liberals is that the left is elitist, controlling, and, indeed, quite conservative. As an essay in *Vanity Fair* claims, "Not to put too fine a point on it, but liberals, in their desperate quest to be taken seriously, are the new conservatives."[41] Public persona is rhetorically negotiated, and not entirely in the hands of the rhetor. In this case, the left has become the subject of an important reversal: although demographically, leadership of the right is just as, if not more, conservative, wealthy, well-connected, and elite, the "Left Can't Meme" meme seems to provide evidence that the so-called left is the unreachable party. In other words, the left's politics and political strategies are elitist and out of touch. The point here is not just that the left is unfunny or to unproblematically uphold these stereotypes. Nor are we suggesting that liberals necessarily become part of the "dirtbag left" so as to counter the Alt-right with lefty lulz. While laughter or lulz may be the goal of the Alt-right, we maintain that, in many cases, laughter is still morally reprehensible in the face of many ongoing issues facing the nation. Yet, the left must still develop memetic tactics that highlight a welcoming, opening ethos that rhetorically tracks, especially given the circulation of viral and memetic content. Without that, criticisms made by the right and others will continue to be successful at making the left, which purports to forward an inclusive and caring set of policies, appear as a fussy, uptight, and even corrupt, bully.

From this perspective, the seriousness of the left becomes a rhetorical hurdle to reaching the lulzy masses. According to the Alt-right, the left fails at memes because it takes things too seriously, because it cannot approach the world with levity, and because it just doesn't "get it." Like a parent disciplining a child, the left is framed as too "triggered" to accomplish anything, except, perhaps, for those in the most elite ranks. For its part, the most visible parts of the left appear to verify these claims. For instance, influential actors with liberal leanings do seem to police memetic content to significant degree, though this self-policing is less often about political correctness—as the Alt-right insists—and more often about an obsession with accuracy. For instance, Dan Hopper implored his readers to stop sharing images and memes that mocked the idea that Melania Trump does not smile around her husband.[42] Hopper lamented the deep dive into Melania's nonverbal communication while insisting that the liberals sharing a photograph of Melania laughing with Barack Obama must understand that the claim that she did not laugh around Donald was untrue. In effect, Hopper refused to engage in memetic behavior that mocked the Trumps because such images were false—Melania somehow does in fact smile in Donald's presence regularly. In this instance, it is seriousness and an obsession with facts—not so-called PC culture—that proves an obstacle to effective liberal memes. As Dana Cloud writes of the left's obsession with facts: "we assume that in any controversy, the person who has the truth on their side will eventually win the day."[43] This assumption has not served the left well and certainly does not bode well for its meme forays. Yet, there are non-institutional liberal meme generators who may light a path forward.

In 2016, media outlets began to report on BSDMS—or Bernie Sanders Dank Meme Stash—a Facebook page dedicated to circulating the "dankest" Bernie Sanders memes. The *Washington Post*, for instance, featured a story on "How Bernie Sanders became the lord of 'dank memes.'"[44] The coverage gestured towards the importance of creating and disseminating memes as a grassroots activity by "frenzied denizens" who "share their pro-Sanders creations far and wide: across Facebook, on Reddit, and in their Twitter and Tumblr feeds."[45] A *Motherboard* article similarly declared Bernie the internet's favorite candidate. "With over 294,000 members," *Vice* journalist Carles Buzz wrote, "Bernie Sanders Dank Meme Stash is indicative of Bernie Sanders' control of the high-level internet."[46] Like Alt-right memes, BSDMS was productive of images that were, like most memes, abstract and concrete, coherent and divisive, collective and singular. As Buzz notes, "This is the problem with 'niche' on the internet. It has a ceiling, and at a point can become an insular cycle. Broad appeal comes from marginalizing the message and reaching audiences that you never thought you could identify with. The community/website/ Facebook group feels less dank, but if the goal is electing the next President of the United States, the message will continue to morph."[47] This analysis is astute insofar as it depicts the tenuous connection between internet culture in the margins (dank) and mainstreaming this content for the benefit of more and different people (less dank). Moreover, journalistic coverage linking Bernie Sanders as candidate with Bernie Sanders, meme icon, demonstrates that democratic candidates had an opportunity to use memetic content to influence the election. That a more institutional, "normie" candidate, Clinton, won the primary seemed to throw a stake in the heart of the Democratic Party's memetic potential with certain meme generators.

Radical grassroots organizations and movements have had some successes in using political memes. Black Lives Matter and Occupy Wall Street displayed innovation and creativity in their social media uses, particularly their uses of memes.[48] Today, various forms of social media, including those utilized by the Alt-right, allow leftist memes to proliferate. On Facebook, for instance, one may join "Sassy Socialist Memes," "Socialist Memes for Anti-Social Teens," "Socialist Memes for Proletarian-minded Teens," "Revolutionary Memes Extreme," "Anarcho-Accelerationist Memes for Egoist Teens," "Crunchy Continental Memes," "New Urbanist Memes for Transit-Oriented Teens," and more. These meme groups have significant traction with large audiences. On Facebook, for instance, "Sassy Socialist Memes" boasts well over a million followers. A recent post, picturing Karl Marx on a trading card as a "revolutionary, legendary creature," and "Human rebel" who enables users to "Seize the means of production!" features over 6,300 reactions, nearly 1,200 shares, and around 900 comments at the time of this writing (See Fig. C.1).[49] These large collectives bespeak the potentiality of memes to work toward new political realities.

Figure C.1: Seize the Memes of Production.

Turning Marx into a meme might be a rhetorically effective way to re-introduce socialist (or otherwise leftist) politics to young people for whom memes are already a central mode of communication. In 2017, *Vice* published an article entitled "How Meme Culture is Getting Teens into Marxism."[50] The tagline is prescient: "On social media, youths are seizing the memes of production to prove that continental philosophy isn't just an academic abstraction."[51] An article in *Teen Vogue* entitled "Who is Karl Marx," introduces Marx through memetic abstraction: "You may have come across communist memes on social media. The man, the meme, the legend behind this trend is Karl Marx, who developed the theory of communism, which advocates for workers' control over their labor (instead of their bosses.)."[52] Marx as meme provides salience across multiple discursive milieus. These meme groups may be the left's counterpart to Alt-right memes, or at least these are images working to activate class politics among latent voters.

At present, most institutional leftist actors seem ill equipped to understand, let alone use, memes as forms of political persuasion. To test this claim, we spoke with the CEO of Authentic Campaigns, a social media firm that has designed messages for Kamala Harris, MoveOn.org, the ACLU, and Governor Dan Malloy. The firm prides itself on crisis response and fundraising, as well as generating innovative digital campaigns for clients. Yet, what we learned in our interview with CEO Mike Nellis is that memes were not part of the firm's overarching or crisis response strategies.[53] Despite potential presidential candidates like Kamala Harris and internet-based advocacy groups like MoveOn.org as clients, memes had yet to be deployed as part of this media company's arsenal. Nellis suggested his work dealt primarily with donors and did not follow the memetic trends of the day.[54] Nellis's candid assessment seems reinforced by the host of democratic and left-leaning political candidates who have not used or have failed in their use of memetic or viral content. The institutional left, then, may be able to learn from the rogue fans of Sassy Socialist Memes and more. The *ad hoc* meme stashes featuring Marx and Bernie Sanders may provide a roadmap to those forms of memetic discourse that have tracked most successfully with voters—younger or otherwise.

Ultimately, those who care about the future of democracy will have to grapple with a change in the location and circulation of public talk. As we negotiate those pressing concerns that have long underwhelmed the promise of democracy, yet another threat looms: the persuasive power of digital propaganda and the memes leading the charge. At present, institutional leftist actors have yet to capitalize on the ways digital persuasion can empower and embolden actors. But, perhaps this institutional failure may allow for more radical or egalitarian memes to dominate social media channels. These memes may profit the democratic establishment, or potentially, open up new alliances that promise even more robust agonism. Our current pessimistic assessment of the Alt-right's suasory methods and considerable wins need not determine future courses of action. Indeed, our actions must acknowledge current limitations and press ever forward to a more radical democratic praxis. This requires we underscore the limitations of the institutional left, including its ability to effectively communicate with latent publics, and, ultimately, seek out those forms of identification that recognize and embolden contingent alliances in the pursuit of radical change.[55]

Beyond the Meme Election of 2016

In the case of the 2016 election, the Alt-right's prize was not only the installation of Donald J. Trump, but the beginning of an unsettling shift of the Alt-right to the mainstream. Trump was certainly significant to some members of the Alt-right because he would institute policies palatable to most of this collective. However, Trump represented a symbolic victory in moving the "Overton Window," shifting the nature of public discourse and political deliberation.[56] When, in 2018, President Trump called undocumented immigrants "animals,"[57] the Alt-right was likely to have cheered, not only because it signaled a policy shift from a centrist democrat (Obama), but because it was an indication that additional xenophobic policies were forthcoming. Yet, there is another set of lessons emerging from the "Great Meme War" of 2016; namely that a group of relatively unorganized, highly motivated internet users had a significant effect through the power of image-based persuasion. Regardless of one's view of the Alt-right, that potentiality bespeaks the importance of memetic modes of rhetorical address. As such, we conclude this volume by offering assessments of how we might embrace the potentiality of memes while curtailing the wanton actions of the Alt-right and others.

First, given the nature of digital propaganda, educators must teach broader media literacy skills in both formal and public educational initiatives. As J. Michael Sproule notes, after World War I and to some extent World War II, there were concentrated efforts to instill media education curriculum in both K-12 and college classrooms.[58] Those institutional campaigns were augmented by public campaigns such as Radio Free Europe and Voice of America. Such curricula emerged against concerns that without appropriate checks, propaganda could undo the very foundations of democratic practice. Today, in response to the news that Russian operatives used memes and advertisements to target voters, there have not yet been significant efforts to legally curb these machinations, nor has a loud demand for media literacy curriculum emerged as a bulwark against outside influences. Instead, at present, politicians and citizens have either ignored or downplayed Russian efforts by focusing nearly singularly on "fake news" rather than the impact of deceitful adversaries on an unprepared populace.[59] Without organized, targeted curricula to combat the spread of digital propaganda, those who use social media and traditional media are left to decipher information from disinformation on their own.

There are already exemplars for how such media literacy programs and policies could effectuate change. The European Union and other targets of Russian tactics began constructing their own protective measures as early as 2015.[60] The EU developed the StratCom Task Force, which reviews ongoing disinformation campaigns and briefs government officials, who then come up with public messaging and broader operations in response.[61] StratCom reports on emerging forms of propaganda to the public alongside wider media literacy initiatives that investigate ownership and advertisement placement.[62] Sophisticated white papers on media literacy and policy changes have already been published by the Atlantic Council and the Carnegie Endowment for International Peace, among others.[63] These proposals are theoretically robust and detail both infrastructure and targeted media literacy. Suggestions from reports encourage a set of changes in the US:

- Ongoing analyses of current disinformation campaigns conducted by the CIA, NSA, and more;
- Public messaging to deter the effectiveness of propaganda;
- Training political officials to recognize potential interference;
- Asking the media to police advertised content and report sources of revenue;
- Inviting social media firms to redesign algorithms to counter threats;
- Explain to the public clearly and concisely the risks of outsider disinformation.

Ultimately, these papers suggest that improved media literacy and strengthened systems against malicious psychological operations are essential to the protection of democracy. Altogether, these specific prompts, among many others, must be addressed and debated by both the public and by those institutional actors with the means to enact these changes. Without broad changes in media literacy and policy, the public is unlikely to protect itself from disinformation campaigns conducted by the Russians, the Alt-right, or any other groups.

As it relates to memes specifically, traditional classroom lesson plans and sweeping public campaigns must teach pupils how memes work. Students must be able to decode memetic messages, learn the specific entailments of their functions, and grasp how memes move across digital networks. While many may assume that students are "born digital," considerable experience with digital media does not translate to media creation skills or media literacy, let alone ethical orientations to the media.[64] Reading work by Limor Shifman, Ryan Milner, Gabriella Coleman, Whitney Phillips, and even this volume provides students with opportunities to understand how pithy memes are also persuasive tools. Without intentional, careful instruction, students may not grasp the multi-faceted ethics of such persuasion. For instance, both of us have taught meme (and media) literacy in our classrooms, instructing students with various political affinities and affectations. After these classes concluded, a few students noted their involvement in 4chan and reddit—especially the boards and subreddits we studied in this project—and suggested that they simply understood memes as forms of lulz. Several students also admitted that taking memes seriously in a classroom setting allowed them to understand how quickly complex memetic content spreads, as well as the myriad ways these memes speak to diverse and diffuse audiences. By engaging an ethical frame, these users acknowledged they had gained memetic literacy and understood the negative impacts of their previous behaviors. More generally, then, students may apprehend and employ memes as effective persuasive devices but may not have considered the extent to which those actions could jeopardize larger communal values. To help students recognize not simply the power of memes but the need for media ethics, we suggest deep classroom and public conversations on the impacts of memetic persuasion. Such conversations not only abet broader media literacy skills but may enable current gatekeepers and innovators to come up with ethical and important solutions for using memes in productive, rather than destructive, ways.

In addition to media policies that abet literacy, a set of legislative and corporate policy changes related to privacy should be pursued. Congressional representatives in the United States have yet to issue laws that further protect consumer privacy in digital spaces, largely leaving individuals to negotiate and master their own privacy controls on social media sites or opt out of usage. Congressional hearings discussing how Facebook sold advertising space and capitalized on data provided by customers failed to provide any substantive basis for policy reform. Indeed, many of the questions posed to Facebook CEO Mark Zuckerberg indicated the ignorance of congressional representatives on matters of digital circulation and profit models.[65] Despite highly publicized hearings that purportedly "grilled" Zuckerberg on how Facebook sold personal data, there has been little political willpower for significant legislative changes. Even the watered-down Honest Ads Act, which would regulate advertisements on social media in the same way as television and radio ads are regulated, has stalled out in its progression.[66] While there is still time for legislation to be passed that might enable US users to have stronger privacy protections and to diminish the effectiveness of all forms of propaganda, there is a lack of political will within Congress or the Trump administration to accomplish these tasks.

In fact, the United States is already delayed in its legislative changes when compared to those recently enacted by the European Union and the United Kingdom. The EU began enforcing the General Data Protection Regulation on May 25, 2018. The policy is a sweeping change that "expands the scope of what companies must consider personal data" and requires firms to track the data it houses on EU residents.[67] The law also offers citizens the ability to delete personal data, gather records on data, and designate how their data can be used. If there is a data breach, the law requires consumers be notified within 72 hours. Other legal changes have set the stage for a series of lawsuits against social media firms that refuse to regulate themselves. In May 2018, the Information Commissioner's Office in the United Kingdom ordered the now defunct Cambridge Analytica to provide David Carroll, a Boston professor, with any information it held on him.[68] Embroiled in bankruptcy, Cambridge Analytica has yet to disclose Carroll's data, but the press for greater control over user privacy continues at a robust pace in the EU and UK.[69] The same momentum in the US remains elusive.

Protections for user privacy and regulation of social media firms would help curb malicious content on a number of social media outlets. Thus, while many of the restrictions passed elsewhere are an attempt to reduce Russian disinformation, those same protections may impede hateful discourse from extremist groups. As we indicated in chapter one, there has already been some, albeit limited, momentum from reddit, Twitter, and 4chan to more strongly control content. Yet, as it relates to the propaganda of the Alt-right, regulating hateful content may diminish its range of influence, but will ultimately not impede the circulation of Alt-right content wholly. Instead, the Alt-right will likely seek out new locales from which it might provoke the mainstream media to cover vitriolic messages. The Alt-right has thus far been relatively successful in working around speech codes that remove its content. When reddit and 4chan cracked down on particular forums, users moved to other sites, such as Gab. The shift may have reduced Alt-right discourse on some sites, but users found other locales to broadcast their political messaging. Moreover, many who espouse Alt-right views have learned how to switch the tone and language of their advocacies to evade hate speech laws, all while decrying purported infringements upon their first amendment rights.[70] Thus, much as with media literacy campaigns, legislative changes are only one small component of a broad set of efforts necessary to combat the Alt-right (or whatever the next iteration of this far right hydra comes to be dubbed).

Third, journalists must change their reporting practices on far right groups while the public re-orients how we read stories about the far right. Encouraging circumspection regarding how journalists cover the Alt-right would help to diminish its ability to impact public discourse. In May 2018, Phillips published a report on media amplification, noting that "just by showing up for work and doing their jobs as assigned, journalists covering the far-right fringe…played directly into these groups' public relations interests."[71] As we maintained in this volume, media coverage commonly augments the Alt-right's agenda and enables a stronger public presence—coverage often seizes public attention and controls the flow of discourse about the collective. Phillips provides a guidebook on best practices to communicate salient far right events without unnecessarily amplifying their work. The entire report is well worth reading as it offers a practical guide for journalists and others. Her suggestions focus on the public good—offering advice to undercut the ways the Alt-right uses the media to magnify its public presence while simultaneously generating profits for media agencies. By contrast, she encourages reporters to narrow the conditions under which they report on the Alt-right, providing advice that suggests journalists: refrain from centering the narrative on "bad actors," understand the strategy of these groups, "be equally aware that extremist groups…are eager to use journalistic norms as a weapon against journalism," minimize the focus on "personal psychology," and avoid using the Alt-right's chosen language and terms.[72] For Phillips, reporters should be well-versed in the practices of both digital culture and the specific groups being investigated. Overall, Phillips invites journalists to consider the social benefit of coverage and weigh that asset against potential harms. Given our analysis in this book, we concur with Phillips' assessments and encourage a broad investment in stronger journalistic norms alongside a more critical orientation to readership.

In keeping with these journalistic guidelines, the insistence that fact-checking can corral the disinformation of the far right or others must be understood as an incredibly limited resistance strategy. Fact-checking seems to be a relatively significant pursuit for journalists and others who have aimed to undo the work of the Alt-right collective by calling out lies and misapprehensions. Yet, as Cloud writes,

> The necessity of mediation means that we cannot simply put "facts" in front of audiences and expect them to respond in a meaningful political way. Instead, the Left should take up some of the compelling rhetorical mediation tools that the Right has long embraced: emotion, embodiment, narrative, myth, and spectacle. Successful mediation is what takes "facts" and turns them into beliefs and, ultimately, common sense.[73]

Cloud's point is to insist that fact-checking and a misplaced reliance on the truth cannot always combat lies effectively. Her solution does not embrace the absence of any truth, but suggests actions and knowledge are rhetorically mediated. What comes to be known as common sense is based on our embodied and emotional sensibilities. Thus, fact-checking may not stem the tide of far right discourses and their stranglehold on the rhythms of public culture, but understanding how to redirect or deploy affective resonances might.

While the Alt-right predicates affective resonances on resentment, affective tactics may bolster communal identification and caring alongside agonism. Kathleen Woodward has suggested that we live within a "new economy of the emotions," in which emotions circulate at a rapid rate.[74] Our emotions are not understood through a "psychology of depth and interiority" but "reduced to intensities and sensations" such as those delivered by "good action films."[75] Memes capitalize on this circulation of sensation and intensities, particularly when they are coupled with the Alt-right's irreverence. But, the sensibilities of Alt-right memetic discourse ought not be appropriated for those with more radical democratic ambitions. Lauren Berlant proposes compassion as an alternative—emphasizing that within vulnerability one can find common points of identification—while rejecting the darker side of compassion that often includes sadism.[76] Berlant is joined by scholars such as Judith Butler who insist that recognition of humanity and a shared understanding of precarity can open up a radical orientation to others.[77] It does not seem far-fetched to imagine that memes that can so viciously draw on emotions of enmity and revenge could also cultivate compassion and connection via novel memetic strategies. Butler even suggests as much with her discussion of imaging strategies elsewhere.[78] Ultimately, we must consider the image's role in the relational dynamics of politics.

The memes that have been so effectively deployed by the Alt-right point to the potentiality of radical democratic relations. To be sure, Alt-right memes ultimately foreclose these possibilities. But, the fact that unorganized and otherwise unaffiliated 4chan and reddit users have so effectively shaped public discourse outside of institutional politics offers a moment of hope. On our view, part of that hope requires that citizens turn away from the politics of enmity and embrace agonism. We are not suggesting a politics of love in response to hate—there is much to reject in the far right, the mainstream right, and certainly various factions of the institutional left. Yet, to despise the Alt-right and revel in castigating its hate-filled discourse only facilitates its ambitions. Instead, as we suggested through our discussion of Chantel Mouffe's theorizations in chapter five, we must embrace agonism. Such agonism means resolutely rejecting advocacies of the far right while refraining from the same mode of vicious enemyship upon which the Alt-right capitalizes. That agonism is abetted when citizens take up the helm of their own democracy. The Alt-right users of 4chan and reddit have used the tools at their disposal to influence public culture and politics. As scholars, we are remiss if we do not vivify the same robust effort to counter far right advocacies and propose new modes of democratic praxis. Moreover, we endorse those who seek to counter such aims to develop their own forms of rhetorical address—through memes or whatever tools are available and effective—to galvanize and align those groups and individuals that might actualize radical democratic politics.

What we must encourage is nothing less than a massive cultural shift—one in which individuals understand and mobilize their own rhetorical role in digital ecosystems. Our missive is not to rehearse the idea that the affordances of the internet engender egalitarianism—far from it. Instead, we must insist that just as with any form of rhetorical address, some modes of persuasion are more effective than others. Internet denizens of all political stripes should heed well the lessons of this volume that prompt us to consider how memes can become productive forms of digital persuasion amplified by algorithmic circulation. The Alt-right has no special formula to influence public culture through memes. Alt-right devotees are simply astute students of rhetoric. Generating innovative digital advocacies that bolster democracy's project is a task that every reader of this volume must now consider. This project must be thoroughly debated and tested to be compelling. Participants must study digital rhetorics, alongside more traditional forms of rhetorical address, to discover their own place and power within networked cultures. We must begin, then, with the conversation this volume has inaugurated. There is no end point. There is only the ongoing and inventive use of rhetorical address to imagine and create new modes of political relation.

Notes

1. "Tucker Carlson," *Know Your Meme*, n.d., accessed May 30, 2018, http://knowyourmeme.com/memes/people/tucker-carlson; "Tomi Lahren's 'Dear Liberal Snowflakes' Picture," *Know Your Meme*, n.d., accessed May 30, 2018, http://knowyourmeme.com/memes/tomi-lahrens-dear-liberal-snowflakes-picture; "Turning Point USA," *Know Your Meme*, n.d., accessed May 30, 2018, http://knowyourmeme.com/memes/people/turning-point-usa; Megan Farokhmanesh, "Did Ted Cruz Just Kill the Best Ted Cruz Joke?" *The Verge*, October 18, 2018, https://www.theverge.com/2017/10/18/16499058/ted-cruz-zodiac-killer-meme-twitter-joke.
2. "NextGen America," *NextGen America*, n.d., accessed May 30, 2018, https://nextgenamerica.org/; "Sassy Socialist Memes," *Facebook*, n.d., accessed June 20, 2018, https://www.facebook.com/sassysocialistmemes/.
3. "4Chan: The Rude, Raunchy Underbelly of the Internet," *Fox News*, April 8, 2009, http://www.foxnews.com/story/2009/04/08/4chan-rude-raunchy-underbelly-internet.html. On this understanding of these sites, see, for instance, Gabriella Coleman, "Anonymous: From the Lulz to Collective Action," *The New Everyday: A Media Commons Project*, April 6, 2011, http://mediacommons.futureofthebook.org/tne/pieces/anonymous-lulz-collective-action; Brian X. Chen, "How Reddit Scooped the Press on the Aurora Shootings," *New York Times*, July 23, 2012, https://bits.blogs.nytimes.com/2012/07/23/reddit-aurora-shooter-aff/; Steve "spez" Huffman, "Let's All Have a Town Hall about R/All," *Reddit*, June 16, 2016, https://www.reddit.com/r/announcements/comments/4oedco/lets_all_have_a_town_hall_about_rall/.
4. Lucas Matney, "Facebook Has a Very Specific Pepe the Frog Policy, Report Says" *TechCrunch*, May 25, 2018, https://techcrunch.com/2018/05/25/facebook-has-a-very-specific-pepe-the-frog-policy-report-says/.
5. Whitney Phillips, *This Is Why We Can't Have Nice Things: Mapping the Relationship between Online Trolling and Mainstream Culture* (Cambridge, MA: MIT Press, 2015), 137.
6. Eric S. Jenkins, "The Modes of Visual Rhetoric: Circulating Memes as Expressions," *Quarterly Journal of Speech* 100, no. 4 (2014): 443; Catherine Chaput, "Rhetorical Circulation in Late Capitalism: Neoliberalism and the Overdetermination of Affective Energy," *Philosophy & Rhetoric* 43, no. 1 (2010): 21.
7. Tiziana Terranova, *Network Culture: Politics for the Information Age* (London: Pluto Press, 2004), 70.
8. Josh Horwitz, "Reddit's Most Popular Meme Forum Was a Hangout Spot for Russian Trolls," *Quartz*, April 11, 2018, https://qz.com/1249579/r-funny-reddits-most-popular-meme-forum-was-a-hangout-spot-for-russian-propaganda-trolls/.

9. Christopher Hooks, "The Jade Helm Fiasco Says More About Texas Than It Does Russia," *Texas Observer*, May 4, 2018, https://www.texasobserver.org/jade-helm-fiasco-says-more-about-texas-than-russia/.
10. Hooks, "The Jade Helm Fiasco Says More About Texas Than It Does Russia."
11. Stephen Young, "Abbott Fell for Russia-Inspired Jade Helm Furor, Ex-CIA Director Says," *Dallas Observer*, May 4, 2018, http://www.dallasobserver.com/news/greg-abbott-fell-for-russian-jade-helm-trap-ex-cia-director-says-10653302.
12. Hooks, "The Jade Helm Fiasco Says More About Texas Than It Does Russia."
13. Kathleen Hall Jamieson, *Cyber-War: How Russian Hackers and Trolls Helped Elect a President* (New York: Oxford University Press, 2018).
14. David D. Kirkpatrick, "Signs of Russian Meddling in Brexit Referendum," *New York Times*, November 15, 2017, https://www.nytimes.com/2017/11/15/world/europe/russia-brexit-twitter-facebook.html.
15. "Jade Helm 15: Image Gallery," *Know Your Meme*, n.d., accessed June 1, 2018, http://knowyourmeme.com/memes/events/jade-helm-15/photos.
16. Massimo Calabresi, "Inside Russia's Social Media War on America," *Time*, May 18, 2017, http://time.com/4783932/inside-russia-social-media-war-america/.
17. See, for example, Cheryl E. Matias, *Feeling White: Whiteness, Emotionality, and Education* (Rotterdam: Sense Publishers, 2016); Kate Manne, "Melancholy Whiteness (or, Shame-Faced in Shadows)," *Philosophy and Phenomenological Research* 96, no. 1 (2018): 233–42; Meta G. Carstarphen *et al.*, "Rhetoric, Race, and Resentment: Whiteness and the New Days of Rage," *Rhetoric Review* 36, no. 4 (2017): 255–347; Joe L. Kincheloe *et al.*, ed., *White Reign: Deploying Whiteness in America* (New York: Palgrave Macmillan, 2000); Cynthia Levine-Rasky, *Whiteness Fractured* (Surrey, UK: Ashgate, 2013); Lee Bebout, *Whiteness on the Border: Mapping the U.S. Racial Imagination in Brown and White* (New York: New York University Press, 2016).
18. Tess Owen, "Police Think Creating the next #HotCop Meme Will Fix America's Policing Problem," *Vice*, May 24, 2018, https://news.vice.com/en_us/article/ywep8v/smilecon-miami-taught-police-how-to-create-the-next-hot-cop-meme.
19. Owen, "Police Think Creating the next #HotCop Meme Will Fix America's Policing Problem."
20. Renee Stepler, "Key Findings on How Police View Their Jobs amid Protests and Calls for Reform," *Pew Research Center*, January 11, 2017, http://www.pewresearch.org/fact-tank/2017/01/11/police-key-findings/.
21. Stepler, "Key Findings on How Police View Their Jobs amid Protests and Calls for Reform."
22. W. Lance Bennett and Alexandra Segerberg, *The Logic of Connective Action* (New York: Cambridge University Press, 2013); Bradley E. Wiggins and G. Bret Bowers, "Memes as Genre: A Structurational Analysis of the Memescape," *New Media & Society* 17, no. 11 (2015): 1886–1906.
23. Judith Butler, *Gender Trouble: Feminism and the Subversion of Identity* (New York: Routledge, 1990), 33.
24. Emma Axelrod, "The Role of Memes in Politics," *Brown Political Review*, March 20, 2016, http://www.brownpoliticalreview.org/2016/03/role-memes-politics/.

25. Brian Feldman, "How One Texas Candidate Is Using Memes and Facebook to Push the State Leftward," *Select All*, March 1, 2018, http://nymag.com/selectall/2018/03/texas-candidate-richard-wolf-memes-facebook-something-awful-chapo.html.
26. mugrimm, "A 23 Year Old College Drop Out Who Lives with His Father Is Running for the Texas House in Dallas Purely on Memes, Bonus: His Name Is Richard Wolf," *Reddit*, March 1, 2018, https://www.reddit.com/r/ChapoTrapHouse/comments/816cbt/a_23_year_old_college_drop_out_who_lives_with_his/.
27. Dawn Chmielewski, "Hillary Clinton Just Burned Donald Trump with the 'Delete Your Account' Meme on Twitter," *Recode*, June 9, 2016, https://www.recode.net/2016/6/9/11896826/hillary-clinton-donald-trump-delete-your-account-meme-twitter.
28. Hillary Clinton in Katie Reilly, "Hillary Clinton Transcript: 'Basket of Deplorables' Comment," *Time*, September 10, 2016, http://time.com/4486502/hillary-clinton-basket-of-deplorables-transcript/.
29. Politico Staff, "Clinton Partially Walks Back 'Deplorables' Comment," *Politico*, September 10, 2016, https://www.politico.com/story/2016/09/clinton-partially-walks-back-deplorables-comment-227993.
30. Farida Jalalzai, for instance, notes "That [Clinton's] unarguably less qualified opponent won suggests the durability of the American presidential glass ceiling; executive institutions and electoral processes remain difficult for women to navigate as the public continues to associate the presidency with men and masculinity." See Farida Jalalzai, "A Comparative Assessment of Hillary Clinton's 2016 Presidential Race," *Socius: Sociological Research for a Dynamic World* 4 (2018): 2.
31. Stephen R. Barley, Beth A. Bechky, and Frances J. Milliken, "The Changing Nature of Work: Careers, Identities, and Work Lives in the 21st Century," *Academy of Management Discoveries* 3, no. 2 (2017): 111–15; Gerald Friedman, "Workers without Employers: Shadow Corporations and the Rise of the Gig Economy," *Review of Keynesian Economics* 2, no. 2 (2014): 171–88.
32. Carla Norrlof, "Hegemony and Inequality: Trump and the Liberal Playbook," *International Affairs* 94, no. 1 (2018): 63–88.
33. Jennifer Grygiel, "The Left Shouldn't Be Too Proud to Meme," *New York Times*, March 5, 2018, https://www.nytimes.com/2018/03/05/opinion/democrats-memes-social-media.html.
34. ZhonPepe, "Why the Left Can't Meme," *Reddit*, June 9, 2017, https://www.reddit.com/r/The_Donald/comments/6g7j14/why_the_left_cant_meme/.
35. Grygiel, "The Left Shouldn't Be Too Proud to Meme."
36. ZhonPepe, "Why the Left Can't Meme."
37. ZhonPepe, "Why the Left Can't Meme."
38. Dr. Stan Kerifeke, "Yes, We Can Meme: A Progressive-Left Playbook for Winning the Internet Culture War," *Amazon*, July 12, 2017, https://www.amazon.com/Yes-We-Can-Meme-Progressive-Left/dp/1521793573.
39. Kerifeke. "Yes, We Can Meme"
40. Kerifeke, "Yes, We Can Meme."
41. Michael Wolff, "No Jokes, Please, We're Liberal," *Hive*, June 2005, https://www.vanityfair.com/news/2005/06/wolff200506.

42. Dan Hopper, "The Petty, Misleading Photos We Need to Stop Sharing," *Cracked*, May 25, 2018, http://www.cracked.com/blog/the-petty-misleading-photos-we-need-to-stop-sharing.
43. Dana Cloud, *Reality Bites: Rhetoric and the Circulation of Truth Claims in U.S. Political Culture* (Athens: Ohio State University Press, 2018), 1.
44. Caitlin Dewey, "How Bernie Sanders Became the Lord of 'Dank Memes,'" *Washington Post*, February 23, 2016, https://www.washingtonpost.com/news/the-intersect/wp/2016/02/23/how-bernie-sanders-became-the-lord-of-dank-memes/?noredirect=on&utm_term=.77e7168c0a82.
45. Dewey, "How Bernie Sanders Became the Lord of 'Dank Memes.'"
46. Carles Buzz, "Can Bernie Sanders' Dank Meme Stash Swing the Election?" *Vice*, February 22, 2016, https://motherboard.vice.com/en_us/article/d7ypwa/bernie-sanders-dank-meme-stash-facebook-page.
47. Buzz, "Can Bernie Sanders' Dank Meme Stash Swing the Election?"
48. Colin Wayne Leach and Aerielle M. Allen, "The Social Psychology of the Black Lives Matter Meme and Movement," *Current Directions in Psychological Science* 26, no. 6 (2017): 543–47; Ryan M. Milner, "Pop Polyvocality: Internet Memes, Public Participation, and the Occupy Wall Street Movement," *International Journal of Communication* 7 (2013): 34; James Alexander McVey and Heather Suzanne Woods, "Anti-Racist Activism and the Transformational Principles of Hashtag Publics: From #HandsUpDontShoot to #PantsUpDontLoot," *Present Tense* 5, no. 3 (2016).
49. "Sassy Socialist Memes—Karl Marx, Revolutionary," *Facebook*, n.d., accessed May 28, 2018, https://www.facebook.com/sassysocialistmemes/photos/a.1393581200962840.1073741828.1393565747631052/2069006316753655/?type=3&theater.
50. Hannah Ballantyne, "How Meme Culture Is Getting Teens into Marxism," *Vice*, April 27, 2017, https://broadly.vice.com/en_us/article/7xz8kb/how-meme-culture-is-getting-teens-into-marxism.
51. Ballantyne, "How Meme Culture Is Getting Teens into Marxism."
52. Ballantyne, "How Meme Culture Is Getting Teens into Marxism."
53. Mike Nellis, Interview with Authentic Campaigns CEO, Phone, May 16, 2018.
54. Nellis, Interview.
55. Ernesto Laclau and Chantal Mouffe, *Hegemony and Socialist Strategy* (New York: Verso, 2001).
56. Derek Robertson, "How an Obscure Conservative Theory Became the Trump Era's Go-to Nerd Phrase," *Politico*, February 25, 2018, http://politi.co/2FunqYx.
57. Linda Qiu, "The Context Behind Trump's 'Animals' Comment," *New York Times*, May 18, 2018, https://www.nytimes.com/2018/05/18/us/politics/fact-check-trump-animals-immigration-ms13-sanctuary-cities.html.
58. J. Michael Sproule, "Authorship and Origins of the Seven Propaganda Devices: A Research Note," *Rhetoric & Public Affairs* 4, no. 1 (2001): 135–43; J. Michael Sproule, *Propaganda and Democracy: The American Experience of Media and Mass Persuasion* (New York: Cambridge University Press, 1997); J. Michael Sproule, "Propaganda Studies in American Social Science: The Rise and Fall of the Critical Paradigm," *Quarterly Journal of Speech* 73, no. 1 (1987): 60–78; Thomas Holt, "Busting Russia's Fake News the European Union

Way," *The Conversation*, May 29, 2018, http://theconversation.com/busting-russias-fake-news-the-european-union-way-93712.

59. Anders Fogh Rasmussen and Michael Chertoff, "The West Still Isn't Prepared to Stop Russia Meddling in Our Elections," *Politico*, June 5, 2018, https://politi.co/2sGvYG0.
60. Holt, "Busting Russia's Fake News the European Union Way."
61. Holt, "Busting Russia's Fake News the European Union Way."
62. Kavitha Surana, "The EU Moves to Counter Russian Disinformation Campaign," *Foreign Policy*, November 23, 2016, https://foreignpolicy.com/2016/11/23/the-eu-moves-to-counter-russian-disinformation-campaign-populism/.
63. Erik Brattberg and Tim Maurer, "Russian Election Interference: Europe's Counter to Fake News and Cyber Attacks," *Carnegie Endowment for International Peace*, May 23, 2018, https://carnegieendowment.org/2018/05/23/russian-election-interference-europe-s-counter-to-fake-news-and-cyber-attacks-pub-76435; Robert Faris *et al.*, "Partisanship, Propaganda, and Disinformation: Online Media and the 2016 U.S. Presidential Election," *SSRN Scholarly Paper* (Rochester, NY: Social Science Research Network, August 1, 2017), https://papers.ssrn.com/abstract=3019414.
64. Michael Thomas, *Deconstructing Digital Natives: Young People, Technology and the New Literacies* (New York: Taylor & Francis, 2011).
65. Dylan Byers, "Senate Fails Its Zuckerberg Test," *CNN*, April 10, 2018, http://money.cnn.com/2018/04/10/technology/senate-mark-zuckerberg-testimony/index.html; Issie Lapowsky, "Mark Zuckerberg's Congress Testimony Day One: Simple Questions, Hard Answers," *Wired*, April 10, 2018, https://www.wired.com/story/mark-zuckerberg-congress-day-one/; Clare Malone, "Congress Needs To Understand Facebook Before Dealing With It," *FiveThirtyEight*, April 12, 2018, https://fivethirtyeight.com/features/is-facebook-too-much-of-a-shape-shifter-to-regulate/.
66. April Glaser, "Facebook Finally Unveiled Its Full Plan to Make the Next Election Less Awful Than the Last One," *Slate*, May 24, 2018, https://slate.com/technology/2018/05/facebook-finally-unveiled-its-plan-to-make-the-next-election-less-awful-than-the-last-one.html; Mary Louise Kelly, "What You Need to Know About The Honest Ads Act," *NPR*, October 19, 2017, https://www.npr.org/2017/10/19/558847414/what-you-need-to-know-about-the-honest-ads-act.
67. Justin Jaffe and Laura Hautala, "What the GDPR Means for Facebook, the EU and You," *CNET*, May 25, 2018, https://www.cnet.com/how-to/what-gdpr-means-for-facebook-google-the-eu-us-and-you/.
68. "UK Watchdog Orders Cambridge Analytica to Hand Over American's Personal Data," *Reuters*, May 6, 2018, https://uk.reuters.com/article/uk-facebook-privacy/uk-watchdog-orders-cambridge-analytica-to-hand-over-americans-personal-data-idUKKBN1I70CB.
69. Natasha Lomas, "Facebook Data Misuse Firm Snubs UK Watchdog's Legal Order," *TechCrunch*, June 5, 2018, http://social.techcrunch.com/2018/06/04/facebook-data-misuse-firm-snubs-uk-watchdogs-legal-order/.
70. Wade Goodwyn, "Alt-Right, White Nationalist, Free Speech: The Far Right's Language Explained," *NPR*, June 4, 2017, https://www.npr.org/2017/06/04/531314097/alt-right-white-nationalist-free-speech-the-far-rights-language-explained.

71. Whitney Phillips, "The Oxygen of Amplification," *Data & Society*, May 22, 2018, 7, https://datasociety.net/output/oxygen-of-amplification/.
72. Phillips, "The Oxygen of Amplification," 15–18.
73. Cloud, *Reality Bites*, 2.
74. Kathleen Woodward, "Calculating Compassion," in *Compassion*, ed. Lauren Berlant (New York: Routledge, 2014), 60.
75. Woodward, "Calculating Compassion," 61.
76. Lauren Berlant, "Introduction: Compassion (and Withholding)," in *Compassion*, ed. Lauren Berlant (New York: Routledge, 2014), 10.
77. Judith Butler, *Precarious Life: The Powers of Mourning and Violence* (New York: Verso, 2004).
78. Judith Butler, *Frames of War: When Is Life Grievable* (New York: Verso, 2010).

INDEX

D

E

F

G

I

J

K

L

M

N

O

P

R

S

W

Y

Z

General Editors
Mitchell S. McKinney and Mary E. Stuckey

At the heart of how citizens, governments, and the media interact is the communication process, a process that is undergoing tremendous changes as we embrace a new millennium. Never has there been a time when confronting the complexity of these evolving relationships been so important to the maintenance of civil society. This series seeks books that advance the understanding of this process from multiple perspectives and as it occurs in both institutionalized and non-institutionalized political settings. While works that provide new perspectives on traditional political communication questions are welcome, the series also encourages the submission of manuscripts that take an innovative approach to political communication, which seek to broaden the frontiers of study to incorporate critical and cultural dimensions of study as well as scientific and theoretical frontiers.

For more information or to submit material for consideration, contact:

Mitchell S. McKinney: McKinneyM@missouri.edu
Mary E. Stuckey: mes519@psu.edu

To order other books in this series, please contact our Customer Service Department:

peterlang@presswarehouse.com (within the U.S.)
order@peterlang.com (outside the U.S.)

Or browse online by series:
WWW.PETERLANG.COM